WORKFORCE ENGAGEMENT

Strategies to
attract,
&motivate
retain talent

Stephen P. Hundley, Ph.D.
Frederic Jacobs, Ph.D.
Marc Drizin

About WorldatWork®

WorldatWork (www.worldatwork.org) is the association for human resources professionals focused on attracting, motivating and retaining employees. Founded in 1955, WorldatWork provides practitioners with knowledge leadership to effectively implement total rewards—compensation, benefits, work-life, performance and recognition, development and career opportunities—by connecting employee engagement to business performance. WorldatWork supports its 30,000 members and customers in 30 countries with thought leadership, education, publications, research and certification.

The WorldatWork group of registered marks includes: WorldatWork®, workspan®, Certified Compensation Professional or CCP®, Certified Benefits Professional® or CBP, Global Remuneration Professional or GRP®, Work-Life Certified Professional or WLCP™, WorldatWork Society of Certified Professionals®, and Alliance for Work-Life Progress® or AWLP®.

WorldatWork.
The Total Rewards Association
www.worldatwork.org

Any laws, regulations or other legal requirements noted in this publication are, to the best of the publisher's knowledge, accurate and current as of this book's publishing date. WorldatWork is providing this information with the understanding that WorldatWork is not engaged, directly or by implication, in rendering legal, accounting or other related professional services. You are urged to consult with an attorney, accountant or other qualified professional concerning your own specific situation and any questions that you may have related to that.

This book is published by WorldatWork Press. The interpretations, conclusions and recommendations in this book are those of the author and do not necessarily represent those of WorldatWork.

No portion of this publication may be reproduced in any form without express written permission from WorldatWork.

©2007 WorldatWork Press
ISBN 9781579631666

Table of Contents

Preface

"Employees are our most valuable asset." "Through these doors walk the world's greatest employees." "We strive to be an employer of choice." "This company is like one big family." "We put our people first."

Phrases like these are seen and heard in lots of organizations—and with good reason. Successful companies realize their employees are one of the most important resources that can assist the organization in creating a sustainable competitive advantage in the marketplace. Employee knowledge generates new products, services and solutions. Employee behaviors can facilitate improved customer service and lead to customer loyalty. And employee attitudes can enhance the overall work experience for others in the organization, including the desire to work hard, help colleagues and maintain positive working relationships. Thus, employees can and do contribute to the organization's ability to succeed and to competitively differentiate itself from rival firms. Maximizing employee potential, however, requires more than catchy phrases and well-intentioned leaders. It requires an ongoing commitment to the concept of workforce engagement.

Workforce engagement involves understanding what employees need and want from their work experience. It also involves creating and implementing organizational practices designed to advance the capabilities of the enterprise through the improved work experiences of employees. These organizational practices are not the sole jurisdiction of the human resources (HR) department, either. Instead, organizationwide understanding, commitment and action are necessary if we are to find, keep and motivate engaged, productive employees. This book will assist in those endeavors.

Workforce Engagement is organized to provide readers with data, concepts and case studies that will enhance their understanding of workforce engagement. This book is organized into five parts:

Part I: Understanding Workforce Engagement
- Introduction to Workforce Engagement (Chapter 1).

Part II: Strategic Issues in Workforce Engagement
- Effective Senior Leadership (Chapter 2)
- Reputation Management (Chapter 3)
- Ethics, Diversity and Safety (Chapter 4)
- Stakeholder Input (Chapter 5).

Part III: Core HR Processes in Workforce Engagement

- Workforce Selection (Chapter 6)
- Organizational Orientation (Chapter 7)
- Training and Development (Chapter 8)
- Rewards and Recognition (Chapter 9)
- Work-Life Balance (Chapter 10).

Part IV: Operational Components in Workforce Engagement

- Performance Management (Chapter 11)
- Tools and Technology (Chapter 12)
- Opportunities for Advancement (Chapter 13)
- Daily Satisfaction (Chapter 14).

Part V: Enhancing Workforce Engagement

- Making Workforce Engagement Work (Chapter 15).

Each chapter contains data highlights from two National Benchmark Studies on Workforce Engagement that were conducted by the Performance Assessment Network (*pan*) in 2004-2005 and 2006-2007. These national benchmark studies present findings and implications for employers from a nationally representative sample of employees—including an understanding of the "levels" and "drivers" of workforce engagement. The intellectual framework for the national benchmarks was developed by Marc Drizin, a co-author of this text and founder of www.employeeholdem.com. Concepts provide the foundation-level knowledge for each workforce engagement component and, in many cases, will enhance readers' understanding of topics, ideas and practices for which they may already be familiar. Case studies are designed to provide analysis and discussion on the often complex issues associated with the chapter topic. The cases, developed under pseudonyms or composites drawn from real organizations, are suitable for use in a variety of management-development training programs or other courses. Thus, the inclusion of data, concepts and case studies provides the reader with evidence, information and analysis useful in considering the myriad of topics associated with workforce engagement.

While no one book can definitively provide all of the solutions to employer-employee issues, we feel this book will appeal to—and be useful for—readers from a variety of backgrounds and contexts. In organizations where workforce engagement is already a priority, readers will likely find the information contained in this book a sound validation of practices in place. For those who are newer to the journey, this book will provide useful suggestions and insights into clarifying and prioritizing activities related to workforce engagement. Leaders and senior-level decision makers, HR practitioners, managers/supervisors and even individual-contributor employees will find relevant information about how their role can best contribute to workforce engagement's success in the organization. Finally, students of leadership, organizational behavior, HR management and other similar disciplines should find this book a useful source of information that augments concepts from other texts.

Workforce Engagement is published by WorldatWork, the total rewards association. In this context, total rewards refers to all of the tools available to the employer that may be used to attract, motivate and retain employees. Total rewards includes everything the employee perceives to be of value resulting from the employment relationship. This book provides a framework for understanding workforce engagement as part of a broader total rewards strategy, and the reader is encouraged to visit www.worldatwork.org for further information and resources about total rewards.

PART I
Understanding Workforce Engagement

Introduction to Workforce Engagement

Chapter 1:
Introduction
to Workforce Engagement

Introduction: What Do We Mean By 'Workforce Engagement'?

From time to time, new concepts and priorities emerge in the business world influencing how organizations operate, how employers and employees interact and how and when change occurs. Looking back at the past 25 years, the terms "management by objectives," "total quality management (TQM)," "zero-based budgeting" and other phrases represented efforts to improve the workplace by emphasizing fundamental principles. Recently, the term "workforce engagement" has gained wide popularity.

This book is about workforce engagement: what it means, why it is important and how it affects individuals and organizations. As the data, concepts and case studies of workforce engagement are explained, some material will be familiar and some will be new. Indeed, as readers will quickly observe, the term "workforce engagement" encompasses many ideas and practices and, by becoming familiar with them, future practices can be enhanced.

The first task, then, is to define what is meant by "workforce engagement."

Workforce engagement is defined as an ongoing process to recruit, retrain, reward and retain productive and effective employees by enhancing understanding of organizational practices and employee priorities, attitudes, behaviors and intentions.

What are the essential elements in this definition? First, as an ongoing process, ideas associated with workforce engagement are continually evolving, with new ideas frequently introduced. Second, workforce engagement applies to every aspect of employment—recruiting, retraining, rewarding and retaining employees—and is not a one-time intervention. Third, workforce engagement takes into account not just individual employee performance, but attitudes, intentions and priorities as well. Thus, the fundamental ideas of workforce engagement encompass philosophy and strategy.

That is, an organizational commitment to workforce engagement involves a set of beliefs about enhancing workforce performance and particular activities to achieve them.

Why Is Workforce Engagement Important?

Since the dawn of the industrial revolution, there has been much attention paid to the employer-employee relationship. Early research efforts focused on maximizing efficiency, organization and production, which was needed as work shifted to the new era of manufacturing. The rise in unions and increased government legislation on workforce matters, coupled with more thoughtful understanding of employee issues on the part of business owners and managers, gave rise to increased attention on employee issues. In recent times, fierce competition—for talented employees and for customers—in a global context has required organizations to re-examine their workforce effectiveness strategies. Indeed, many organizations continue to introduce, refine and improve workforce engagement approaches, many of which are a synthesis of past practices that have consistently been acknowledged as effective in finding, keeping and motivating employees.

It might be easy for some people to look at workforce engagement, yawn and assert that "nothing is new," and that the premises of workforce engagement are just another scheme to increase worker productivity. The very meaning of the words "workforce" and "engagement," however, contradict that point of view. "Workforce" refers to everyone employed in the organization and explicitly includes managers and individual-contributor employees, and "engagement" refers to commitment, not simply productivity. It should be obvious then that understanding the fundamentals of workforce engagement is imperative for those concerned with all aspects of employment issues and processes.

What Are the Four R's of Workforce Engagement?

The Four R's of Workforce Engagement:

- Recruit—finding the right talent, for the right job, at the right time
- Retrain—equipping employees with the knowledge and skills to continuously perform meaningful work
- Reward—recognizing achievements through monetary, performance-management and other means
- Retain—keeping the right talent, in the right job, for the right amount of time.

Recruit

When organizations recruit employees, they seek to *find the right talent, for the right job, at the right time.* Inherent in this process is a sound understanding of the job, its specific requirements and the relationship the job has to the overall organization. Once that information is defined, organizations can tap recruitment sources that will likely yield the best candidates. The continued and anticipated marketplace demands for the company's products or services are the main factor in determining the need for additional talent. Other considerations impacting an ability to effectively recruit talent include the level of competition in the market, the present composition of the organization's employee resources and the availability of skilled individuals in the labor markets in which the organization conducts business.

Retrain

After recruiting talent, organizations need to *equip employees with the knowledge, skills, perspectives and experiences to continuously perform meaningful work.* Even when employees enter the organization with significant work experience or educational attainment, it is crucial that the company provide training about the organization's way of doing business. Equally important, however, is the need to ensure that such training is ongoing, thus permitting employees to continuously learn the competencies needed to remain a viable, value-adding member of the team.

Reward

The ability to *recognize individual, team and organizational achievements by monetary and other performance-management incentives* is the centerpiece to an effective employee-reward system. While pay is important, numerous studies conclude that simply rewarding employees with cash is not sufficient to motivate them to achieve sustainable performance. Worse, however, is the unintended consequence of potentially "trapping" an employee who might want to leave the organization, but feels that he or she would be unable earn as much elsewhere. Thus, rewarding employees should be a holistic endeavor, in which cash compensation is one of several major components that also include benefits, access to training, development and other professional opportunities, organizational perks and positive feedback.

Retain

One of the measures of workforce stability is an organization's turnover rate. *Keeping the right talent, in the right job, for the right amount of time* is necessary if the organization is to realize success in designing products and services, relationships with customers and business partners and growing the base of intellectual capital within the company. There are real and hidden costs associated with employee turnover. Real costs include the actual financial consequences of losing talent, having to recruit and retrain a new employee and the lost productivity and revenue that result when an unanticipated vacancy occurs. Hidden costs include the lower morale that could emerge given the instability of the organization's employees, the potential for poor or inconsistent service to customers and the loss of intellectual capital that is hard to replace. Although employee retention should be a key organizational goal, it is important to view retention in the context of occupational or industry trends or norms.

What Factors Contribute to an Understanding of Workforce Engagement?

Historical Factors Contributing to Workforce Engagement:

- Increased automation and efficiency in manufacturing settings
- Relationship between employee satisfaction and customer satisfaction
- The rise in the number of service- and knowledge-based industries, organizations and occupations
- Technological and structural advances that change employee work and managerial control
- Changing nature of employer-employee relationships.

Increased automation and efficiency in manufacturing settings

Automation requires manufacturing employees to be multitasked, flexible, adaptable and able to increasingly troubleshoot maintenance-, quality- and production-related functions. As machines have moved from mechanical to electrical to digital, they have become more complex and faster. Operating manuals, too, have become technically complex and require higher-order reading, comprehension, critical thinking and concentration skills. The ability to produce goods in a just-in-time environment is also underscored by an emphasis on manufacturing excellence (e.g., Malcolm Baldridge Quality pursuits and ISO certifications) and cost-effectiveness.

Relationship between employee satisfaction and customer satisfaction

Organizations that truly invest in their employees tend to reap the results of that investment through increased sales, more frequent and deeper relationships with customers and longer-term financial success. Many marketing and customer-service studies have validated the notion that when employees are satisfied about their working conditions, that satisfaction translates into better service to customers. Better service can lead to higher sales, greater customer retention, an increase in market share and sustained profitability.

Rise in the number of service- and knowledge-based industries, organizations and occupations

From the dawn of the industrial revolution through the 1960s, the majority of organizations produced a tangible product of some type. Since the 1960s, however, there have been significant increases in the service sector of the U.S. economy, while there has been a steady decline in traditional manufacturing environments. This shift has resulted in a changing workforce: one less defined by brawn and more defined by brains. Financial planning services, consulting, retail, travel agencies and hospitality are all examples of primarily service-based industries that have grown in the last half of the 20th century. With the rise in information technology (IT) capabilities, there has also been an increasing shift toward knowledge-based work. This is characterized by individuals who develop content and use information to add value to products, business processes or services. Knowledge-based workers leverage technology to perform routine and recurring tasks, thus allocating their time to developing customized solutions, solving problems, creating new products and making more informed decisions.

Technological and structural advances that change employee work and managerial control

In the mass production environments of yesteryear, it was common to have large open work areas where employees worked in close proximity to each other. Supervisory span of control could be larger, because supervisors could move with relative ease from employee to employee to provide close supervision. The expansion of knowledge-based work has changed the nature of employee work and managerial control. In the wired world, where employees may work at a distance or use technology to be self-directed and self-managed, supervisors increasingly take on the role of "coach" or "consultant" to their direct reports, many of whom may possess business or technical knowledge equivalent to or greater than that of the supervisor.

Changing nature of employer-employee relationships

The notion of lifetime employment with one organization is a thing of the past. As the "employment contract" has been rewritten, primarily to provide flexibility to corporations, the level of commitment displayed by employers and employees has diminished. Employers rarely make long-term employment guarantees to employees, and employees often define loyalty now in terms of staying with the company months or years versus decades. Talented employees have a world of choices when it comes to seeking prospective employment. They are socialized to accept that changes to their organizational affiliation are a necessary part of developing a successful career and may continuously seek other opportunities to meet personal or professional objectives.

Emerging Factors Contributing to Workforce Engagement:

- Employees bring their body, mind and feelings to work
- Worldwide competition and the emergence of global labor and consumer markets
- Scarcity of talent in several fields
- Rapid nature of change that affects organizations and individuals
- The realization that employee loyalty only goes so far.

Employees bring their body, mind and feelings to work

Beginning with the publication of Frederick Taylor's *The Principles of Scientific Management* and the subsequent implementation of techniques to improve efficiency and productivity, there was an emphasis on organizational outcomes, not necessarily employee satisfaction. Employees were assigned tasks with little regard for safety or satisfaction, were rarely consulted about working conditions and were expected to leave personal issues at the door.

A more modern perspective has emerged in the last generation, one that recognizes the complexity of people's lives and the impact of one's personal circumstance on job performance. Therefore, managers have come to recognize that employees do not automatically "shut off" their outside lives upon entering the organization's front door. Organizations have also come to value employees and their ideas as intellectual property, something the organization can use as a means of competitively differentiating easily substitutable products in a crowded marketplace.

Worldwide competition and the emergence of global labor and consumer markets

The U.S. economy shifted from manufacturing to one dominated by service and knowledge industries because of the ability for companies to produce goods in other parts of the world at a fraction of the cost. Many firms have continued to outsource not only production jobs, but also service and knowledge work, to these lower-cost labor environments, leaving workers in developed nations with the need to redefine their skills and professional identity. Additionally, more sophisticated shipping, transportation, telecommunications and technological infrastructure around the world have also led to an increased global demand for many products and services. Companies that did business in regional or domestic markets just a few years ago are now serving customers in every corner of the globe, often providing sales, technical support and service on a 24-hours-per-day, seven-day-a-week basis.

Scarcity of talent in several fields

Anticipated job growth will occur predominantly in service- and knowledge-based industries during the next 10 years, including education, health care, professional and business services, information technology, leisure and hospitality and financial services, to name a few. An aging population, combined with declining birthrates, will dramatically decrease the number of participants in the U.S. workforce. This will provide significant challenges to an organization's ability to recruit and retain quality employees. For some industries, the pursuit of substitutable labor will be found through exporting work to emerging markets around the globe, while some industries will seek to import foreign labor (often at lower wage rates than comparable U.S. talent) to meet business and consumer demands.

Rapid nature of change that affects organizations and individuals

In recent years, organizations and employees have experienced a significant number of changes impacting the nature of work performed, customers served, technologies used and products produced. These changes have been the result of mergers and acquisitions, new systems for improved business processes, cost-cutting measures, government regulations and increased competition, among others. Through staff reductions due to downsizing or automation, or both, organizations are redefining jobs so that the same amount of work is being done by fewer people. This has resulted in an unprecedented amount of change to the scope and complexity of work for individual employees. While presumably beneficial to the fiscal health of the organization, such changes are also potentially burdensome to employees, many of whom feel overwhelmed and undervalued by the organization.

The realization that employee loyalty only goes so far

Most people agree that, in general, employee loyalty is a good thing. After all, when employees are loyal, turnover decreases and relative organizational stability can be achieved. In some cases, however, marginal, difficult or improper-fit employees exhibit "loyalty" to their organization. These are employees the organization cannot or will not fire, or these are employees that, for one reason or another, cannot or will not leave the company. Although employee loyalty is good, it should not be viewed as the ultimate measure of workforce effectiveness. Instead, employees need to be engaged in meaningful work and that is also valued by the organization. Employee loyalty alone is insufficient in a competitive marketplace. Thus, there is the need for organizations to identify, implement, monitor, evaluate and improve specific practices that contribute to workforce engagement.

What are the Organizational Practices Contributing to Workforce Engagement?

Organizational Practices Contributing to Workforce Engagement:

- Strategic Issues—Effective senior leadership; reputation management; ethics, diversity and safety; and stakeholder input

- Core HR Processes—Workforce selection; organizational orientation; training and development; rewards and recognition; and work-life balance

- Operational Components—Performance management; tools and technology; opportunities for advancement; and daily satisfaction.

Workforce engagement encompasses organizational practices that permeate all levels of the organization, from senior leaders to individual-contributor employees. Thirteen components of workforce engagement have been identified and are grouped under three broad umbrellas: strategic issues, core HR processes and operational components.

Strategic Issues

Strategic issues are top-level, organizationwide approaches that support workforce engagement. These include: effective senior leadership; reputation management; ethics, diversity and safety and stakeholder input.

Effective senior leadership is defined as the ability of organizational leaders to articulate a meaningful strategy; recognize the relationship between workforce engagement and organizational success; model effective leadership behaviors; and create a high-performance culture.

Reputation management is defined as the ability of organizational leaders to shape and manage the organization's reputation internally and externally; identify and describe strengths of the organization's products, services and solutions; and exercise positive corporate social responsibility.

Ethics, diversity and safety is defined as the ability of organizational leaders to create a culture of ethical conduct and decision-making; comply with laws and policies; respect and manage diversity; and ensure a safe work environment.

Stakeholder input is defined as the ability of organizational leaders to seek regular feedback from customers, business partners and others; benchmark with other organizations on effective practices; measure employee perceptions; and improve work and other organizational experiences.

Core HR Processes

Core HR processes are activities that help acquire, orient, develop and reward an engaged workforce. These include: workforce selection; organizational orientation; training and development; rewards and recognition; and work-life balance.

Workforce selection is defined as the ability of HR professionals to assist the organization by designing meaningful job and work experiences; outlining hiring criteria and competencies; developing effective recruitment methods; and implementing appropriate selection processes.

Organizational orientation is defined as the ability of HR professionals to assist the organization by developing processes for effective employee integration; educating employees about organizational values and business practices; and developing relevant orientation, mentoring and coaching programs.

Training and development is defined as the ability of HR professionals to assist the organization by assessing needs and establishing priorities for training; designing appropriate performance-improvement approaches; and implementing and evaluating training and development activities.

Rewards and recognition is defined as the ability of HR professionals to assist the organization by rewarding performance through a variety of approaches; recognizing employee contributions to organizational achievements; ensuring fair treatment in reward practices; and developing strategies for employee involvement.

Work-life balance is defined as the ability of HR professionals to assist the organization by creating approaches for employees to balance personal, work and community responsibilities; developing flexible approaches to work, as feasible; and managing stress, promoting wellness and avoiding employee burnout.

Operational Components

Operational components are the managerial and supervisory responsibilities necessary for workforce engagement. These include: performance Management; tools and technology; opportunities for advancement and daily satisfaction.

Performance Management is defined as the ability of managers and supervisors to identify relevant dimensions of employee performance; set challenging and meaningful expectations; monitor and evaluate performance; and provide regular and constructive feedback to employees.

Tools and technology is defined as the ability of managers and supervisors to allocate resources necessary for employee work; provide tools and techniques for job performance; ensure ergonomically correct work environments; and appropriately structure workflow, interactions and processes.

Opportunities for advancement is defined as the ability of managers and supervisors to promote from within or provide lateral mobility to employees; identify, develop and, in some cases, release marginal, difficult or improper-fit employees; and effectively handle downsizing, outsourcing or discontinuation of work.

Daily satisfaction is defined as the ability of managers and supervisors to recognize what motivates employees to come to work each day; ensure working relationships are positive; allow for autonomy and discretion in job performance; show respect to employees; and maintain a high-performance, enjoyable workplace.

What are the Employee Perspectives Contributing to Workforce Engagement?

Employee Perspectives Contributing to Workforce Engagement:

- Priorities
- Attitudes
- Behaviors
- Intentions.

Organizational practices represent one side of the workforce engagement scale, while employee perspectives form the other side. Indeed, individual employees each hold specific priorities, attitudes, behaviors and intentions about their work. These perspectives help influence the extent to which employees will be retained by and engaged in the organization, or if they will seek to leave.

Employee *priorities* are defined as the degree to which an individual seeks participation in the workforce; values participation in the workforce; and views work as one of his or her primary activities. Priorities are informed, in part, by personal, circumstantial and environmental considerations. For example, a new mother may seek to remain at home with her child rather than return to work, thus redefining her priorities related to work. Intrinsic motivation, or the personal enjoyment or fulfillment one receives from performing a job, also informs an employee's workplace priority. Additionally, extrinsic pressures, for example debt and other financial issues, may compel participation in the workforce.

Employee *attitudes* are defined as the extent to which an individual feels positively or negatively about the organization, his or her job and workplace relationships; enjoys or dislikes coming to work on a daily basis; and views organizational practices as being relatively consistent with his or her personal values, beliefs and expectations. These attitudes are informed, in part, by specific organizational policies, business processes and people with whom an individual must interact. Individual perceptions about the organization's treatment of its employees, compared to the perceptions of how other organizations treat their employees, also impact employee attitudes. Finally, the nature of work performed by the individual can contribute to a positive or negative attitude.

Employee *behaviors* are defined as the specific ways in which an individual performs work consistent with job requirements, organizational needs and industry standards; seeks to work effectively with various stakeholders (for example, co-workers, supervisors, customers, suppliers and business partners); and adheres to expectations, policies and practices of the organization. Behaviors are informed, in part, by a sound fit between the individual and his or her organization, job and responsibilities; explicitly defined expectations for performance processes and outcomes; ongoing, constructive feedback; and access to appropriate training and development opportunities.

Finally, employee *intentions* are defined as the likelihood that an individual remains with or departs from the organization in the foreseeable future; seeks advancement opportunities either within the organization or from elsewhere; and continues exhibiting behaviors necessary for effective job performance. Such intentions are informed, in part, by the priorities an individual holds about work in general and the job and organization in particular; the attitudes an individual holds toward the organization, the job and his or her workplace relationships; and the behaviors an individual exhibits through his or her performance.

Two National Benchmark Studies on Workforce Engagement
The 2004-2005 National Benchmark Study on Workforce Engagement

pan is in the business of improving the recruitment, selection and retention processes of private, not-for-profit and government organizations. Through the use of online tools including continuous talent-management systems, pre-employment tests and assessments and workforce surveys, *pan* helps businesses improve customer loyalty and retention by concentrating on the *human resources* of an organization.

Basic explanation/background of the model of workforce engagement

Much of the thought behind the workforce engagement assessment is based on a background of customer satisfaction and loyalty. In regard to customer feedback, there were generally positive customer perceptions related to the product or service quality, value for the money, marketing/advertising, delivery, ordering, depth and breadth of product line, repair services, reputation of the company, etc. In the areas of customer care, technical support and account management, customers seemed to have the most negative reaction to their supplier. In doing follow-up focus groups with employees, much of the problems customers were having were a result of faulty hiring and selection processes, inferior training or substandard human resources practices. Moving from an employee survey tool built out of Deming principles and TQM, to measuring employee satisfaction, the foundation used for developing the workforce engagement assessment is based on strong theoretical and research science and decades of HR experience dealing with these issues daily.

Meyer and Allen, in their book *Commitment in the Workplace*, put forth three types of employee commitment: *normative commitment,* where employees feel obligated to stay; *continuance commitment,* when employees feel trapped and feel they have to stay; and *affective commitment*, when employees stay because they want to. It is this affective commitment, or the feeling of personal and psychological attachment to an organization, that creates the employee attitudes necessary for workforce engagement. However, attitudes, by themselves, are not enough. Employees also need to behave in ways that benefit the organization. Employee behaviors and actions necessary for business success include:

- Recommending the organization as a good place to work
- Staying with the company for the next two years
- Doubting negative information heard about the company in the press
- Being highly motivated to work hard
- Going the extra mile for customers
- Working hard as a team member

- Participating in training and development opportunities
- Advocating for the company even after employment ends.

It is the combination of behaviors and attitudes that help create workforce engagement, and when employees are engaged, they are much more likely to behave in ways the benefit customer loyalty, retention and business success. The components of workforce engagement needed to encompass the entire employee life cycle.

To inform the workforce engagement assessment, research was conducted on best practices being used by a host of HR practitioners like Hay Group, Watson Wyatt, Walker Information, Gallup and Hewitt. In addition, leading industry associations and organizations such as the Society for Human Resource Management, HR.com, WorldatWork, the American Society for Training and Development and the American Management Association provided insight through national and international studies conducted with companies worldwide. Also, decades of experience with hundreds of HR consultants and clients and hundreds of thousands of employees worldwide provided a unique perspective to the building of the workforce engagement assessment by experts at *pan*.

An initial list of 500 workforce engagement items was compiled in an effort to explain the various work factors that impact employee engagement. Once the list was compiled, similar or like items were eliminated or incorporated into other attributes. The remaining 200 attributes were grouped again into like items, and natural separations into various employee/employer "touch points" were created. An additional item reduction was completed, and a 150-question Workforce Engagement Assessment was finalized for initial field testing. Companies nationwide were invited to participate as beta test sites, and decisions on which organizations would be included in the validation studies were made to ensure a representative sample for the validation study.

Four research projects were conducted to validate and ultimately improve the causal model built into the workforce engagement assessment. A high-tech manufacturing company headquartered in Ohio was used as the initial beta test site and was chosen due to the unique history of the company, employees located in the United States and Canada and a diversity of white- and blue-collar jobs. A 50-percent sampling of its 5,000 employees was included in the initial research effort, and a response rate of 85 percent was accomplished through an Internet-based data-collection methodology.

Statistical analysis was conducted to determine the linkage between the 13 workforce components (workforce selection, organizational orientation, training and development, etc.) and the engagement level of the employees. In addition, each of

the individual questions was subjected to factor analysis as part of the initial validation and modeling process. Although no individual attributes were deleted, those that
showed no correlation to the overall component question, or to workforce engagement, were noted for later review. In addition, questions were moved and substituted
in an attempt to improve the overall model fit.

A medical services company of 600 employees was used as the second beta site and
was selected because of its diverse workforce, large geographic dispersion of offices
and leadership position in its industry. The same survey used with the initial beta
client was used in this second beta application. A 95-percent response rate was achieved
using an Internet-based methodology. The same statistical analysis was used on this
second set of test data, and after a review of the first and second data set, a number
of individual attributes were deleted, moved and substituted in an attempt to improve
the overall workforce engagement model fit.

These changes were incorporated into the third test, a national benchmark of 2,600
employees across industries conducted by *pan* in late 2004. A reduced 100-item set
questionnaire was used, comprised of 13 workforce engagement components and those
specific questions that provided the strongest linkage to worker engagement determined in the initial analysis of the data. Partnering with Greenfield Online, one of the
largest online panel companies in the world, *pan* used its consumer-based panel of 3.1
million members to select an appropriate sample for the national benchmark.

Certain over-quotas were achieved during the survey phase, including federal
and state/local government workers and employees in Indiana (the state in which
pan is headquartered). Final assessment results were weighted by gender, industry
and geography to most closely match the demographics of the national workforce
(according to the Bureau of Labor Statistics, August 2004). To qualify to participate in this nationally representative benchmark study, panelists were required to
be 18 years of age or older and work part or full time in an organization with at
least 50 employees. Research has shown that companies with less than 50
employees tend to have very different group dynamics than those in larger organizations. More than 20 demographic questions were asked in this national
benchmark study including the following:

- Tenure in the job
- Tenure with the company
- Age
- Gender
- Given a pre-employment test or assessment
- Position in the company

- Division
- Department
- Participated in company-sponsored social event
- Industry
- Geography (state/census region)
- Size of company
- Households with children
- Households taking care of loved ones other than a child
- Commute of more than 50 miles to work
- Travel internationally for work
- Number of promotions in the last three years
- Participated in company-sponsored training or education
- Ethnic background
- Education
- Union representation.

Additional statistical analysis was conducted on the national benchmark data to validate the initial two projects and test the new revised workforce engagement survey. As expected, this new survey provided the benefit of a shortened questionnaire that could be completed in just 20 minutes and a more reliable model of workforce engagement, which provided more assurance for *pan*'s clients that improving the issues addressed in the survey would improve the engagement of their employees and subsequently their behaviors and actions.

Finally, a fourth company, a professional services firm of 400 employees, administered the workforce engagement assessment, achieving a response rate of nearly 80 percent. The same survey used in the *pan* national benchmark was used for this organization, and analysis corresponded with earlier projects.

The Levels of Workforce Engagement

As noted, workforce engagement is a combination of the attitudes of employees and their likelihood to exhibit the kinds of behaviors that make companies successful, specifically their likelihood to stay, go the extra mile for customers and recommend the organization as a great place to work. To better understand the dynamics of engagement inside an organization, *pan* divides employees into three engagement groups: fully engaged, reluctant and unengaged employees.

Fully engaged employees have a strong personal or psychological attachment to their organization and will act in ways that benefit their customers and their organization. These employees are the most likely to "stay longer, work harder and recommend the organization as a good place to work." They are the stars that will not only meet customer requirements, but will exceed them on a consistent basis. However, do not assume that employee tenure necessarily equates to engagement. Numerous research studies have shown that just because employees stay with a company, it does not necessarily mean they are behaving in ways that continue to help the company be successful.

In the *pan* 2004-2005 national benchmark study, less than half of all employees were fully engaged (46 percent). Financial services and retail had the lowest levels of engagement (43 percent), while education services had the highest level, topping out at 50 percent. The age of the employee also shows differences by engagement, with those aged 18-24 and 55 and older most engaged (51 percent) and those aged 25-34 being least engaged (43 percent). The size of company also seems to matter, with employees working in companies with less than 1,000 people being significantly more engaged than employees who work in companies with more than 1,000 people.

Reluctant employees may act in ways that benefit their company. Some employees may have other priorities that impact their ability to fully commit to their organization, such as new moms who want to stay home with their children, spouses who are leaving town and taking their spouse (the employee) with them or a team member who just wants to change careers. These kinds of situations normally account for a small percentage of reluctant team members.

Far more serious are those reluctant workers who do not have a strong commitment to the organization and therefore are much less likely to go the extra mile for customers. These are the employees who are reluctant to leave and to work hard. They may be scared to find other employment because they feel as if they do not have the skills necessary to find another job or other jobs may not be available. Most worrisome are those employees trapped with "golden handcuffs" that keep them retained because *they have to be*, not because they *want to be*. Although a company will retain these employees either way, this "subtle difference" makes all the difference in the world to clients and the level of support they receive from employees.

In the *pan* 2004-2005 national benchmark study, nearly one quarter of all employees were reluctant (23 percent). Not surprisingly, federal government had the highest levels of employees feeling trapped (28 percent). Interestingly, the federal government has employee tenure 2.5 times the average nongovernment employee, showing that the federal government has a *retention* strategy, not one based on commitment or engagement.

Senior executives feel significantly less reluctant than other positions in the company (17 percent for senior executives versus 24 percent for middle management, supervisors and individual contributors), while employees in MIS/IT feel the most trapped in their job (30 percent).

Unengaged employees may be the least desirable of all the workforce engagement groups. These employees do not have a positive relationship with their company and have sent their résumé out to competitors. In some cases, they may try to harm existing relationships with customers or suppliers, or may try to steal company secrets. Even if they have "one foot out the door," one foot still resides in the company, making the management of this portion of the workforce vital, as well.

In the *pan* 2004-2005 study, nearly one-third of all employees were unengaged (31 percent). Financial services had the highest level of feeling unengaged (37 percent), while the federal government had the lowest levels of employees feeling unengaged (22 percent). Employees who received work-related training and development were significantly less unengaged than those employees who had not received training (25 percent versus 39 percent), while union employees were significantly more unengaged than nonunion employees (36 percent versus 29 percent).

The 2006-07 National Benchmark Study on Workforce Engagement

Using similar methodology employed in 2004-2005, an administration of the National Benchmark Study on Workforce Engagement was again conducted for 2006-2007. With more than 1,800 employees representing public, private and not-for-profit organizations, the 2006-2007 benchmark results paint a darker picture for today's employers than the study conducted two years ago:

2004-2005: 46 percent fully engaged, 23 percent reluctant, 31 percent unengaged

2006-2007: 40 percent fully engaged, 24 percent reluctant, 36 percent unengaged.

In 2006-2007, only 40 percent of all employees are fully engaged with their organization, a significant decrease in engagement from 2004-2005's level of 46 percent. This two-year drop in engagement comes at a time when national unemployment rates have been falling and the competition for talent has again been heating up. This drop in workforce engagement was witnessed in every industry, from state and federal government to health services, from retail trade to manufacturing. No industry was immune. The Mid-Atlantic region (New York, New Jersey and Pennsylvania) showed an improvement in workforce engagement; however, the Mid-Atlantic region was ranked as the worst census region in 2004-2005, so perhaps some improvement was inevitable. The East South-Central region (Alabama, Kentucky, Tennessee and Mississippi), on the other hand, had the strongest engagement level in 2004-2005 and showed even stronger performance in 2006-2007.

Engagement dropped among men and women, across the various levels of company and job tenure, all age groups (except in 35- to 44-year-olds where engagement remained the same as in 2004-2005), across companies from 100-2,500 employees in size, across all levels of employee education and with senior executives, middle managers and individual contributors. Whether union or nonunion or those working full or part time, the drop in engagement and the corresponding increase in the levels of the workforce feeling unengaged cut across the national landscape.

With nearly as many employees pushing against their company as pulling for them and one in four feeling reluctant to leave and reluctant to work hard, the 2006-2007 national benchmark not only puts employee engagement and retention more at risk, it puts customer satisfaction, repeat purchase and the company's financial health at risk as well.

There were few, but interesting, differences in the drivers of workforce engagement compared to the 2004-2005 benchmark study results. First and foremost, there were no changes in the "primary drivers" of workforce engagement in the 2006-2007 study:

1. Daily satisfaction
2. Ethics, diversity and safety
3. Reputation management.

    However, there were changes to the "secondary drivers":

4. Stakeholder input (new in 2006-07)
5. Effective senior leadership (moved down one position from 2004-2005)
6. Training and development (new in 2006-07)
7. Organizational orientation.

Work-life balance, which was the weakest secondary driver of workforce engagement in 2004-2005, was not a driver of engagement in the 2006-2007 study, nor was *tools and technology.* In terms of the items most impacting the top three drivers of engagement (daily satisfaction; ethics, diversity and safety; and reputation management), there were few if any noticeable differences in what issues were most critical to the employees.

For more information about the 2006-07 national benchmark results, please go to www.employeeholdem.com.

Summary

This chapter has introduced workforce engagement as a complex topic, one that involves an understanding of many things, including historical influences on work, organizational practices and employee perspectives. It is also important to note that even if organizational leaders created, implemented and nurtured an engaging workplace, employees may still not be fully engaged in their jobs. As the previous section outlined, individuals have their own priorities and intentions about work, in general, and their own attitudes and behaviors about their job and organization, in particular.

Because it is impossible to fully know what motivates and infuriates employees, workforce engagement is an art and a science and requires continuous commitment and attention of everyone in the organization. Thus, organizational leaders, HR professionals, managers and supervisors and individual employees each play a role in creating the conditions under which an engaged workforce can emerge.

As the case study that follows highlights, many individuals have differing experiences and expectations about the employer-employee relationship and how that relationship enhances or impedes their level of engagement. The case illustrates that employees of the same organization often have vastly different perceptions about, experiences with and expectations of their employer. These differences are further exacerbated during times of organizational change and evolution, making some of the principles discussed earlier in this chapter a necessary and challenging proposition for organizational leaders.

The Dynamics
of Workforce Engagement
'Thinking About Tomorrow'

Introduction: Apprehension About Change

There was a constant drizzle, so the four people stood under the large canopy covering the entrance to the downtown Stylish Suites Hotel where they had been told they would be picked up by the shuttle van. None of them knew who else was going, or even how many people would make the trip, and it would be somewhat awkward to say hello if they were not, in fact, co-workers at the bank. They stood in silence, not looking at one another, for at least 10 minutes until a shuttle van pulled up with a sign saying "Federated Commercial Bank." As all four moved toward the van, they began to smile as they realized they all worked for the same bank and were going to the same destination.

After exchanging names and describing their jobs at the bank, they settled in for what was expected to be a three-hour trip. The trip was significant for all of them because they were going to be meeting their counterparts at Apex National Bank, which acquired Federated. During the merger transition that would take almost a year, groups of four to six Federated staff members were traveling to Apex Center for a day of meetings almost every day of the week. The selection of people to go on a particular day was random, based on the schedule of their counterparts as well as workload and deadlines at Federated. Most people voiced apprehension about the meetings and some speculated that the selection process was intentional, not random, and rumors abounded about the significance of the visits and the selection of participants.

For all those working at Federated, this was a period of transition, and there was a pervasive sense that change was imminent. Some people welcomed the idea of change, but many were unsettled, even threatened, by what might be new routines, different job descriptions, new supervisors and even separation from the company.

The merger and consolidation of the banks that constituted these two "mega banks" was dizzying. The Federated banking system was only 7 years old and was the result of three existing banks that operated eight branches. Apex traced its roots to the Constitution National Bank (CNB), one of the first commercial banks in the United States, founded in 1802. Beginning in the 1960s, CNB acquired several regional banks, then merged with the Mercantile Bank of Boston. It became the seventh largest bank in the country 1987 when it became Apex National Bank. With the recent the acquisition of Federated, Apex was the United States' fourth-largest bank.

The rapid expansion of Apex led to financial success, and the future appeared bright. Business success, however, came at a price. Attempts to integrate business systems to eliminate redundancy often failed or were more costly than estimated. Personnel policies at once independent banks were brought into conformity, sometimes at the expense of employee morale. And, although corporate revenue and profits increased, the overlap of branches across the country resulted in the elimination of almost 12,000 jobs, 10 percent of the total workforce.

The four Federated employees on the shuttle van were aware of these issues and were especially concerned about the overlap of branches between Federated and Apex. Almost a quarter of Federated branches were within a five-mile radius of existing Apex branches. And, equally significant, the two corporate offices were less than 200 miles from each other, and it was widely assumed that, over time, all corporate operations would move to the Apex Center.

As they sat in the van, the four people began to talk to one another about their jobs, their priorities and their futures as they faced the changes that would inevitably come as a result of the merger.

The Federated Employees on the Shuttle Van

The four passengers were diverse both in terms of personal characteristics and job descriptions. Here is a summary of those people.

Eduardo Del Santos. A 46-year-old Cuban American, Del Santos worked for Federated for six years and previously worked for 12 years at another bank that was then acquired by Federated. He was successful at the bank and received several promotions. He is associate director of auditing for Federated's mortgage division. As the merger approached six months earlier, he was told by his supervisor that Apex was going to offer him a similar position, but with greater responsibilities in its corporate offices. He would probably need to relocate, but he was offered an excellent professional opportunity.

The idea of relocating was daunting. He and his family had strong roots in the community: his children were active in their schools and church; his wife had a part-time job she loved; and he just finished his 10th year as coach of a little league team. Neither moving nor commuting for four to five hours a day was appealing to him.

Roberta Block-Henderson. With an MBA in marketing, Block-Henderson came to Federated 11 years earlier to head the marketing division of its credit-card division. Her division always met its sales goals but, over time, the bank became more interested in its commercial operations, and the credit-card division's budgets remained relatively static. Block-Henderson thought her high energy level was one of her greatest assets, and she felt somewhat underutilized. The idea of the merger had some appeal to her because there might be greater professional opportunities at Apex.

At the same time, Block-Henderson was at a potential career juncture. The mother of two children, 6 and 3, she enjoyed the prospect of spending more time with them, and she estimated that she might be able to meet her financial needs by freelance consulting, freeing up more of her time.

Paul Hunt. Hunt was a retired police lieutenant who attended law school at night. Federated hired him five years prior to head the office of investigations that was responsible for locating depositors whose accounts had become dormant, or to locate relatives of depositors who died intestate (without a will). Two years after he was hired, Federated decided to outsource those functions, and Hunt was transferred to the refinance division, reviewing mortgage contracts.

During the next several years, Hunt's job performance was adequate, but just barely so. His lackluster job performance was accompanied by a lack of vitality and interest in his work. He was asked several times if he wanted to transfer to another position in the bank, but he said that he had "the perfect job" in the bank when he started and he would never find another one that good. Hunt was not asked if he thought the work of his office should be outsourced and he felt that his expertise had been ignored.

Carol Carlyle. As director of information systems, Carlyle supervised a large staff and was frequently consulted by senior management about a wide range of policy and operational issues. Her first job in the banking industry was at a small regional bank. After four years, the bank was bought by a larger bank seeking to expand its operations in that area. Six years later, the bank merged with Federated. Now, after 15 years, she was going to be working for her fourth employer without changing jobs. Carlyle managed her staff well and maintained state-of-the art operations, even in a rapidly changing field.

Despite receiving excellent performance reviews, better-than-average salary increases and generous budget allocations, she gradually became disaffected with the bank. After the first merger, she was asked by the senior vice president if she would be interested in taking over as director of the bank's ATM operations, a job that would broaden her responsibilities beyond her technology expertise. Nothing materialized, and the vice president became increasingly vague about why nothing happened. Eventually, of course, the bank merged with Federated, and that possibility "fizzled." At Federated, there was an associate vice president for technology and information systems, and although she supervised nearly twice as many people as she had before, she reported to an *associate* vice president rather than to *the* senior vice president.

Carlyle was also frustrated by the glacial pace of change at Federated. As a single parent, she wanted to leave by 4 p.m. several days a week. Policies about flex time were vague, and she had gone to her supervisor and to the director of HR on several occasions to request a policy change, or at the very least, approval of her request as an exception. It seemed as if delay was the norm, and nothing happened. A year ago, the director of HR told her consultants were being brought in to develop a "master plan" for HR. Nothing happened, and now that the merger with Apex occurred, nothing probably would in the foreseeable future.

Thinking About Tomorrow: Reflections from the Shuttle Van Passengers

As they rode together, they felt more comfortable with one another and began a dialogue about their jobs and their future at Apex, if there was one. It was easy to be candid in that setting because none of them worked in any proximity to the others, and all of them spoke honestly and without "holding back" their opinions and feelings.

Carlyle spoke first.

"To be perfectly honest, at this point in my career, I don't care if I work for Federated or Apex. These big conglomerates are basically the same. They make promises and forget them. They ask for your priorities and then move on to asking someone else without even considering what you have said. I really believe that some executives think that talking about doing something is the same as doing it."

She shared some of the experiences that brought her to that conclusion and then said, sadly but without anger, that she wished her bosses understood that "it was easier to accept being disappointed than it was to experience being ignored."

Hunt said, "I agree. I worked my tail off to get that J.D. degree and I always thought my motivation and commitment were big selling points. But I have become a minimalist." "What do you mean when you say 'minimalist'?" someone asked. "They provide me with minimum information about their plans for me and I give them a minimum amount of my effort and energy," he responded.

Block-Henderson spoke next.

"Let me tell you something. I think I have been successful here at Federated and I certainly can't complain about the increases I have received. But this feels like some kind of dating relationship where things are terrific for a while and then the guy says, 'You're wonderful, but I have decided that you aren't that special, but let's stay friends.' At some point I stopped being special, but no one ever told me what had changed. Now, I am treated well, but the 'magic' isn't there."

When Hunt said that Block-Henderson was describing his weekly conversations with his daughter in graduate school, everyone laughed, but it was evident that she had struck a responsive chord as everyone seemed to recall similar experiences they had had in their professional lives.

Hunt continued, "From my point of view, both of you women have gotten a fair shake. The bank may not be sending you flowers every month, but you've got decent jobs. But this bank doesn't give a damn about me, and nobody would even blink if I quit. They made big changes, took away a great job, shoved me somewhere where I don't belong or want to be and then—can you believe it—they want me to be grateful!"

Del Santos looked pensive and after a long pause, he said, "From what you say, I think it was a bad break for you that events happened as they did, but trust me on this, some companies would let you know your job was eliminated by having a different person sitting in your office some Monday morning. I worked for a bank for 12 years and when they announced the merger with Federated, they also gave every single employee 30-days' notice because they thought it would be 'fairer' to not encumber Federated with the employees of the old bank. I got two-and-a-half days' severance for every year I worked there."

No one spoke for a few minutes until Del Santos broke the ice by saying, "Hey, it's all right. I landed on my feet and ever since then, I have learned not to expect too much. Years ago, your boss had a name and a face, but now 'corporate' isn't a person, it's a mechanism."

Hunt said, "I have one more thing to say and then I'll shut up for the rest of the ride. Everybody gives the public sector a bum rap and people say it's 'bloated' and 'ineffi-cient', and maybe it is. But, you know what's going on, what to expect and what kind of job security you have. I came to work every day for 25 years and worked hard because I knew I was protected, not by a supervisor who liked me, but by the system."

Carlyle looked around at the other passengers and said, "Look, we have another few hours on this van, so I think we should make some lemonade. We know that there are big changes coming to the bank, some good and some probably not so good. In all probability, some of us will be unemployed within a year. So, let's not talk about bad things that have happened. Let's think about tomorrow and how each of us can be prepared for whatever comes."

The Unanswered Questions: What Can We Expect and What Do They Expect?

As the shuttle van moved them closer to their destination, each of them appeared lost in thought. Carlyle, who seemed to have become the de facto leader of the group, said, "I guess I'm the one with the most experience in these mergers and changeovers. It also makes me the most resilient because I've seen it all before. And, I think there is something important I can share with you.

"What really matters is not those wonderful words everyone throws around: dedication, commitment, responsibility and loyalty. What matters is whether people believe they are being told the truth. For better or worse, people want clarity and candor. Look, how many times have you read about some big company assuring its workers that everything is 'OK' on a Monday and then filing for bankruptcy protection on Thursday? What makes me feel loyal is honesty."

Del Santos nodded vigorously as he spoke. "You know, that's what I have been feeling ever since the news of this merger was announced. I was offered a job last year with Commonwealth Banks, and it was a good job, really good, but I would have had to move and relocate my family. I talked to Ed Benthurst (one of Federated's senior vice presidents), and he told me to stay with Federated because I had a secure job and would never have to move. When the merger with Apex was announced I asked Ed if he knew about it, and he said he did but couldn't break confidentiality by telling me. And now, I may have to move anyway and I gave up a really good deal."

"So," Carlyle said, "now you don't feel that you have to honest with them because of what happened." "Exactly," he said, as the others shook their heads in agreement. Block-Henderson, who had been relatively quiet, said, "It's really a simple proposition, kind of like 'do unto others.' They want us to put all of our energy into work, to make it a priority, but they hold back information and don't think we have a need to know the big picture. Frankly, I think somebody already knows what is going to happen to each of us, and we are just going through this little melodrama before we get the news."

"What I don't understand," Case said, "is why this is such a big deal to everyone. To me, it's all about expectations: they tell me what they want and they pay me for doing it. I want a paycheck, a job that I'm able to do, the security of knowing that if I do a good job, I have a job, and the potential to get recognition and advancement if I want to. End of story."

Carlyle, who had the most experience as a supervisor, felt it was important for everyone in the van to have a positive attitude as they went through the series of meetings at Apex. She decided that she had to help put things in perspective. "None of us knows what will happen as this merger goes forward. Some of us may end up working for Apex, and some of us may move on to other jobs. The important thing to remember is that there are implicit and explicit expectations and values between employers and employees. Everyone benefits when those expectations and values are clearly understood. As employees, we have expectations and obligations and so do our employers. Let's not think about what's been wrong or will be wrong; let's think about tomorrow and how greater clarity can be achieved by employers and employees."

As the van continued moving toward the Apex headquarters, the passengers sat quietly, considering all that had been said, each of them contemplating an uncertain future. Carlyle thought about what she said and wondered if she had been helpful to the others. All she could be certain of was that the relationship between employer and employee was something everyone worried about and that there were few "right" answers.

Conclusion: What Do We *Really* Want and What Do They *Think* We Want?

Block-Henderson felt that among the four she was the one who had given the most serious thought to leaving, and she felt that she had to say something about what her mother had always called the advantage of having "a bird in the bag." She said, "Well, it sounds as if none of us is exactly thrilled with what is happening and how our jobs are likely to change. But what's the alternative? If we go to work for another company, the same thing could happen in a few years. I've thought about trying to make a go of it on my own, as a consultant, but that's risky, and the older I get, the less I feel like taking risks."

They were nearly at the Apex headquarters, and their time together was coming to an end. Del Santos said, "Let me have the final word. It all boils down to this: The real problem is that what employees want and employers want are constantly changing. Let's be honest here. Circumstances change, priorities change and what we want today may not be what we want next year. Our bosses are the same: they *think* they know what we want, but what they *really* know is what the 'experts' have told them and often that is not what the majority of the workforce wants, needs and hopes for. What I'm saying is that there's no conspiracy to deliberately ignore what employees want in order to feel truly engaged in their work. It's damn complicated and, you know what, there are no easy answers."

Questions for Consideration and Discussion
'Thinking About Tomorrow'

1. What do these four people have in common in regard to their employment at Federated? Are there common elements in their experiences at Federated that help explain their dissatisfaction?

2. Can you identify the specific reasons why each of these employees has become dissatisfied? What short- and long-term strategies do you think could be effective for each of them?

3. If each of these individuals becomes an employee of Apex, what issues do you think should be addressed for each of them to increase the likelihood that they will be engaged in their new jobs?

4. At the end of the case, Del Santos says that there are "no easy answers." What do you think are the three or four strategies and ideas that are most likely to help employers and employees understand the complicated issues related to employee engagement?

PART II

Strategic Issues in Workforce Engagement

Effective Senior Leadership

Reputation Management

Ethics, Diversity and Safety

Stakeholder Input

Chapter 2:
Effective Senior Leadership

Introduction: What Do We Mean By 'Effective Senior Leadership'?

Effective senior leadership is the ability of organizational leaders to articulate a meaningful strategy; recognize the relationship between workforce engagement and organizational success; model effective leadership behaviors; and create a high-performance culture. The effective senior leadership component of workforce engagement reflects the extent to which employees perceive their senior leaders have a vision for the company and understand the value of the employee. Perceptions of effective senior leadership are influenced by the way employees are valued and rewarded, how well they know and understand the strategic direction of the organization and if senior leaders have high personal integrity.

Highlights From the 2004-2005 National Benchmark Study on Workforce Engagement

Study after study has shown the importance of strong leadership (or the lack thereof) in an organization. Market share, share of wallet, perceptions of ethical fitness, stock price and profitability are known to be impacted by the quality of senior leadership. More often than not we hear about these linkages as companies are spiraling out of control.

In many cases, senior executives are purposely the public face of the company. Whether it is Jack Welch, Kenneth Lay, Phil Knight or Martha Stewart, much of a company's reputation, both good and bad, is built around its senior leaders. And the survey results from the 2004-2005 *pan* study may help explain why nearly two employees voluntarily leave their job every second of every business day.

According to the *pan* study, slightly more than half of all employees agreed their senior leadership was effective, about a quarter were neutral and a quarter disagreed. Given the importance senior leadership has on workforce engagement, it is not at all surprising that when employees were fully engaged, nearly eight in 10 of them agreed about the effectiveness of senior leadership, while for those employees who were unengaged, only one in six agreed.

Perceptions of senior leadership effectiveness decrease as the tenure of the employee increases, a worrisome finding in the **pan** research. Two out of three employees who have been with their organization for less than a year feel positively about the effectiveness of senior leadership, while fewer than one in two employees with their employer for more than 10 years feels the same way. Perhaps due to the historical relationship between business and unions, union employees are significantly more negative in their perceptions of senior leadership than nonunion employees.

One of the reasons why senior leadership effectiveness is suspect may be because only half of the employees in the **pan** study agree that senior leadership has a clear vision for the future and are satisfied with the strategic direction of the company. Again, the longer employees stay with their company, the more negative their impression becomes. The department in which the employee works can also impact these perceptions; employees in finance are significantly more positive in their perceptions than employees in operations and MIS/IT regarding their satisfaction with the strategic direction of the organization.

Only four in 10 employees feel that senior leadership treats them like their most important asset and sadly, the same number disagree. Government employees tend to be most negative in their assessment, with a higher percentage of federal and state/local employees disagreeing with the statement than agreeing to it. One of the most interesting findings from the **pan** Workforce Engagement Benchmark was the differences in the data based on whether or not the employee had participated in a company-sponsored social event in the past year. Nearly twice as many employees who participated in a company-sponsored social event felt they were treated like the company's most important asset versus those that had not participated (47 percent versus 27 percent). This clearly provides an inexpensive way for companies to build the engagement of their employees.

Of all of the benchmark survey data related to senior leadership, perhaps the most disturbing is the fact only half the employees agree that their senior leaders are people of high personal integrity. As we will talk about in more detail later, ethics is a "top down," not a "bottom up," process. Day-to-day employees who have to deal with the majority of ethical dilemmas will look to senior leadership as a role model of ethical behavior. If employees believe their management would "do the right thing, the ethical thing," they will follow suit. Otherwise, they will cut ethical corners to increase profit. In addition, the way employees feel about the ethical fitness of their senior leaders is the strongest driver of the effective senior leadership component, yet another reason that leaders must "walk the talk."

Union employees are significantly less likely than nonunion employees to feel good about the personal integrity of senior leaders (37 percent versus 53 percent), while senior management rates their performance significantly more positively than do the individual contributors (78 percent versus 45 percent). The youngest employees seem to have the most favorable opinion of senior leadership ethical fitness, with two in three feeling positive and one in six feeling negative. However, agreement falls to the 50-percent level once an employee reaches 25 years of age or older, a continuation of a telling trend in the data. Thus, whether it is WorldCom, Adelphia, IMClone, Quest, Xerox, Enron, Arthur Anderson, Global Crossing or any other scandal-plagued company, ethical problems start and stop in the corporate boardroom with senior leaders.

Highlights From the 2006-2007 National Benchmark Study on Workforce Engagement

Although slipping one slot in its impact on workforce engagement, effective senior leadership still plays an important part in the likelihood for employees to act in ways which benefit their organization. Yet again, fewer employees are satisfied with the effectiveness of their company's senior leadership than in 2004-2005, slipping from 53 percent to 50 percent in 2006-2007.

Showing a continuing decline that started in 1997, less than half of all employees agree *senior leaders are people of high personal integrity*, while one in five disagrees. As the ethical fitness of senior leaders is the strongest driver of this workforce component, another weakening in the perception of employees does not fare well for company leaders. As seen in 2004-2005, perceptions of the senior leader's ethical fitness wane as an employee's tenure in the organization increases, proving these executives are not seen as doing more than "talking the talk."

Showing the linkage between engagement and the employee's perception of the ethical fitness of his or her senior leadership, nearly four times as many fully engaged employees believe in the integrity of senior leaders than do unengaged employees (73 percent versus 19 percent). Half of all employees feel their senior leadership has a clear vision for the future and are satisfied with the strategic direction of the company. However, a third of all senior leaders cannot agree they are satisfied with the direction of the company, a startling discovery.

The weakest performance in this workforce component in 2006-07 followed a pattern developed in 2004-2005; now just more than a third of all employees agree that senior management treats employees like their most important asset and, in fact, nearly the same number of employees disagree (35 percent):

- 52 percent of employees in companies with less than 100 employees agrees with the statement. However, just 23 percent of those employees working in companies with 2,500-5,000 employees feel the same.
- Tenure again shows a disturbing trend. As the employee's tenure with his or her company decreases, the positive perceptions of being treated like the most important asset decrease.
- Six in 10 East South-Central employees agree, twice as many as employees in the Pacific region.
- Nonunion employees were twice as likely to agree as were union employees (40 percent versus 19 percent).

The importance of having effective senior leadership is critical to customers, employees, shareholders, suppliers and community leaders. If employees lose confidence in their senior leaders, engagement will suffer.

Why are Effective Senior Leaders Important?

Peruse any bookstore's business section and one is likely to uncover several titles pertaining to leadership. The fascination by, interest in and criticism of leaders— in business, political, sports, entertainment and other arenas—underscores the impact people in leadership roles have on their respective spheres of influence. When viewed through the lens of workforce engagement, leadership takes on paramount importance. Indeed, effective senior leaders are those who find, keep and motivate productive employees who help the organization succeed. To understand how this happens, it is important to consider what defines effective senior leaders and differentiates them from others within the organization; the competencies associated with effective senior leaders; what employees want from effective senior leaders and how effective senior leaders impact workforce engagement.

Effective Senior Leaders are Defined as Those Individuals Who:

- Set the organizational agenda.
- Hold legitimate power and use authority judiciously.
- Communicate successfully with various stakeholder groups.
- Inspire and earn the confidence of those around them.
- Assume responsibility for the organization's performance, reputation and effectiveness.

Effective senior leaders *set the organizational agenda*

One of the most important activities in which leaders engage is determining the organization's priorities during a given time frame. These priorities often center on what products to produce, which customers to serve, which technologies to leverage, what financial targets to hit, what markets to compete in and other ways to provide a sustainable competitive advantage, thus ensuring organizational survivability over the long haul. Senior leaders are engaged in high-stakes activities that, generally, produce high-stakes outcomes. Thus, their work differs from other employees primarily due to the agenda-setting nature of crafting enterprisewide goals, objectives and measures of effectiveness for the month, quarter and year.

Consider how differing organizational agendas have shaped the rivalry between airplane makers Boeing and Airbus. While U.S.-based Boeing largely dominated the aircraft market for decades, in recent years European rival Airbus has made significant inroads in new product development, new airplane orders and increased market share. Airbus leaders are banking on air travel of the future that requires a super-jumbo jet, the double-decker A380, to transport massive amounts of passengers between large hub airports. At Boeing, meanwhile, senior leaders there have staked their future on the demand for a midsized, long-range airplane—the Boeing 787 Dreamliner—that assumes airlines will want to fly passengers on more point-to-point routes that bypass busy hub airports in favor of more flexible travel arrangements.

The contrasting organizational agendas of Airbus and Boeing demonstrate the complexity of decisions and options that senior leaders must make. It also highlights the ultimate responsibility these leaders have to their customers, employees, investors and communities. Thus, the amount of physical, financial, intellectual and human resources over which they exert control and responsibility is one of the single biggest distinguishing characteristics between senior leaders and other employees. Another difference, of course, is the nature of power held by organizational leaders.

Effective senior leaders *hold legitimate power and use authority judiciously*

Senior leaders are sanctioned by the virtue of their role to hold significant, legitimate power within their companies. Unlike employees at other levels, leaders are granted the authority to make decisions about strategy, business processes, people, technology and financial matters, to name just a few. Leaders often use such power to advance the aims and purposes of the organization. There are times, however, when leaders leverage their power in ways that are inappropriate, unethical or even illegal. The rise in the number of "whistleblower" cases during the last few years is indicative of power abuses and feelings of invincibility among some leaders.

Fortunately, the renewed focus on ethical decision-making practices, transparent corporate governance, public policies dealing with fiscal reporting and executive accountability and leadership development programs that emphasize a servant/stewardship leader philosophy all conspire to equip leaders with an understanding of what is necessary in carrying out their duties.

Effective senior leaders *communicate successfully with various stakeholder groups*

A significant portion of a senior leader's time is spent communicating with others about the organization's capabilities and performance. This communication is largely done to encourage further support for and investment in the organization's future. To communicate effectively, senior leaders need to identify what information is important, who the organization's stakeholders are and the appropriate methods for communicating that information to stakeholders.

The nature of information communicated about an organization typically centers on its products and services, financial performance, future growth plans, environmental impact issues or specific information that is provided during a crisis. Organizational stakeholders generally include investors, employees, customers, suppliers, partners and the communities in which the company is located or conducts business. Finally, methods for communication to stakeholders include informal exchanges, electronic communications (e.g., Web sites; e-mails; listservs), press releases, marketing and advertising campaigns, meetings, quarterly and annual reports and filings with various government and regulatory agencies.

While most mid- and large-size organizations employ corporate communications professionals to handle day-to-day communication requirements, senior leaders are largely the external and internal face associated with an organization's identity. Certainly one of the most prominent examples of leader-as-communicator is Bill Gates, founder and CEO of Microsoft, the world's dominant software manufacturer. Gates and his executive team regularly provide communication concerning the state of Microsoft, future trends in the industry, the role technology (in general) continues to play in our lives and, in the past, were called to explain and defend Microsoft's alleged monopolistic and anti-competitive practices. While an extreme example, Microsoft's senior leaders highlight an important role that further differentiates them from employees at other levels of the organization. Closely associated with communication is the ability to inspire others to behave in ways that are beneficial to the organization's ongoing success.

Effective senior *leaders inspire and earn the confidence of those around them*

Mother Teresa, Dr. Martin Luther King Jr., Pope John Paul II, Gandhi, Jimmy Carter and others are widely recognized humanitarian leaders who have truly inspired others to perform acts of service and social justice. Although these leaders are widely acknowledged for their inspirational impact, organizational leaders, too, accomplish great things by inspiring others around them. Typically, inspirational leaders exhibit tremendous charisma, in which they show concern for people as individuals, are passionate about their vision, are perceived as change agents and display a strong sense of purpose and self-confidence. Additionally, inspiring leaders also tend to be positive people who have the ability to think in new ways and exert influence by compelling followers to buy into their vision. While inspiration and charisma are important ingredients for success, the accountability for organizational performance is another distinguishing characteristic of success.

Effective senior leaders *assume responsibility for the organization's performance, reputation and effectiveness*

Leaders are held accountable for organizational performance by a number of constituents. Corporate boards expect leaders to exhibit business acumen and strategy-setting and strategy-execution skills; shareholders expect an appropriate return on their investment; employees want to work for an organization that is stable, fair and provides them a sense of purpose in their work; vendors and suppliers expect the company to be a good business partner; communities want the organization to be a good corporate citizen; and customers expect to receive quality and value for the products, services and solutions offered by the organization.

The major factors that lead to organizational growth and success are discipline around employee development, leadership, performance standards and effective execution of the organization's strategy. Business and leadership literature suggests that leader behaviors, management practices, organizational structure and organizational culture are some of the greatest determinants of corporate success. Ultimately, leaders are held accountable for an organization's success. In most private-sector, for-profit companies, "success" is largely defined as a healthy bottom line and/or the ability for the organization to maximize the shareholder's return on investment.

True organizational performance, however, has increasingly been viewed as encompassing measures beyond just money. Robert Kaplan and David Norton's book, *The Strategy-Focused Organization,* explains that, to survive and thrive in a competitive marketplace, successful companies measure their progress in four distinct yet related areas: financial; customer; internal business processes; and employee learning, growth and development. This broader view of organizational performance, known as the Balanced Scorecard, necessarily emphasizes fiscal health, yet recognizes the less-quantitative areas (customer, process, employee) as equally important to long-term success. Thus, the ability to demonstrate effectiveness in each of these areas requires leaders to possess certain competencies that embody the knowledge, skills and abilities associated with effective senior leadership.

What are the Competencies Associated with Effective Senior Leaders?

Effective Senior Leaders Should Be Able To:

- Articulate a meaningful vision and strategic direction for the organization.
- Identify and model behaviors that support workforce engagement.
- Reflect on and improve their own leadership practice and its accomplishments.
- Cultivate a high-performance culture and meaningful work environment.
- Encourage and value employee loyalty.
- Encourage and value quality, service and a focus on customers.

Effective senior leaders are able to *articulate a meaningful vision and strategic direction for the organization*

Perhaps one of the most important competencies associated with effective senior leaders is their ability to articulate a meaningful vision and strategic direction for the organization. Unfortunately, this is one competency that needs work, especially as it relates to workforce engagement. According to a recent survey conducted by the Society for Human Resource Management (SHRM) and the Balanced Scorecard Collaborative, a majority of organizations claim to have a clearly articulated strategic direction, yet less than half believe that direction is clearly communicated to employees.

Effective senior leaders are explicit and intentional in their planning, coordination, communication and execution of the organization's strategic direction. Thus, a clearly articulated strategic direction includes—although is not limited to—the following three broad areas: *who we are* (mission, vision, values); *how we perform* (competencies, goals, objectives); and *what we manage* (assumptions, resources, constraints).

Who We Are: Mission, Vision and Values

Mission

An organization's mission is, simply put, why it exists. Why is the organization operating? Whom does it serve? What does it accomplish? For example, most colleges and universities have a variation on the following mission: to engage in teaching, research and service activities in a prescribed geographic area and serving a prescribed population. Admittedly, this mission is broad and encompasses three disparate yet related areas: teaching, research and service—missions that more often than not seem to operate in conflict rather than in concert. Most private sector companies' missions are more tightly focused, a luxury afforded to organizations that perhaps have narrower constituencies to serve than do colleges and universities.

Savvy leaders understand the importance of the organization's mission. They ensure that the mission is short, simple (but not at the expense of minimizing its importance) and widely embraced, understood and communicated throughout the organization's hierarchy. Business unit leaders can play a role in ensuring their activities reflect the broader corporate mission, and the elements of the corporate mission should be evident in the mission of each business unit.

Vision

If the mission tells us why the organization exists, the vision tells us what the organization wants to become. What are the aspirations of the company? Where does it envision itself in three to five years? Ten years? Twenty years? A vision serves as a lofty benchmark against which mission-related activities should be focused. A bank, for example, might have as its vision "to become the financial institution of choice for customers in the state." Inherent in this mission are the stretch goals of becoming a dominant force, while also operating in a marketplace characterized by competition. Typically, senior leaders craft the vision for the organization, with appropriate input from key stakeholder groups—employees, board members, shareholders, etc. The vision should be somewhat related to the mission, although the present-day mission should not overly restrict the possibilities that a promising vision can hold for the company.

Values

Missions tell us why we exist, visions tell us where we want to be and values tell us what the organization holds near and dear to its heart. Values are all of the publicly espoused elements—such as teamwork, diversity, quality and innovation—that the leadership of an organization articulates as important underpinnings to the mission. Sometimes values come off sounding like a litany of leadership sound bites. However, effective leaders know that to carry out the mission and move toward fulfilling the vision, values are needed to guide decision-making within the organization.

One prime example of a value that many employee-centric organizations uphold is the importance of investing in their human capital. This type of value is supported operationally at some organizations by investments in people through training, tuition assistance benefits and flexible employee scheduling to accommodate going back to school.

How We Perform: Competencies, Goals and Objectives
Competencies

Competencies are those things that the organization does as good as if not better than anyone else. They also help inform the competitive advantage the organization may enjoy relative to its competitors. Presumably every organization has at least one thing it does better than others. Michael Treacy and Frederic D. Wiersema, in their book *The Discipline of Market Leaders*, provide a useful framework for a discussion of organizational competencies. They posit that every successful organization focuses its efforts in one of three areas of excellence: best total cost, best total service and best total solution.

Best total cost infers that the organization delivers substantial savings to its customers through unparalleled purchasing power enjoyed by its economies of scale. Wal-Mart is a useful example, because its core competency focuses on providing low prices to its customers. Best total service is a core competency enjoyed by organizations such as Nordstrom and the Mercedes-Benz division of DaimlerChrysler. These companies are not competing on price—far from it. Instead, their efforts focus on adding value through unmatched service, for which they can command—and get—a premium price. Finally, best total solution outlines the core competencies enjoyed by organizations who provide a one-stop-shopping approach to their business. Microsoft provides total solutions for customers— whether they are individual or corporate. Microsoft's products and services, combined, offer many users a near-total solution to their computing needs.

Treacy and Wiersema are quick to point out that while successful companies may focus on only one main area of excellence (best total cost, best total service or best total solution), those same companies are also pretty darn good in the other two areas as well. For the purposes of driving organizational initiatives forward, including leveraging resources to support the organization's mission, these organizations have to focus on one thing and consistently do it better than others. In doing so, however, they cannot minimize or completely ignore the other areas, but when hard decisions need to be made, activities that support core competencies serve as key drivers in decision-making and resource-allocation processes.

Goals

If competencies tell us what organizations do as good as if not better than anyone else, goals are those things that provide focus to activities during the next six to 24 months and contribute to the improvement of those competencies. Developing specific goals beyond the six- to 24-month window is not very pragmatic, as changes in a number of areas (technology, economic factors, consumer demand, competitive changes, etc.) are likely to force the revision of goals that are too long-term in orientation. Ideally, goals should directly relate to the competencies. For example, if excellence in teaching and learning is a competency of colleges and universities, one goal related to that competency might be to increase the number of students enrolled in baccalaureate programs on campus.

Objectives

While goals outline the broad plans for improving upon competencies, objectives are the specific ways those goals will be carried out and hopefully accomplished. It is likely that there will be multiple objectives associated with one goal. Continuing the example from above, the competency is teaching and learning, and the goal is to increase the number of students enrolled in baccalaureate programs on campus. A number of objectives would likely emerge to help facilitate the accomplishment of this goal. For example, the institution could offer classes at more convenient times; discount tuition for selected programs; partner with employers to offer courses at business locations; or engage in a new marketing and advertising campaign aimed at attracting new students. All of these are objectives that support the goal and contribute to the improvement of one of the organization's core competencies.

What We Manage: Assumptions, Resources and Constraints
Assumptions

Every organization operates under a series of basic assumptions about what must fundamentally happen for the organization to succeed. In all organizations, there is a sense that the entity is a going concern—an accounting term used to infer that the organization's existence is assumed to be indefinite. By viewing the organization as a going concern, leaders actively make plans for the future, undeterred by the thought that the organization might come to an end at some point down the road.

In the private sector, profitability is viewed as a fundamental basic assumption. Few for-profit organizations can remain viable for too long operating in the red. As a result, the profit motivation for these organizations is assumed. It should be noted that some have argued that "making money" is, indeed, the mission of an organization. Profitability should not be viewed as a mission, because there would be no way to discriminate between the differences in focus of the organizations mentioned earlier, such as Southwest, Wal-Mart and Microsoft. Instead, profitability, like going concern, is thought to be a basic assumption inherent in the operation of the organization.

Additional assumptions might include an acknowledgement that there will always be competition in the industry; that technological (and other) changes will continue to occur at a rapid pace; and that customers in the future will still demand (and want) the product, service and/or solution provided by the organization. In the absence of having a basic assumption satisfied, the organization is faced with serious trouble. Mission, vision and strategic directions can be severely threatened when assumptions are not met. As a result, assumptions should not be viewed as a well-removed adjunct from the organization's mission, vision and strategic directions; the degree of certainty of the former directly impacts the organization's ability to effectively perform the latter.

Resources

Resources are all of the ingredients present in an organization that drive it toward fulfilling its mission, reaching its vision and carrying out its strategic directions. Examples of resources include physical, financial and HR; technological resources; quality of products, services and/or solutions; the positive attitudes and motivations of individuals, work teams and units; and competitive advantages enjoyed by the organization (its core competencies).

In strategic planning processes, one of the first steps is conducting a situational analysis—commonly referred to as a SWOT analysis (Strengths, Weaknesses, Opportunities and Threats). Resources, coupled with core competencies, can be viewed as strengths of the organization; they are, indeed, its greatest asset and can contribute immeasurably to its ongoing success. Resources can be articulated at the corporate- and business-unit levels, and they need to be identified, solidified and nurtured to maximize their effectiveness.

Constraints

If resources drive an organization toward mission fulfillment, constraints are, conversely, the ingredients that hold the organization back from achieving its full potential. Like resources, examples of constraints include: physical, financial and human constraints; technological limitations; product lines, business processes and policies that are disconnected from the organization's mission and purpose; and employees who lack the attitude or motivation to fully contribute to the organization's strategic directions.

Ultimately, the strategic direction of an organization—*who we are; how we perform; what we manage*—provides the framework for leaders, employees and other stakeholders to make decisions that guide the organization toward success. In addition to the strategic directions framework, effective senior leaders need to identify and model behaviors that support workforce engagement.

Effective senior leaders are able to *identify and model behaviors that support workforce engagement*

Leaders are highly visible people who have considerable influence within their organization. As such, employees look to leaders to see if there is congruence between what they say and what they do. Much has been written about the styles and orientations of leaders and the role of leader behavior in shaping the culture of an organization. In general, a leader's style can range from highly autocratic to highly participative, and his or her orientation can range from a strong orientation toward productivity to a strong orientation toward people.

In highly autocratic leadership styles, much of the decision-making, control and power rest with the leader. Leaders who use this style retain their authority and sparingly grant discretion over organizational matters to their subordinates. Although indicative of command-and-control, hierarchical organizational structures, the autocratic leadership style can be effective in any type of setting under certain circumstances. There are times when employees want and need leaders to retain a high degree of authority and control. Autocratic leadership might be best employed, for example, when crises emerge, when legal or regulatory pressure exists, when time constraints require quick action or when there are significant knowledge disparities between the leader and employee.

By contrast, participative leadership styles actively involve subordinates in decision-making, provide subordinates with the ability to exercise appropriate control over resources and grant subordinates the necessary power and authority to accomplish their tasks. Leaders who use this style tend to delegate to their subordinates and empower them to perform in ways that have a positive impact on the organization. Participate leadership styles are best employed when there is a high degree of maturity and sense of responsibility on the part of the employee, when an employee possesses specialized knowledge or technical skill (especially knowledge or skill that the leader does not possess) and when the leader wants to develop employee capabilities for engagement, retention or upward or lateral mobility purposes.

Closely related to leadership styles are the orientations a leader has relative to an emphasis toward productivity or an emphasis toward people. When a leader focuses on productivity over people, he or she places a premium on getting the specific tasks accomplished, with limited regard to the thoughts or feelings of employees. Demands from customers, competitive or financial pressures, correction of errors and strict adherence to deadlines are all ingredients that may compel a leader to emphasize productivity. Conversely, leaders who exhibit an orientation toward people are more concerned with their workforce's affairs and how their employees think, feel and perceive the work environment. Leaders who have a strong people orientation tend to place value on interpersonal relationships with and among employees and want to create an environment that fosters personal expression and development of the workforce. The competing and coexisting tensions that exist between being concerned with productivity versus being concerned with people illustrate the true complexity and fluidity of a leader's role.

An understanding of leadership styles and orientations is helpful to realize ways leader behaviors contribute to workforce engagement. In reality, of course, most leadership styles and orientations are necessarily flexible and are adaptable to the situation, context and experiences of the leader and the employee. Knowing when, how and under what conditions to use a particular leadership style or orientation is one measure of a leader's effectiveness in managing his or her workforce.

Effective senior leaders are able to *reflect on and improve their own leadership practice and its accomplishments*

Understanding successful strategies, lessons learned and pitfalls to avoid are important components to effective leadership. However, leaders (and others) often seem too busy focusing on the future to take stock of past performance and the behaviors and practices that led to that performance. Effective leaders regularly reflect and improve on their leadership styles and orientations to gauge the effectiveness of their approaches. The rise in the number of leadership coaching programs in the past decade is evidence of the attention being paid to reflection and personal improvement endeavors at the highest levels of organizations. These programs emphasize not only the results a leader accomplishes, but an analysis and understanding of the steps taken, rationale and justifications applied, people involved and the impact of these things on the ultimate outcome. The goal is to assist the leader in making explicit that which is implicit. In other words, create an awareness of how and why leaders behave in the ways they do and the consequences of these actions. Such honest assessment of leadership strengths and challenges is necessary to assist the leader in creating a culture that exceeds performance expectations and provides employees with an enjoyable work experience.

Effective senior leaders are able to *cultivate a high-performance culture and meaningful work environment*

Fortune regularly lists companies that create the most total shareholder returns over a sustainable period of time. The list includes many well-known companies such as Starbucks, Johnson & Johnson, Wal-Mart, Southwest Airlines, FedEx, Dell, General Electric and Proctor and Gamble, among others. Each of these organizations achieves superior financial performance through the cultivation of high-performance cultures and meaningful work environments for employees.

High-performance cultures do not just happen. Leaders play the most important part in identifying the need for high performance and in creating the internal understanding of the need to achieve it. Such cultures are typically characterized by the organization's ability to anticipate and embrace change; use core competencies, structures and employees as competitive strengths; develop goals that stretch performance beyond minimal, acceptable standards; focus on adding significant value to products, business processes and relationships with customers; and reward people who are contributing to high-performance outcomes and coach, discipline or dismiss those who are not.

One of the necessary ingredients of a high-performance culture is work that is meaningful and engaging for the employee. Meaningful work permits employees to use a variety of knowledge, skills and abilities in the performance of their job duties. Meaningful work also provides employees with the tools, resources and training opportunities to enhance their success. Employees who perform meaningful work see the results of that work and understand the significance of their role in the organization. Leaders in high-performance cultures tend to their workforce issues as much as—if not more so—than any other variable, for they realize that the key to long-term, sustainable performance rests with their employees. Thus, in addition to creating a meaningful work environment that leads to high performance, effective senior leaders also encourage and value employee loyalty.

Effective senior leaders are able to *encourage and value employee loyalty*

Employee loyalty is the ability for employees to be retained by and committed to an organization. While this differs from engagement—in which the employee continuously adds value by performing meaningful work that is needed by the organization and is enjoyable for the individual—employee loyalty, in general, is a good thing. Effective leaders understand and value employees who demonstrate their loyalty by longevity of service, getting the job done and seeking a high sense of personal satisfaction from and affiliation with the organization. Such understanding and value translates into organizational practices that reward employee retention and commitment.

Recognizing employee loyalty poses a fine line for a leader to walk. While it is important to value loyalty, a leader needs to be mindful of not creating a culture of employee dependence. Such dependence on the leader or the organization, poses the risk of employees becoming "trapped" in their job or not keeping themselves viable on the open market; or in performance that is characterized by poor self-confidence; or the potential for diminished or risk-averse decision- making. Overall, however, loyal employees can go a long way toward assisting the leader and the organization in serving its customers.

Effective senior leaders are able to *encourage and value quality, service and a focus on customers*

We live in an era that is characterized by the commoditization of products and services and where it is sometimes difficult to tell the difference between easily substitutable product alternatives. When Pepsi adds a new flavor, Coke is not far behind. When Ford offers a new feature, Chevrolet ups the ante by improving upon that feature. When Circuit City lowers prices on DVD players, Best Buy follows. Thus, in a marketplace crowded with rival firms offering indistinguishable products, it is all the more important for organizations to emphasize quality, service and a focus on their customers.

Savvy leaders know customers have a multitude of choices and, in general, a product's features and benefits alone may not be enough to satisfy demanding consumer tastes. As a result, flawless execution of service, coupled with quality and value for the money, is key to attracting and retaining customers. Closely related to quality and service excellence is strong customer-relationship management techniques. Customers buy products and services from companies, but form relationships with the people in those companies. Leaders, therefore, must understand that to maximize relationships with customers, their most important relationship must be to the employees who serve the customers. Employees, too, are as demanding as external customers and, increasingly, they, like customers, have a host of choices when it comes to their participation in the workforce. As a result, effective senior leaders need to fully understand what employees want and need from them.

How Can Effective Senior Leaders Impact Workforce Engagement?

Senior Leaders Can Impact Workforce Engagement Through:

- What they say
- People they hire
- Decisions they make
- Opportunities they pursue
- Legacies they leave.

Senior leaders impact workforce engagement through *what they say*

Employees and other stakeholders listen to what leaders say and, in general, are apt to believe the messages that emanate from the highest levels of an organization. Leadership credibility, however, rises and falls based on the alignment between what is said and what is done. It is not enough for a leader to merely say that employees are an organization's most important asset; he or she must believe it and must continuously act in ways that are consistent with that sentiment.

Leaders who place a premium on their workforce and its ability to competitively differentiate the organization from rivals are likely to espouse employee-centric messages in their internal and external communications. Such leaders recognize that it is employees who develop ideas, create innovations, serve customers and permit the organization to carry out its mission. These leaders are quick to praise employees for successes enjoyed by the organization and are equally quick to defend their employees against unruly customers, belligerent customers or other similar sources.

Perhaps most telling are the leadership messages communicated by Wegmans Food Market, a perennial Fortune "100 Best Companies to Work For" winner. In its stores, the supermarket places a sign that states "Employees First; Customers Second." Robert Wegman, chairman of the supermarket chain started by his father and uncle in 1916, said of the recognition, "This is the culmination of my whole life's work. When I became president of our company in 1950, after working in our stores for a number of years, I was determined to make it a great place to work." His first step was to raise all salaries, and within a couple of years, he implemented fully paid health care. Later, the company added a defined contribution retirement plan, a 401(k) plan and an employee scholarship program, which has given nearly $54 million in tuition assistance to 17,000 employees since it began in 1984. The consistent recognition by *Fortune* is external validation of what the supermarket's employees already know: beyond just lip service, Wegmans truly creates an environment where employees are valued.

Senior leaders impact workforce engagement through *people they hire*

One of the most significant ways a leader can shape the organization's culture is through the people that he or she brings aboard the organization. Good leaders shore up their "bench strength" by identifying individuals who help to round out the leader's skill set, while also being a good fit with the organization's core values and purpose. In many cases, leaders hire direct reports who are dissimilar to them, with the goal of having robust capabilities that can be tapped to serve the organization. Each of the major airlines has had at least one CEO turnover since the Sept. 11, 2001, terrorist attacks. At Southwest Airlines, American Airlines and Continental Airlines, all of the current CEOs are products of each airline's finance or operations division and were hired by their predecessors—many of whom were not financial experts, but were larger-than-life executives with a flair for marketing and external relations. While the style of all new CEOs is notably different from their predecessors, their understanding of the airline industry and the specific corporate cultures of each organization were initiated by good hiring decisions on the part of past leaders. Developing such a talent pipeline is a critical component of leadership and represents a key decision that effective leaders make.

Senior leaders impact workforce engagement through *decisions they make*

Leadership involves a series of complex, often interrelated, decisions. Effective leaders must continuously decide issues regarding finance, marketing, technology, research and development, strategy, communications and, of course, matters pertaining to their workforce. Often, a leader will help shape the culture and structure of the decision-making process itself. In highly centralized organizations, for example, decisions are typically made from the top and are superimposed on the business units and departments throughout the enterprise. Such a process requires varying levels of input by and consultation from managers and individual contributor employees. By contrast, decentralized decision-making enables managers and employees at the levels closest to the customer to decide how to respond to market-driven issues and pressures. In these cases, leaders provide the overarching strategic direction and appropriate control mechanisms to give guidance to how decisions are carried out.

Beyond setting the culture and structure for decision-making in an organization, the actual decisions made by leaders signal their relations with employees. Labor costs are typically the single largest expense in most organizations, sometimes accounting for upward of 70 percent of the total organizational budget. Ironically, most leaders only allocate between 2 percent to 3 percent of their total payroll to the continued training and development of their workforce, despite the significant cost the workforce encumbers. Similar decisions about the allocation of resources, financial or otherwise, send powerful messages to employees about how well they are valued by leaders. Other examples of how leadership decision-making influences workforce engagement include when, how and under what circumstances change is communicated; the methods for rewarding and recognizing employees; and the extent to which employees, themselves, are regularly involved in or consulted about decisions that have a direct bearing on their jobs.

Senior leaders impact workforce engagement through *opportunities they pursue*

Closely related to leadership decision making are the organizational opportunities that leaders choose to pursue. Such opportunities can serve to underscore a leader's commitment to and investment in his or her workforce. Conversely, opportunities that a leader chooses to pursue may also signal a high degree of self-interest at the expense of overall employee morale.

Some of the opportunities leaders can choose to pursue include products and services to offer; markets to penetrate, concentrate on or abandon; technologies in which to invest; organization structural, reward and development considerations; and mergers, acquisitions or alliances in which to participate. Each of these activities has a direct or indirect impact on how work is performed and on the overall culture of the organization.

Senior leaders impact workforce engagement through *legacies they leave*

One enduring aspect of a leader's work that tends to be different from that of an individual-contributor employee is the scope and magnitude of the leader's legacy. The reputation of the leader and the organization; the quality and effectiveness of the succession plan; the financial contributions made to the organization and the community; and the imprint on the corporate culture and organizational values are all variables that form the type of legacy a leader can leave.

Sam Walton, founder of Wal-Mart, left his legacy in each of the areas listed above.

His organization emerged as a true industry leader, largely credited to the early innovations and persistence of Walton. Wal-Mart's notorious promote-from-within practice helped ensure a sound leadership team firmly rooted in an understanding of and appreciation for Wal-Mart. The economic imprint Wal-Mart has made—on its employees, its shareholders, its communities and even the entire U.S. economy—is virtually unrivaled. Finally, the grassroots, entrepreneurial corporate culture and hometown values of Sam Walton exist, in varying degrees, even today. While most leaders will not leave a legacy as profound as that of Walton, the actions they take, especially around values, decisions and succession planning, can leave a lasting mark on the organization and its employees.

Summary

This chapter highlighted why effective senior leaders are an important component in shaping employee perceptions of the organization and represent a true driver of workforce engagement. Activities undertaken and competencies associated with senior leaders were highlighted, with particular emphasis on the strategic nature of leadership planning and decision-making. Senior leaders also have to signal their commitment to employees in word *and* deed. Unfortunately, as the case study which follows highlights, often lip service is not backed up with concrete actions that support well-intentioned leaders.

Case Study:
Effective Senior Leadership and Workforce Engagement
'But Not as I Do'

John Talcott smiled as he walked toward the back of the room, shaking hands, nodding and softly saying "thank you" as people remarked, "great job," "congratulations" and "well said." He had just finished giving the luncheon address at the annual meeting of the Association of Chief Operating Officers, one of the city's most well-known organizations for business leaders. His topic was "Are We More Successful When We Count People Or When We Make People Count?"

An accomplished and affable speaker, Talcott was respected for his success as president of Consolidated Brands, a leading distributor of "house brands" of canned and bottled goods. In the past seven years, he took a modestly successful company and streamlined its operations and increased its profitability. Among his accomplishments: implementation of new marketing and control procedures, development of a 10-year strategic plan and creating the position of vice president for HR.

His speech today was about the importance of making the human resources function more than simply a benefits and hiring office. He reiterated his belief that "engagement" and "commitment" were abstract terms with tangible meaning and consequences. It was a familiar message, one he had stated on numerous occasions, but today's audience seemed to respond with special enthusiasm. As he reached the back of the room, the association's president, himself the head of a large insurance company, said, "John, that was terrific. It was a great speech and we should all be doing what you say! Thanks a lot."

Back in his office, Talcott felt restless and after a few minutes, walked to the conference table at the corner of his office where he kept papers, reports and files that needed his attention. He took a large blue binder from one corner of the table, went back to his desk and started to read. It was entitled "Strategic Directions for HR: A Six-Year Plan." He involuntarily moved his head as he looked at the bottom of the cover page: *For Implementation in July 2003.* Almost two years. Where had the time gone? What happened?

When Talcott arrived at Consolidated in 1997, HR was not a cohesive entity, but a series of independent offices, each carrying out specific functions that were not coordinated with other personnel activities. There was a benefits office, payroll office, and hiring and training office, among others. Within six months, an integrated HR office was established, and within a year, he hired a vice president for HR.

Change came quickly, at least initially. The new vice president moved quickly to set up an employee assistance program (EAP), brought in consultants to evaluate and recommend changes to the benefits program and created a new performance-appraisal system which included a mandatory training program for all supervisors. Although these were welcome changes and improvement, there were few tangible results. The retention rate was essentially unchanged, as was the rate of absenteeism among hourly workers.

By the end of his third year as president, systems were more efficient. However, Talcott felt that the changes were "piecemeal," and there was no systematic plan to make workforce engagement a priority with seamless and effective policies and procedures.

He had great confidence in Nicole Raines, the vice president for HR. He asked her to work with company personnel and outside consultants to develop a strategic plan. He said, "Give me something that will move us beyond 'lip service' to a meaningful commitment to employees." After 15 months, the "Strategic Directions" report was on his desk, but it arrived when the company's third-largest customer decided to have its labeling and packaging work done in Mexico. Talcott spent several months reallocating resources, cutting budgets and launching a national marketing initiative to find new corporate clients.

After dealing with that, Talcott turned his attention to problems that were cropping up in the new information-processing system that was being installed. It was not user friendly, employees said, and some data were lost and other information had to be backed up manually. Despite his interest, the report was on Talcott's desk for nine months before he read and absorbed the recommendations. In late 2002, he told Raines and his other vice presidents that he was ready to move ahead with the strategic plan for HR.

But, inevitably, there were other operating problems that demanded his attention and presence. He found it difficult to attend planning meetings, and sometimes proposals that required his approval sat on his desk for many weeks before he reviewed them. Time passed. Small changes happened, but the broad and ambitious goals of the strategic plan existed only on paper and not in practice. In November 2003, he told the vice presidents that although he was disappointed that more progress was not made, he understood how busy everyone was and that he, too, had let some important HR issues slide in the press of other business. He said, "Next year I am going to find the time and I hope you will too."

The phone rang and Talcott took a congratulatory call from a friend who had heard him speak several hours before. When the call ended, he looked out the window and thought to himself, "If only I could do it as well as I say it."

Questions for Consideration and Discussion
'But Not As I Do'

1. John Talcott's speech ostensibly highlighted the philosophy that a company's human capital is its most important asset and that human relations should play a central role in helping organizations succeed. To what extent does Talcott practice what he preaches? Does Consolidated Brands truly value its employees or does Talcott offer well-intentioned lip service alone?

2. In what ways can and should senior leaders play a role in workforce engagement issues? To what extent do their words and actions contribute to a culture that values employee commitment, retention and satisfaction?

3. Suppose you were hired as a consultant to provide advice to Talcott and his vice presidents about ways they could make workforce engagement more central to the work at Consolidated. What advice would you provide? How would Talcott know if he were successful in implementing your advice?

4. How can busy organizational leaders balance the often competing and coexisting tensions of fiscal and operational performance with the needs of individual employees? To what extent do leaders have greater concern for productivity versus greater concern for people? When might people concerns be most paramount?

Chapter 3:
Reputation Management

Introduction: What Do We Mean By 'Reputation Management'?

Reputation management is the ability of organizational leaders to shape and manage the organization's reputation internally and externally; identify and describe strengths of the organization's products, services and solutions; and exercise positive corporate social responsibility. The reputation management component of workforce engagement reflects the extent to which employees perceive the company is viewed as reputable and admirable in the marketplace and the extent to which the organization is viewed favorably internally, as well.

Highlights from the 2004-2005 National Benchmark Study on Workforce Engagement

Customers want to buy from and employees want to work for companies with a solid reputation. For customers, a company's reputation can be as important as the quality of products and services; it can help differentiate between a competitor's "me too" product. As Warren Buffet once commented, "If you lose money for the firm, I will be understanding. If you lose reputation, I will be ruthless." In the *pan* Workforce Engagement Assessment national benchmark, only two-thirds of all employees believed the reputation of their organization was excellent, while one in eight disagreed.

With *Reputation Management* being a top-five driver of workforce engagement, employers have to measure and manage their internal and external branding.

Engaged employees are two to three times as likely as unengaged employees to feel that their organization's reputation is excellent, highlighting the impact among reputation, engagement and positive job performance.

In his work with Harris Interactive, Dr. Charles Fombrun, professor emeritus of the Stern School of Business and executive director of the Reputation Institute, has demonstrated the link between strong corporate reputation and increased product purchases from customers, more positive investment behavior from shareholders and improved market capitalization. Just as important, their work has shown the linkage between a company's reputation and its ability to recruit and hire talented employees.

The average employee has 13 to 15 jobs during the course of his or her career, seven by the time he or she is 30. As employees continually move from job to job, the companies they previously worked for become more and more important to their prospective employers. Therefore it is in the employee's best interest to work for companies with solid reputations, as it can give them a leg up on other applicants when they are looking for their next job. And, because most companies in most industries are still engaged in the war for talent, it is beneficial for their previous company to be seen as a "great place to work."

Perhaps more today than in the past, a company's reputation starts in the CEO's office. *The Economist* once stated, "On average, a CEO accounts for about 14 percent of a company's financial performance." *Fortune* opined, "Despite the size and complexity of modern corporations, the person in charge still sets the tone, defines the style and becomes the company's public face. If you want to analyze a corporation, read its financial statements. If you want to plumb its soul, talk to its chief executive."

The last 10 years have shown us the impact ethics can have on the reputation of an organization. The last five years have shown us how senior leaders, especially those in the "c-suite," can impact their company's ethics. In the 2004-2005 *pan* study, only half of employees agreed that their senior leaders were people of high personal integrity, while one in five disagreed. Burson-Marsteller, one of the world's largest public relations firms, stated, "50 percent of a company's reputation is attributable to the CEO's reputation."

Beyond the effect the CEO has on a company's reputation, there are other factors that can make or break a company's reputation. Not surprisingly, a critical matter is the quality of the company's products and services, and in the *pan* study, nearly three quarters of all employees felt that their company's products and services were highly regarded. There were minimal differences in responses across all of the demographic questions asked, but there were a couple of note. First, state/local government employees were the least positive, with less than half agreeing that their products and services were highly regarded and one in six disagreeing, a level of disagreement twice as high as any other industry. Second, only half of all union employees agreed that their products and services were highly regarded compared to nearly eight in 10 nonunion employees.

Employees (and customers) also want to form relationships with leaders in their industry. A slightly lower percentage of employees, 70 percent, felt they worked for an industry leader. Younger employees felt more positively, as did workers in companies with more than 2,500 employees. State/local government employees and those in education services were least positive (46 percent and 59 percent, respectively). Employees who received work-related training/education in the last year were significantly more likely to feel positively than employees who had not received training and, again, nonunion employees were significantly more positive than union employees

The concept of corporate citizenship has taken on an increased importance in recent years, as organizations realize that there are benefits from "doing well." In work done by Walker Information, studies have shown that employees who believe their organization does a good job giving back to the community (they call it a high Corporate Philanthropy Index) are much more likely to stay longer, work harder and recommend the organization as a good place to work than employees who feel otherwise. In the PAN study, two-thirds of all employees believe their organization is a good corporate citizen. Perceptions of corporate citizenship drop as the tenure of employees increases, perhaps because they see how (or if) the company "walks the talk." Financial-services employees are the most positive of any industry group, with more than eight in 10 expressing support for the corporate citizenship of their organization, while local/state government employees rank last among industries (51 percent positive).

Finally, in the area of reputation management, more than half of all employees agreed that their organization treats employees well (56 percent), while one in five disagreed (20 percent). Again, the length of time an employee has been employed shows significant variance in employee perceptions. More than 70 percent of new employees believe their company treats employees well; this drops to 60 percent of employees with their organization one to two years, 55 percent for those who have been with their employer three to 10 years and less than 50 percent of employees with their organization 10 years or more. Smaller companies tend to perform better than larger ones, senior management is significantly more positive than individual contributors and only four in 10 union employees feel their organization treats employees well.

Companies understand the benefits of being a "Best Place to Work" or a "Most Admired Company." Customers want to buy products from companies that are leaders and innovators in their field. Local governments want to attract and retain these same companies and do so through local tax abatements. Shareholders are more likely to stay invested in an organization with an excellent reputation, even during a business downturn. And employees want to associate with companies that look good on their resume. But as Ben Franklin said, *"Glass, china and reputation are easily cracked and never well mended."*

Highlights from the 2006-2007 National Benchmark Study on Workforce Engagement

The third strongest driver of workforce engagement and the last of the primary drivers, reputation management's performance dropped slightly over the last two years, from 67-percent positive to 64-percent positive. Although not considered a significant decrease, it follows the same trend as the other two primary drivers of workforce engagement: weaker results over the last two years.

An area that changed from being a strength to leverage an opportunity for improvement is *This organization is a leader in its industry*, where only two-thirds of employees agree with the statement while one in eight disagrees. One of the interesting findings concerning this question relates to the position in the company. In nearly every other question asked in the survey, executives/senior managers are significantly more positive than are middle managers, supervisors and individual contributors. In fact, in many cases, the higher you go up in the organization, the more positive the responses. However, this question shows little/no change among the four groups:

- Executives: 65 percent agree, 12 percent disagree
- Middle Management: 66 percent agree, 13 percent disagree
- Supervisors: 62 percent agree, 15 percent disagree
- Individual Contributors: 65 percent agree, 12 percent disagree

Again, nonunion employees rate the reputation of the organization more positively than do union employees. In fact, they are significantly more positive and much less negative across every measure of reputation management asked in the national benchmark study. The most striking difference is in *This company treats employees well.*

- 55 percent of nonunion employees agree with the statement while only 36 percent of union employees agree
- Only two in 10 nonunion employees disagree with the statement, while three in 10 union employees disagree

When performance in each of the primary drivers of workforce engagement—daily satisfaction; ethics, diversity and safety; and reputation management—all show declines in the perceptions of employees, is it any wonder why engagement dropped from 46 percent to 40 percent and the number of unengaged workers increased from 31 percent to 36 percent, both considered significant changes from 2004-2005?

Why is Reputation Management Important?

An organization's reputation, simply put, is a reflection of how the enterprise is viewed by others. The advances in technologies, including the Internet, have made real-time information instantly available to global audiences. Newspapers, press releases, chat rooms, online newsgroups, Web blogs and e-mail make is possible for users to communicate information, opinion, experiences and even rumors or untruths about an organization to its many stakeholder groups. Thus, now more than ever, the ability for an organization to proactively and continuously shape and manage its reputation is necessary if it is to be successful in attracting and retaining customers, investors, business partners and employees.

Organizational reputations are, in essence, perceptions others hold about the organization, and those perceptions are likely to change over time. Reputation is never an absolute measure, as people constantly make either implicit or explicit comparisons between companies, or use their own personal values, attitudes, needs, wants, desires and past experiences as a guide to making decisions. Customers frequently hold the "what have you done for me lately" syndrome when pondering repeat purchases or larger orders with a firm. Employees, too, are likely to have the "most recent experience" mindset when making determinations about working harder, recommending the organization and exercising responsible behaviors at work. As such, organizations face a tough challenge in shaping and managing their reputation. Reputation management is a necessary strategic issue for many companies, and increasingly the demands of a variety of stakeholder groups compel senior leaders to make this an ongoing organizational priority.

Among the many variables that contribute to corporate reputation are the quality of its products and services, financial performance, employment issues, ethical practices, environmental policies and social responsibility. Individuals who do business with, work for, supply to and invest in the organization all have a stake in how the organization is managed. More importantly, stakeholders want the organization's perception in the marketplace and community to be positive, and companies have a responsibility to their myriad stakeholder groups to keep the firm's reputation generally well received by the public.

Reputation management is important not only to the leadership of an organization, but to the myriad of stakeholder groups who are also affiliated with the enterprise. Customers, business partners, suppliers, shareholders and employees are all interested in an organization's reputation in the community, industry and marketplace. Customers want to buy products and services from an organization with a positive reputation. Business partners and suppliers want to do business with an organization that has a positive reputation. Shareholders and others, such as state and local governments, want to invest in organizations that enjoy a positive reputation. Finally, employees want to work for an organization that has a good reputation. both internally and externally. Thus, there are a number of reasons why shaping and managing the organization's reputation is an important strategic consideration.

Shaping the Organization's Reputation is Important Because:

- If the company does not shape its own image, others are likely to shape the image for it.

- Organizational reputation is a key driver in getting stakeholders interested in the firm.

- Positive reputations can lead to expanded sales, product lines and strategic partnerships.

- Good reputations might provide the organization assistance in times of crisis and latitude with requests.

- Prospective employees are attracted to and current employees want to stay with organizations that have good reputations.

- Companies with good reputations enjoy the "benefit of the doubt" from media and investors.

If the company does not proactively and continuously shape its own image, others are likely to shape the image for the organization

Corporate reputations can be shaped unintentionally by several entities, sometimes with less-than-favorable results. Customer complaints spread through word of mouth or, increasingly, via Internet forums where companies' products and services get reviewed, rated and commented on by customers. *Competitors* showcase salient differences in products, quality, service, price, benefits, features and experience. *Media outlets* choose to cover and report items of their own choosing. *Employees* may provide inconsistent or inaccurate information to the public. *Individuals* and *groups* may demonstrate against a position, policy or action of the organization. *Government agencies* and *policymakers* might create or enforce legislation against an organization or industry or might seek to make an example out of an organization engaged in an unfavorable practice. Finally, *financial analysts* may upgrade or downgrade the organization's stock value or write reports commenting on the firm's leadership, strategic direction, product potential and level of creditworthiness, among other things.

Organizational reputation is a key driver of getting stakeholders interested in the firm

Customers want to buy from reputable organizations, and employees want to work for successful firms. In most cases, if the stakeholder does not have any direct experience with a company, the only thing he or she can rely on is the reputation the organization has in the industry, the marketplace or the community. This is accomplished through, among other things, reading articles, hearing news reports, listening to word of mouth from customers and employees, responding to image campaigns from the organization and remembering past actions—positive and negative—taken by the company.

In today's marketplace, studies have indicated that a company's reputation can account for a significant portion of its shareholder value. Shareholder value is informed, in part, by the gap between what the company is worth on paper (assets, liabilities, equity, etc.) and what shareholders believe to be the true value or potential of the company.

In the mid-1990s, for example, many "dot com" companies were highly valued by investors, largely for the promises built on a business model that made critical assumptions about consumer willingness to do business in an e-commerce environment. The investments built on the organization's name, past experiences, leadership capabilities and anticipated demand for online products or services contributed to the perceived value placed on high-tech companies. Given the industry context and the promise for the future, many e-commerce companies quickly soared in market value due to significant investment capital. While some organizations were ultimately successful in the e-commerce environment, many technology-driven companies ultimately did not live up their promise, based on a lack of potential customers and sketchy business models. Toward the end of the 1990s, the "dot bomb" happened, and many of these firms lost their marketplace value. Investor confidence in the industry was shaken, and several companies ended up foregoing e-commerce, reinventing their business models or ceasing operations completely. Thus, while an organization's reputation might initially attract investors, its continued ability to meet and exceed their expectations is the only way to sustain the reputation.

Positive reputations can lead to expanded sales, product lines and strategic partnerships

Customers have shown their willingness—even their desire—to do business with firms they perceive to have sterling reputations in the marketplace. How customers are treated by employees, how customers view the quality of products, how customers feel about the organization's policies and practices and how favorably customers hold the overall image of an organization are all ingredients that will likely lead to continued customer loyalty. As organizations better manage their relationships with customers, there is the strong likelihood that expanded sales will increase. Customer-relationship management initiatives, such as creating customer profiles, maintaining frequent, customized and personalized communications with customers, and continuing to add products and services that are desired by customers are all ways to enhance the organization's reputation.

Another way a positive reputation aids an organization is through its ability to form strategic partnerships with other organizations. Strategic partnerships create value for customers by bundling complementary products and services from two or more companies and providing a seamless experience for the customer. These partnerships may also lead to production and distribution efficiencies for organizations and are likely to create value for shareholders, too. Strategic partnerships are well-crafted arrangements that explicitly articulate how two or more firms will work together to design products, market to and serve customers and distribute goods and services. The willingness of organizations to enter into strategic partnerships with each other is predicated, to a large degree, on the reputation of each firm.

Good reputations might provide the organization assistance in times of crisis and latitude with requests

In the best of times, organizations enjoy the benefits of good reputations: increased sales, the attraction and retention of talent, good publicity, the support of communities and willing investors. It is in times of crisis, however, when an organization's positive reputation can really pay off. When a company needs to renegotiate with vendors, suppliers or creditors, a track record of success and a positive marketplace reputation can go a long way toward facilitating the creation of new business terms or contracts. Additionally, when an organization faces a decision that requires latitude on the part of another—for example, seeking exemptions to zoning requirements, tax abatements, exceptions to policies—the company's overall reputation and history as a good corporate citizen are ingredients in the decision-making process.

Prospective employees are attracted to and current employees want to stay with organizations that have good reputations

Talented employees want to work for a winning organization. Companies are viewed as winners, in part, due to their reputation as a good place to work, a good place from whom to purchase and a good place with whom to do business. Organizations that are viewed as industry leaders and who exhibit characteristics of "employers of choice" attract well-qualified, hard-working and cream-of-the-crop employees. Companies with stellar reputations also tend to enjoy relationships with their employees that translate into workers that stay longer, work harder and refer the organization as a good employer.

Companies with good reputations enjoy the 'benefit of the doubt' from media and investors

When an organization faces a public-relations crisis, the media and investors often put the crisis in the context of the organization's overall and long-standing reputation. A good reputation can buy an organization a tremendous amount of benefit of the doubt from the media. Newspaper editors, TV reporters and consumer watchdog groups are likely to give organizations with good reputations a potentially fairer hearing in the press than organizations that are repeat offenders of fiduciary responsibility, consumer trust, employee loyalty and community goodwill. Investors, while generally concerned with the maximization of their return on investment, have also shown a willingness to stick by an organization that temporarily has difficulties, but has an overall positive reputation. Indeed, numerous organizations' reputations have either helped or hurt their long-term viability.

How Have Reputations Helped or Hurt Companies?
Companies with Positive Reputations
Johnson & Johnson

In 1982, Johnson & Johnson faced a public-relations crisis when seven people died from ingesting Tylenol capsules laced with cyanide. When it quickly became apparent that product tampering resulted in the deaths, Johnson & Johnson developed a two-pronged approach to handling the crisis. First, the organization immediately reached out to law enforcement, the medical community and consumers and instituted a nationwide recall of the product. Once the impending crisis had passed, Johnson & Johnson spent money on developing safer, tamper-resistant packaging, shared this knowledge with others in the industry and relaunched Tylenol. The company put the health and welfare of its customers first, was candid with the public from the beginning of the crisis and worked to restore consumer trust. Within a year of doing the right thing, strong market share recovered for Johnson & Johnson, and the company has continued to enjoy a positive reputation from consumers, policymakers and the media.

Nordstrom

Although Nordstrom is now known as an upscale department store chain, it began as a shoe retailer in Seattle. From that origin, it has developed and maintained a positive reputation as one of the best women's shoe stores in the United States, in addition to offering a wide range of other products. Shoppers are willing to pay a premium for otherwise cheaper shoes available elsewhere. Why? The sales experiences, in which employees treat customers like royalty, is one reason; the after-sales care, support and customer-centric return policies are another. Nordstrom is also known for its excellent ability to attract top employees, as a result of the overwhelmingly positive reputation it has as a sales organization and as an employer.

Harley-Davidson

It is not too often that an organization enjoys such a positive reputation that customers literally brand their bodies with the company's logo—in the form of tattoos. For Harley-Davidson, customers have developed an almost cult-like following of the organization's products. The upscale, high-end motorcycles are excellent, but Harley-Davidson has taken its customer relationship strategy one step further: riding a Harley-Davidson has less to do with the act of getting from point A to point B on a motorcycle and more to do with a lifestyle associated with the product. Customers flock to Harley-Davidson rallies, participate in Harley-Davidson ride groups, wear Harley-Davidson clothing and adorn their motorcycles in Harley-Davidson custom products. This company does an excellent job of managing its image with customers and actively involving customers in the ongoing shaping and managing of its reputation.

Companies with Mixed Reputations
Nike

Like Harley-Davidson, Nike enjoys the product-as-lifestyle reputation with customers. Nike shoes are high quality, and the company created an extremely positive reputation through early product innovation and marketing tie-ins linked to sports stars. This positive reputation, however, is off-set by negative stories that emerged concerning where and how Nike shoes are made. Reports of sweatshop conditions, human rights violations, the use of child labor and other disconcerting practices have been the subject of media scrutiny, consumer watchdog groups and college-student activists. Thus, while Nike enjoys a positive product reputation, its overall corporate reputation suffers from the perception of its organizational practices.

Martha Stewart Brand

Excellent products, wide-ranging media and consumer goods, and a strong and loyal following of customers all conspire to make Martha Stewart one of the most well-known personal brands in the United States. Stewart's legal problems, including a short prison term, made headlines throughout 2004 and impacted not only Stewart the person, but also the brand, the corporation's employees, investors and business partners. The full effect of these circumstances on the sustained success and ongoing value of the Martha Stewart brand remains unknown. However, the reputation of the company has certainly been adversely impacted as a result of the media attention and legal difficulties faced by Martha Stewart.

Microsoft Corp.

The true Goliath in its industry, Microsoft is the biggest, richest and most successful brand in its category. The company is seen as innovative, charitable, good to its employees and active in the communities in which it operates. However, because of the almost monopolistic nature Microsoft commands in its industry, the company has been subjected to numerous investigations and lawsuits related to antitrust issues brought by government entities. Some individuals also dislike the near-dominance Microsoft has over the daily functioning of technology-related work using the company's ubiquitous software products.

Companies with Negative Reputations

Philip Morris Cigarettes

It is difficult to find companies who are still in business even after suffering a generally negative image in the marketplace over a sustained period of time. Nonetheless, Philip Morris is a prime example of an organization that has suffered a declining reputation, largely thanks to actions it took—or didn't take—relative to the manufacturing and distribution of its cigarettes products. For years, the company denied that cigarettes had addictive qualities, denied that it knew of a direct link between smoking and cancer, denied that it actively courted teenagers as customers through appealing marketing campaigns and denied the effects of secondhand smoking. Philip Morris faced constant litigation, charges from consumer watchdog groups, intense media and government scrutiny and, ultimately, a backlash as being perceived as acting against the public good. Through awareness, education and outreach campaigns, the company has attempted to improve its image in recent years. This occurred primarily after evidence of its prior knowledge about the harmful nature of its product came to light and as a result of settlements reached with numerous government agencies. The net result, however, is that Philip Morris continues to face a daunting reputation management task in the marketplace.

Internal Revenue Service (IRS)

While technically a U.S. federal agency and not a company, the IRS nevertheless is another example of an organization that generally is perceived by the public as having a poor reputation. Some people simply do not like to pay taxes and thus blame the IRS as a result of their personal philosophy. Many taxpayers find the bureaucratic nature of the agency frustrating, while others find the complex and ever-changing tax code and regulations to be very nonuser friendly. The fear, warranted or unwarranted, of tax audits from IRS officials is another reason the agency faces a poor reputation in the public. This fear was further exacerbated in 1997, when hearings were televised of testimony from employees about abuses of power within the IRS. To combat its consistently negative image, the IRS has, among other things, established a taxpayer advocate, whose role is to assist individual and business taxpayers in settling disputes with the IRS and to try to repair the larger, systemic flaws that cause trouble for taxpayers and IRS employees. In spite of efforts like this, the IRS still faces a generally negative public reputation.

What Activities are Associated with Reputation Management?

Reputation Management Involves the Following Activities:

* Branding and value creation
* Internal marketing
* Research and competitive intelligence
* Intellectual property protections
* Corporate communications
* Investor relations and corporate governance
* Community outreach and philanthropic endeavors
* Corporate social responsibility
* Daily interactions among and between stakeholders.

Branding and Value Creation

Branding is the process of creating value for products, services and solutions for the purpose of eliciting a positive response to and widespread awareness of the organization. As a result, managing an organization's brand is one of the most critical components to reputation management. While integral to advertising, branding should not be confused with or discounted as a mere marketing ploy. Instead, branding involves a series of activities that are designed to align how the organization's products, services and solutions are encapsulated and communicated to customers and other stakeholders. A fundamental component of branding seeks to define the organization's value proposition. The value proposition is, simply put, the reasons why customers should buy from the organization. In other words, what value does the customer derive from doing business with the company?

Creating value for customers as part of the branding process involves understanding what customers want and are willing to pay for. Typically, companies compete for customers by providing low prices, having outstanding quality/service or providing total solutions; rarely does an organization excel at creating value for customers in all three arenas simultaneously. Wal-Mart, GEICO, JetBlue Airways, Super 8 Motels, Payless Shoes and E-trade are all organizations that compete in the marketplace using lower prices as their principal competitive differentiator. Organizations that compete by providing outstanding quality and service as a means to differentiate include The Ritz-Carlton, Nordstrom, Lands' End, Singapore Airlines, Bath & Body Works and Godiva Chocolates. Finally, organizations that provide total solutions to customers in a chosen market include FedEx (logistics), Microsoft, Citigroup (financial services), Marriott (hospitality management), Walt Disney Co. (entertainment) and Office Max (supplies and procurement). Understanding what a customer wants—and is willing to pay for—is key to determining how best to position the organization in the eyes of the customer.

Another way branding and value creation can be understood is by identifying the tangible and intangible attributes associated with an organization. Tangible attributes are the specific benefits, features and differentiators offered by a product or company. Because of the increasing ease with which customers can find alternative or substitutable products, using tangible attributes as a value-creation activity may be shortsighted. Product innovations that provide a lead today can be easily matched and, in some cases, surpassed by competitors in a relatively short time frame.

As a result, branding and value creation is perhaps best maximized when customers elicit positive intangible attributes—the sustainable images, feelings, expectations and perceptions—about a specific product or company. These intangible attributes vary from customer to customer, of course, but the notion of customers having a high personal attachment to or relationship with the organization underscores their importance. It has often been said customers buy products from companies, but form relationships with the people selling them those products. In an era when consistently and proactively managing relationships with customers might be the truest way to earn their loyalty, it is important that employees know what these customers want, need and value from their interactions with the organization. Thus, there is a continual need to engage in internal marketing to educate employees about the organization's branding and value-creation activities and their role in contributing to these activities.

Internal Marketing

As its name implies, internal marketing involves communicating important messages about the organization's products, services and solutions to the very people who are the face of the company: its employees. Educating employees about the organization's branding and value-creation activities is important for several reasons. First, employees need to understand how, why and on what basis the organization is competing for customers. Second, employees need to know the organization's value proposition. This entails being able to describe strengths, features and benefits of the company's products and being able to articulate how and why customers should choose to do business with the organization. Perhaps most importantly, internal marketing emphasizes how and why employees are a critical component of attaining loyalty from and managing relationships with the organization's customers.

Beyond stressing information about products and customers, internal marketing also tends to the issue of how and why employees should want to work for, be retained by, grow with and perform well for the organization. Just like customers, employees form personal attachments to organizations—perhaps even more so than customers, given the near-daily interactions and relationships with co-workers. Providing specific, explicit and continuous communication about employee-centric plans, policies, practices and processes is necessary if employees are to be committed to the organization. Often, however, organizations just assume employees inherently know this type of information or tend to only communicate it during orientation or an annual performance-appraisal meeting. To be truly effective, internal marketing should regularly emphasize the reasons the organization values and invests in its employees. This will help, in part, to energize employees and garner their commitment to serving the organization and its customers.

Finally, internal marketing should also equip employees with an understanding of the financial and other realities confronting the organization. Sometimes referred to as "open book management," this approach seeks to educate employees at all levels of the organization about fundamental concepts (finance, marketing, sales, etc.) that drive organizational performance. Additionally, this approach shares candid information about the organization's performance in key areas and elicits feedback from employees on ways to improve effectiveness. One key to making employees feel more engaged is to share specific information about the big-picture perspective, including industry news, financial forecasts, new technological or other innovations planned, feedback from customers or business partners and information gleaned from research and competitive intelligence data-gathering processes.

Research and Competitive Intelligence

Researching and understanding the competitive landscape is also part of reputation management. Competitive intelligence involves gathering, analyzing, interpreting and summarizing the actions of rival organizations and the implications of those actions. It is designed to be a legal, ethical and ongoing process that can yield significant information about how companies operate within an industry. This type of process typically involves creating competitor profiles; developing financial analyses; conducting a situational analysis, including the identification of strengths, weaknesses, opportunities and threats; planning for various scenarios and contingencies; and, where applicable, engaging in mystery-shopping exercises.

Beyond sophisticated planning and analytical tools and processes, however, research and competitive intelligence can also involve more traditional activities. Attending conferences and trade shows, talking to other professionals and consultants in the industry, reading newspapers and industry periodicals, subscribing to electronic resources, participating in association activities and, in general, observing trends and characteristics of rival firms in the marketplace are all part of understanding the industry. Such an understanding can translate into significant savings and profitability for organizations. For example, NutraSweet estimated it saves $50 million a year thanks to competitive intelligence endeavors; Texas Instruments used its analyses to pursue an acquisition before a rival could; and Merck anticipated and outmaneuvered the competition by crafting a counterstrategy to a rival's new drug.

Additionally, the value of research and competitive intelligence can yield significant results for leaders as they manage the organization's reputation. By understanding the activities and planned actions of competitors, an organization can respond by aligning its products, services and solutions to meet or exceed the expectations of its customers and other stakeholder groups. In many cases, the ability of an organization to forecast what others might do and develop interventions that seek to add value can be the key to customer loyalty.

Intellectual Property Protections

In some organizations, part of reputation management involves safeguarding against the research-and competitive intelligence-gathering activities of others. This is especially true in organizations that have developed specific business practices, processes or technologies for which there is a high degree of value placed on that intellectual property and for which the intellectual property yields significant competitive advantage. Indeed, the ability to protect against the unwarranted infringements on copyright, patents, trademarks, service marks and other proprietary information represents a major challenge in companies.

Corporate Communications

To present a unified, coherent and consistent voice of the organization to its many stakeholder groups, most companies use the corporate communications function. Activities such as generating press releases, maintaining Web sites, engaging in legislative relations, fielding media requests, holding press conferences and handling public-relations events are all part of the scope of corporate communications. These activities are a vital component of reputation management, as they provide an organization-initiated and organization-managed approach to shaping and managing its reputation externally.

Investor Relations and Corporate Governance

Like the corporate communications function, investor relations focuses on proactively and accurately conveying important organizational matters to a vital constituency: shareholders. Investor relations officers are typically charged with providing the investment community with past financial data and reporting on the outlook of future business strategy. As such, the investor relations function plays an important role in reputation management. The level of domestic and international individual and institutional investments in organizations requires more strategic management of these relationships. Additionally, the increased scrutiny of financial reporting, disclosures of conflicts of interest, certification of earnings and other compliance requirements associated with fiscal stewardship make investor relations even more of a strategic priority. Finally, the renewed emphasis on corporate governance also plays a role in reputation management. Transparent business, financial and management practices, governed by a board of directors with appropriate independence and objectivity, are key to installing confidence in the investment community and others regarding the organization's ability to engage in ethical decision-making at the highest levels.

Community Outreach and Philanthropic Endeavors

One way an organization enhances its reputation in the marketplace is through outreach and philanthropic endeavors. These activities are designed to connect companies to their communities and, increasingly, to show how companies are adding value to the overall quality of life in places where they live, work and do business. Some ways organizations engage in these endeavors is through employee volunteerism; donations of products; sponsoring civic clubs and organizations; participating in community events; investing in local art, sporting and cultural complexes; providing internship and other job-shadow and workplace experiences for students; and, in general, being viewed as a good corporate citizen.

Corporate Social Responsibility

Closely related to being viewed as a good corporate citizen is the notion of corporate social responsibility and its role in determining an organization's effectiveness in areas beyond just those associated with money. Social corporate responsibility seeks to judge performance on how an organization treats its people and the environment, in addition to sound fiscal outcomes. The "triple bottom line" emphasizing financial, social and environmental considerations has received increasing attention as communities, employees, investors, policymakers and customers demand a more holistic accounting of an organization's actions. In many quarters, no longer do the ends justify the means. Organizations that commit to corporate social responsibility actively assess, monitor, evaluate and improve their practices in an effort to maintain and improve their reputations and relationships with a variety of stakeholder groups.

Daily Interactions Among and Between Stakeholders

While each of the preceding activities plays an important part, perhaps the most significant ingredient influencing reputation management is the daily interactions that members of an organization have with each other and with their multiple publics. Employees want an environment that values and nurtures their contributions. Customers want value for the money and service that treats them with respect. Investors want honest, accurate information on which to base their decision-making. Vendors and suppliers want a business partner they can trust to treat them fairly. And communities want organizations to be good stewards of their role. Organizational reputations are managed strategically but are typically made and broken operationally; that is, the daily interactions between employees and others can do a lot to enhance or undermine the overall reputation of the enterprise.

Summary

This chapter addressed fundamental concepts related to reputation management. Why and how shaping and managing the organization's reputation is important was also addressed. Examples of organizations with positive, mixed and negative reputations were profiled, and activities associated with reputation management were identified and described. Reputation management is thus a complex and ever-evolving phenomenon, and it has a direct bearing on an organization's ability to find, keep and motivate productive employees. As the case study that follows highlights, reputation management extends even to the employment process. How a firm addresses controversial issues and discloses realistic plans for its employees, among other things, impacts how the organization is viewed by prospective employees.

Case Study:
Reputation Management and Workforce Engagement

'I Hope Others Can Benefit From My Experiences'

Cascadia		Financial
	Services	

Established in 1873 as the United Bank of Oregon

Dear Mr. McNaughton:

Thank you for inviting me to speak at the college's Career Day Orientation for graduating seniors. As you know, I will be retiring later this year after 31 years as a corporate recruiter for Cascadia Financial Services (and its corporate "premerger" predecessors).

For the past 19 years, I have recruited on your campus, and I estimate that there are hundreds of your graduates who have come to work at CFS. I feel that I know a great deal about the education your students receive and what they look for in their first post-college jobs.

Being a corporate recruiter has been a fulfilling career for me, but one with many challenges. As I will try to convey to your students, recruiters do more than find people to get the job done; their most important task is to represent the company's values and actions to prospective employees accurately and honestly.

Attached is a not-yet-finished draft of my presentation.

Sincerely,

E. Victor Denville

Career Day Presentation
Renfrew State University
Draft

When hearing that I have spent my career as a corporate recruiter, some people immediately say, "Boy that must be some cushy job. You go to a campus, students clamor to meet you and impress you, and you have your choice of five or more applicants for each job. What a picnic." Sometimes, if I am in a lighthearted mood, I say, "You are very wrong. Usually I have a choice of *10 or 20* applicants for each slot. Sometimes I don't even bother meeting them. I just pick out names that I like." Well, that's usually a conversation stopper until they see that I am kidding.

I want to tell you what it has been like to be a recruiter for a large corporation, what issues and challenges I have faced and what I actually do when trying to decide whether or not to make an offer to the eager, earnest and very, very nervous graduating students I interview.

Sitting in the interview room, I imagine each candidate in a race that involves successfully leaping over three different hurdles. The first hurdle is the answer to a very simple question: *"What do you know about Cascadia Financial Services?"* Applicants who look at me nervously and say "It is a bank, right?" have already stumbled. Others stumble when their answer is, "I know its corporate headquarters are in Seattle and the person I am dating...."

If applicants get beyond the first hurdle by demonstrating they know something about Cascadia, how it operates and how it is different from other banks, I move toward the second hurdle, more questions: *"What do you know about yourself in terms of the work environment that would enable you to work most effectively? Do you prefer working independently or in teams? Would you have a more positive response to a task-oriented, get-the-job-done environment or a 'take your time, do it right' culture?"* People who say that they want a job in banking stumble almost immediately because there are banks and there are banks. At one time, Cascadia was a regional bank; now it is a national bank and—believe me—there is a big difference between the two.

Those who are still standing at the third hurdle face the toughest challenge. My question to them is: *"If you came to work at Cascadia and you worked there for 10 years, what would you like people to say about the company where you had worked for so long? Imagine overhearing two strangers talking and one of them said, 'What do you think of Cascadia? Not as a business or whether it makes a profit, but what it cares about, what's important to the people who work there?'"*

Let me be candid. Your ability to answer that question is evidence of your ability to be introspective, your capacity for self-reflection and— in my experience—an effective predictor of compatibility between employee and employing organization. I am going to give you three examples that illustrate how important it is to understand if your *values* overlap with the values of the organization. My three examples are drawn from my own experience, and all of them concern the ways in which individuals deal with situations when their values are in conflict with company policies, practices and priorities.

The first example occurred when I was in my fourth or fifth year with Cascadia. I was teamed with our senior recruiter, Ted Bates, who was legendary for his ability to recruit "top talent." We were meeting with the finalists who were probably going to receive offers from us that day. Someone asked if new employees were required to travel during the initial three-year period before employees were eligible for the next rung on the corporate ladder. The person said, "I really don't like traveling and don't want to work somewhere if I am going to be required to do a lot of traveling." Ted said, "We like to keep people close to home during the three-year 'orientation' to our business. In fact, very few of each year's trainees travel at all. In the fourth year the amount of travel people do depends on the assignment they are given."

When we left the meeting, I said, "Don't we require everyone promoted after the third year to do some traveling so we can gauge how well they do in those environments?" "Sure we do," he said, "but that's not what the person asked; the question was whether we require new employees to travel. We don't." I said, "But, after that initial period, a person can't succeed without traveling. Wasn't your answer misleading?" "Look," he replied, "Cascadia works hard to attract 'the best and the brightest.' If I have to 'glide' over some facts to get the people we want, I can live with that. Can you?"

As you can tell from seeing me stand here tonight, I could—and did—live with it. I rationalized that it really wasn't lying, and it was for a good reason because Cascadia wanted to hire the best, most talented people.

The second incident occurred six years ago. The media were having a field day telling and retelling the story that Cascadia was being sued for concealing and condoning repeated incidents of sexual harassment in three of our largest regional offices. It was the peak of our recruiting effort, and I was asked about those allegations over and over again. Some women refused to be interviewed to protest what they believed had happened. I didn't know how to answer questions about those charges. I talked to a very senior executive at the company and he said, "Keep denying everything. Talk about 'innocent until proven guilty.' Talk about anything, but admit nothing. We are trying to arrange a settlement, but until we reach agreement with those women, deny, deny, deny."

I did what I was told because I am a team player, but it was hard for me because these young people were asking me to tell them "the truth." They trusted me and I was betraying that trust. It was something of a shock to me that my own company, the place where I had worked for so long, was actually asking me to lie to people.

My third example is one you are probably familiar with because it happened just last year. A handful of senior executives at Cascadia were indicted by the feds for insider trading, and that was big news because tens of millions of dollars were involved. But it was another aspect of the story that troubled me. In addition to the senior executives, almost two dozen junior and middle-management personnel were also indicted for the attempted "cover-up." Some claimed to have been pressured to go along; others claimed to have participated because they wanted to "please" their bosses. More than half of them said that there was a pervasive attitude that it was OK to cut ethical corners if you could get away with it.

There have been some plea bargains, and the trials will begin in a few months, so we will have to wait and see what happens then. But, here's the dilemma. Remember that third hurdle I discussed? It was being able to answer questions about what a company cares about and what's important to the people who work there.

Well, what should I, or any recruiter, or any corporate spokesperson do in such situations? How should I respond when a prospective employee asks me what it's like to work for Cascadia? If someone at a recruiting session asked, "Is it true?" I could candidly say, "I don't know, and we will have to wait until we hear what a jury thinks." But what if one of you asks a different question: "Do you think it *could* be true?"

In such a situation, should I remain loyal and upbeat, putting forward the argument about "a few bad apples" or should I articulate my fears that, yes, it could be true and, yes, it could have happened the way it is being reported?

I wish I had answers to these difficult questions. People always ask me for hints, suggestions and ideas about how to impress a recruiter. I don't have answers to give them or you, but the questions I am asking can very much determine your futures. By telling you all of this, I hope you and others can benefit from my experiences in your own emerging careers.

Rick McNaughton finished reading the draft of the speech Vic Denville sent him. It was powerful and thought provoking, and he sat back and reflected on how prospective Cascadia employees and others now beginning their careers would react and respond.

Questions for Consideration and Discussion
"I Hope Others Can Benefit From My Experiences"

1. Given the content of Vic Denville's proposed speech, what concerns, if any, would you have about working at Cascadia? How might these concerns impact your interest in Cascadia as a potential employer?

2. To what extent does Cascadia have a reputation management problem? In what ways have the leaders at Cascadia chosen to shape and manage how their organization is viewed by others? To what extent do you feel this is an effective or ineffective approach?

3. Suppose you were hired as a consultant by Cascadia's leaders to advise on how to improve reputation management activities. What, specifically, would you advise and why? What should Cascadia keep doing? What should it change?

4. When an organization has had negative information reported in the media, how can recruiters, HR professionals, managers and others best handle inquiries about the negative information from current employees and candidates for employment? What approaches should they take? What type of information should they disclose? Why?

Chapter 4:
Ethics, Diversity and Safety

Introduction: What Do We Mean By 'Ethics, Diversity and Safety'?

Ethics, diversity and safety considerations involve the ability of organizational leaders to create a culture of ethical conduct and decision-making; comply with laws and policies; respect and manage diversity; and ensure a safe work environment. The ethics, diversity and safety component of workforce engagement reflects the extent to which employees perceive the company is hiring and promoting a diverse workforce, providing a pleasant and safe working environment and ensuring a culture of ethics.

Highlights from the 2004-2005 National Benchmark Study on Workforce Engagement

It was not until early 2000 that the wave of ethical scandals made daily news. It continues today, and the parade of companies is impressive: Ford-Firestone, Enron, Adelphia, Xerox, Global Crossing, Tyco, Royal Ahold, Worldcom, Citigroup, Arthur Anderson, Martha Stewart, etc. Employees want to know that their organization is ethical, is not willing to place profits in front of ethics and holds people accountable if they violate company standards.

As a top-five driver of workforce engagement as determined in the *pan* 2004-2005 study, ethics, diversity and safety is a critical element in the relationship employers have with their employees. Just six in 10 employees believe their organizations are highly ethical, while one in six disagree. Government employees tend to have the least positive perceptions of their organization's culture, with slightly more than half agreeing they work in a culture of ethics. Information services, financial services and health services are seen as the most ethical, with nearly two thirds of the employees stating they feel their organization is highly ethical.

However, financial services and health services are regulated industries where "compliance" is required for accreditation. Compliance ensures that a company does what is required; an ethical culture ensures that companies do the right things because they are the right things to do. Nonunion employees are less likely than union employees to believe their organization is highly ethical (two-thirds versus one-half), one of the reasons that union employees are significantly more unengaged than nonunion employees.

Overall, employees who believe their organization is highly ethical are significantly more likely to be fully engaged than employees who believe otherwise, highlighting the linkage between ethics and engagement. When employees feel that their organization puts profits in front of ethics, cuts corners in ethics and compliance issues to increase profit, does not employ senior leaders who are people of high personal integrity and does not offer a confidential avenue to voice ethical concerns, their level of engagement drops significantly. More importantly, so does their desire to go the extra mile for customers, critical to continued business success.

Only half of all employees in the *pan* study agree that company policies are carried out in a fair and just manner, while one quarter disagrees. State/local government employees are most pessimistic, with nearly as many employees disagreeing (34 percent) as agreeing (40 percent). Employees working in operations are least positive, with only 46 percent agreeing the company carries out policies fairly and 30 percent disagreeing.

A common pattern re-emerges when reviewing the tenure of the employee in the organization: the longer an employee is with the company or has been in the job, the lower the perceptions are of fairness. Interestingly, part-time employees have a slightly more positive impression, perhaps due to having fewer interactions with the company than their full-time brethren. Senior leaders are the most positive of any demographic group measured in the *pan* study, with three-quarters agreeing that policies are carried out in a fair and just manner. However, less than half of all individual contributors feel the same way. Of interest, employees who are caring for either a child or a child or loved one are more positive about policies than employees who are not caring for a child or loved one at home.

In addition to ethics, companies are increasingly aware of the benefits of having a diverse workforce. It is not just cultural or racial differences that make a diverse workforce, it is also religion, age, education, sexual orientation and even the way people think that add to a company's diversity. Promoting a diverse workforce allows companies to match the diversity of their customer base and provides internal benefits as well: it strengthens the ethical values of the organization; it has a positive effect on recruitment and retention; reduces conflicts at work, resulting in a more positive working environment and stronger workforce engagement; and ultimately enhances the reputation of the organization.

The 2004-2005 *pan* study shows that employers have significant improvement opportunities in relations to diversity. Slightly more than half of all employees agree that their organization treats employees with respect and appreciation. Less than six in 10 (57 percent) believe that differences among individuals are respected and valued at their organization. On a more positive note, seven out of 10 employees feel safe from fear, intimidation and harassment. However, a review of the demographic differences uncovers familiar patterns. Senior executives are significantly more positive related to diversity, with eight in 10 feeling good about their progress. This drops to six in 10 middle managers and supervisors, and only half of the individual contributors.

Older employees are much more negative in their perceptions than younger workers, and union employees are significantly more pessimistic in their perceptions of diversity than nonunion employees. And only four out of 10 state/local government workers are satisfied with their organizations' progress on diversity.

Finally, employees expect to be happy with the physical working conditions of their job and want to be satisfied with the physical safety and security of their workplace. In this area, employers are performing well. Eighty-one percent of all employees expressed confidence in their physical safety at work, with older employees again being more negative then younger employees. Nonunion employees express greater confidence in their safety than do union employees, as do employees who have participated in work-related training and education, again showing the positive impact of the training and development "halo effect" on the perceptions of employees.

Some companies do the right things because they are the right things to do. Others do the right things for employees because they understand the positive impact these actions have on employee retention and customer satisfaction. The *pan* results show that most companies need to significantly improve their efforts in ethics, diversity and safety.

Highlights from the 2006-2007 National Benchmark Study on Workforce Engagement

Again the second strongest driver of workforce engagement, the overall performance as perceived by the employees continues to weaken. In fact, only half of all employees believe *People in their organization are treated with respect and appreciation,* while one quarter disagrees.

Disappointing, but not surprising, is the data related to the perception of an organization's ethics. Less than six in 10 employees agree their *Organization is highly ethical* (58 percent), compared to 63 percent in 2004-2005, a statistically significant decrease during the last two years. Smaller companies (with less than 250 employees) view their corporate ethics much more favorably than companies with more than 5,000 employees. Manufacturing and state government perceive their organizational ethics least favorably, while those in business and financial services view their organizational ethics most favorably.

As in 2004-2005, only 60 percent of employees in 2006-07 feel valued as an employee, while another 21 percent disagree with that statement. Feelings of being valued tend to be higher in:

- Companies with less than 250 employees (71 percent feel valued as an employee)
- Executives/senior management (83 percent feel valued)
- Employees with one promotion in the last three years (70 percent feel valued), two promotions in the last three years (73 percent) and three promotions in the last three years (82 percent)
- Workers who received work-related training and education (66 percent)
- Those who participated in a company-sponsored social event (66 percent)
- Leisure and hospitality employees (70 percent)
- Employees who live in the East South-Central Region (81 percent)
- Those who have been with their company or in their job for less than one year (68 percent).

While nearly seven in 10 newly hired employees feel valued as an employee, the percentage falls as their tenure with the company and the tenure in their position increase. Perhaps new employees are looking at the world through rose-colored glasses, and the problem is those glasses do not stay rosy very long.

Why are Ethics, Diversity and Safety Important?

At first glance, it might appear odd to have the seemingly disparate concepts of ethics, diversity and safety linked together. In many instances, however, all three concepts are upheld by the same overriding goal: *creating an honest, safe environment that treats people with dignity and respect.* When viewed through this lens, then, it is easy to see why organizations that truly value their employees' well-being will likely seek to ensure that ethical behavior is encouraged, diversity and inclusion are respected and cultivated and safe work environments are provided.

There are literally hundreds and hundreds of books and articles devoted to the subjects of ethics, diversity and safety in the workplace. This chapter highlights important broad issues associated with each concept and identifies some of the requirements needed to enhance workforce engagement. Thus, the material presented should be used as an overview of ethics, diversity and safety, a review of current practices and a springboard for further action.

From a workforce engagement standpoint, attending to matters of ethics, diversity and safety is crucial—as noted, these concepts are a key driver of workforce engagement. This means that current and prospective employees view the organization's practices in these areas with a critical eye and that organizations succeeding in ethics, diversity and safety are likely to find and keep top talent. Organizations that ignore or back-burner these issues will find themselves unable to compete for the talented and productive employees everyone so desires. Thus, in addition to focusing on these matters because they are the "right" things to do, there is a bottom-line mandate to create ethical, diverse and safe environments that attract and retain employees.

Although there are many definitions surrounding the word "ethics," one enduring and encapsulating meaning is "obedience to the unenforceable." This highlights the notion that individuals and organizations behaving ethically are doing so of their own volition and are not merely complying with a rule, law or regulation. Given the ambiguous nature of ethical decision-making, it is crucial that senior leaders set the tone by talking the talk *and* walking the walk. They can do the former by clearly and continuously articulating their commitment to sound ethical principles and behaviors; the latter can be accomplished, in part, by creating policies, practices and approaches to assist employees in ethical decision-making.

Diversity seems to be the watchword of the workforce these days—and rightfully so. In the United States and elsewhere, changes to demographic patterns are continuing to infuse organizations with more women; minority members; immigrants; older workers; differently abled individuals; and people with diverse personalities, viewpoints and lifestyles. One admittedly simplistic way of thinking about a complex issue like diversity is to define it as "the differences that make us unique." The ability to find, keep, motivate and manage this dynamic workforce is one of the biggest challenges and opportunities facing leaders, managers, HR professionals and others. Therefore, it is important for organizations to know how and why they value diversity, to understand and embrace similarities and differences and to create inclusive approaches to meet the needs of diverse employees.

Finally, safety involves ensuring a work environment free from injury, illness, psychological stress, fear, intimidation and harassment, among other things. It also emphasizes employee well-being through healthy work spaces and provides a secure place that seeks to avoid loss of proprietary knowledge or physical assets. Thus, to attend to issues of ethics, diversity and safety, there are several specific and explicit actions that organizational leaders can take to meet the requirements of these initiatives.

What are the Organizational Requirements to Support Ethics, Diversity and Safety?

Organizational Requirements for Ethics, Diversity and Safety Include:

- A commitment to ethics, diversity and safety from senior leaders

- Widespread understanding and acceptance of ethics, diversity and safety as organizational priorities

- Organizational capacity and infrastructure for ethics, diversity and safety

- Ongoing monitoring and evaluation of ethics, diversity and safety initiatives

- Continuous learning and improvement related to ethics, diversity and safety.

A commitment to ethics, diversity and safety from senior leaders

To be truly effective, senior leaders must commit themselves to the spirit and practice of ethics, diversity and safety initiatives. Such commitment extends beyond mere lip service and includes specific organizational policies, tasks and responsibilities. It also involves recognition on the part of senior leaders as to why and how these initiatives are important.

A commitment to ethics, diversity and safety signals to others—internally and externally—the organization's emphasis on performance. Such practices also contribute to talent attraction, retention and motivation; customer satisfaction; reputation management; and overall financial and operational performance. Performance in this context not only refers to *outcomes* (return on investment, stock price, market share, productivity gains, etc.), but also to the process of achieving performance (decision-making, inclusion, safe and effective practices, etc.). Thus, the ends do not justify the means in organizations with a commitment to these practices.

Widespread understanding and acceptance of ethics, diversity and safety as organizational priorities

Another organizational requirement is the widespread understanding and acceptance up, down and across the entire organization of the commitment to ethics, diversity and safety. Managers and employees must buy in to the notion that if they are to be members of the organization they must realize that the organization is serious about these concepts. They must also be informed that adhering to ethical decision-making, treating others with dignity and respect and performing work in accordance with safety regulations are not voluntary conditions of employment. Rather, most organizations have translated the "how" employees should work into defined performance expectations. This permits any corrective action or counseling interventions to be treated as behaviorally based performance-management issues for employees and helps move the sometimes ambiguous meaning surrounding ethics, diversity and safety into a more objective, observable domain.

Organizational capacity and infrastructure for ethics, diversity and safety

To move beyond mere lip service, senior leaders need to develop the capacity and infrastructure for ethics, diversity and safety. Capacity refers to the willingness of the organization to grow, adapt and embrace conditions under which ethical behavior can be performed, diversity and inclusion can be realized and safety can be maintained. One way to build capacity for these matters is through the identification and allocation of physical, financial, technological, informational and other resources to support ethics, diversity and safety. Infrastructure is the development of specific policies, practices and procedures aimed at providing direction and assistance to organizational members; the assignment of responsibility, authority and accountability for these initiatives; and tracking and reporting mechanisms to ensure compliance and monitor progress.

Ongoing monitoring and evaluation of ethics, diversity and safety initiatives

One way to monitor progress on ethics, diversity and safety initiatives is to explicitly define the performance indicators and metrics used to identify and gauge effectiveness in these areas. An example of a measure for ethics might be the number of conflicts of interest employees disclosed or were uncovered during a given time frame. For diversity, one measure might be scores on employee opinion surveys regarding the organization's perceived commitment to diversity. Finally, an example of a safety measure might be the number of job-related injuries that require workers' compensations claims be filed. Regardless of the performance indicators developed, data collection, analysis, interpretation and reporting on progress in key areas must occur at regular intervals.

Continuous learning and improvement related to ethics, diversity and safety

Attending to matters of ethics, diversity and safety requires an ongoing commitment by senior leaders and others in the organization. This commitment can be manifested, in part, by the identification of lessons learned, pitfalls to avoid and best practices related to these concepts. Widespread dissemination of information relevant to employees about the issues of ethics, diversity and safety helps to ensure that these areas are continually showcased as being a relevant, strategic and ongoing part of the organization's agenda for doing business. Additionally, regularly investing in training, professional development activities and other means to support employees can help infuse the organization's culture with continuous learning and improvement related to ethics, diversity and safety.

How can Ethical Decision Making be Encouraged?

Encouraging Ethical Decision Making Involves:

- Understanding and applying approaches to ethical decision-making
- Creating an environment that fosters honesty, transparency and accountability
- Ensuring appropriate control and reporting mechanisms are in place
- Rewarding ethical behavior and correcting or punishing unethical behavior.

Understanding and applying approaches to ethical decision making

Given the recent scandals related to unethical and, in some cases, illegal practices on the part of senior leaders in U.S. businesses, ethics continues to be a subject with significant importance and consequence in organizations. Many companies have recommitted themselves to ensuring ethical principles are upheld and that employees are trained in how to behave ethically. One of the most frequently occurring activities that can test a person's ethical framework is when decisions—no matter how large or small—are made.

Classic decision-making models tend to espouse a logical and linear approach to reaching a conclusion: (1) define the problem; (2) gather information; (3) identify alternatives; (4) select the best alternative; (5) implement the decision; and (6) evaluate the outcome. While a useful framework for understanding activities associated with good decision making, such models overlook or minimize the influence of personal and organizational values and their role in decision making.

Personal values influence decision-making based on how people view ethics. A utilitarian view, for example, focuses on making a decision based on providing the greatest good to the greatest number of people. Another view is based on the belief that individuals have certain rights and liberties granted to them by the Bill of Rights and other documents. As such, decisions can be made to uphold, protect or expand those rights. Closely related to this concept is the justice view, which seeks to consistently and fairly apply or enforce rules and regulations to ensure equity. In addition to personal values, decisions are often influenced by the organization's espoused and practiced values. A commitment to quality, a focus on the customer and a risk-averse culture are all examples of how organizational values, in addition to personal ones, play a part in ethical decision-making.

Creating an environment that fosters honesty, transparency and accountability

Recent public policy interventions, such as the Sarbanes-Oxley Act, compel organizations to create environments that foster honesty, transparency and accountability for decisions. One way to facilitate honest decision-making is to acknowledge the difficulties in the process and the faulty rationalizations people tend to use as a cover for a poor decision (e.g., "It isn't hurting anyone," "Everyone's doing it," "It's for a good cause"). Establishing guidelines for decision-making and training employees on how to best follow those guidelines helps to signal the organization's seriousness of purpose.

Another way to foster honesty and transparency is through open-book management. This concept provides relevant financial information to employees and educates employees on important matters in the organization. By showing employees the impact, causes and effects of decisions made on financial and operational performance, open-book management seeks to treat employees like owners and equips them with information to aid in improved decision-making.

Identifying and disclosing of harmful, unsafe or high-risk activities signals to stakeholders the ethical nature of the organization and its willingness to subject itself to public scrutiny. Sound corporate governance is another way of providing oversight to leadership activities. Boards of directors and others have an obligation (and, increasingly, a legal mandate) to ensure the organization is behaving ethically, serving shareholder and other stakeholder interests appropriately and disclosing fiscal and other matters of relevance in a timely manner. Thus, engaging in independent auditing, validation and evaluation on key organizational practices is yet another way to foster honesty, transparency and accountability.

Ensuring appropriate control and reporting mechanisms are in place

While making employees more autonomous (as part of their job does contribute to meaningful work), such discretion in performing work does not negate the need for appropriate management control, approval and oversight. Therefore, organizations need to establish and enforce clear guidelines that give employees latitude in carrying out job duties but also seek to limit unethical practices. Providing for appropriate controls for resource allocation, access to information and decision making is one way to safeguard the organization against unnecessary risk.

Two other ways to encourage adherence to ethical principles and behaviors include open-door policies and internal whistle-blowing protocols. Open-door policies permit the employee to have access to persons or departments beyond their own immediate supervisor to discuss issues of concern, seek clarification on work assignments and report unethical or problematic behaviors. Closely related to open-door policies is an internal whistle-blowing protocol.

Whistle-blowing protocols involve having means through which employees can candidly and confidentially report to the organization observed violations of the law, regulations or ethical standards. Some organizations establish a toll-free hotline, in some cases administered by a third-party organization, in which employees can anonymously make reports. An organizational ombudsperson, a person typically charged with resolving disputes or investigating claims, may be another source for internal whistle-blowers. One fact remains, though: if employees don't feel like there are mechanisms to initially report ethical or legal violations internally—without fear of reprisal—they will most assuredly engage in whistle-blowing to federal agencies, media outlets or other external organizations.

Finally, making sure that the organization's policies and performance expectations do not unwittingly encourage lapses in ethical behavior is also important. Sometimes the pressures to produce are so great—and the consequences for underperformance so severe—employees may want to do almost anything to avoid disappointing a manger. While this does not technically excuse the behavior, it may help to explain why employees are tempted to cut corners, make false reports, misrepresent things to customers or managers or hide mistakes. Savvy managers create the right amount and scope of performance challenges for employees, but do so in a manner that still upholds standards of ethical behavior.

Rewarding ethical behavior and correcting or punishing unethical behavior

To truly institutionalize the organization's commitment to ethical behavior on the part of its employees, appropriate rewards, corrections and punishments must occur.

First, when unethical activities are identified or uncovered, corrective action should be the intervention. This could be in the form of a policy clarification or creation, additional training on ethics, peer or third-party review of the situation or job aids and other tools to assist in improved decision making. Second, should repeated or severe ethical lapses occur, disciplinary action—up to and including termination—is needed. Finally, employees who demonstrate their own personal stewardship in ethical decision making should be rewarded. This is especially true when the outcomes of an ethically based decision prove costly or unpopular. Because employees tend to do what is rewarded, providing specific, salient recognition for ethical decision-making is also needed to shape and direct the behavior of employees.

How Can Diversity and Inclusion be Respected and Cultivated?

Respecting and Cultivating Diversity and Inclusion Involves:
- Making the "business case" for diversity
- Understanding differences and promoting inclusion among and between individuals and groups
- Identifying the needs of and providing resources for a diverse workforce
- Auditing, evaluating and improving workplace climates for diversity.

Making the 'business case' for diversity

The many laws devoted to articulating the employer-employee relationship in the United States and elsewhere were largely created as an outgrowth of poor past practices, primarily on the part of managers, owners and others in positions of power. Such practices tended to overlook or minimize worker concerns and well-being and, in some cases, exploited workers for the financial gain of managers or owners. The need for public policies that deal with how to treat employees emerged because some—not all—organizations in the past did not treat their employees fairly or appropriately. If organizations had all along treated employees well because it was the right thing to do, the many laws, rules and regulations directing these efforts simply would not be needed.

When speaking about diversity issues in organizations, it *should* be enough to say diversity is respected and cultivated because it is the right thing to do. Some organizations, in fact, actually believe and practice this sentiment. Others, it would seem, need to have a "business case" for diversity as an outline or rationale for such practices. Thus, in the spirit of assisting with that endeavor, the following reasons are given (in addition to the reason listed previously: *because it is the right thing to do*).

First, diversity issues are important to attract, retain and motivate talent. Top employees want an environment that permits their creativity and productivity to be unleashed. Thus, they seek environments that are inclusive of diverse people, perspectives and approaches to solving problems and generating solutions. Second, diversity is important because internal labor markets should reasonably mirror external labor markets. Canvassing and cultivating all the talent in the metropolitan statistical area helps ensure the organization avails itself of the best and brightest, not to mention has a workforce representative of the community in which it lives, works, invests and transacts business. Finally, diversity issues are important because diverse customers require new, innovative and diverse solutions.

Customers have shown their willingness to do business with organizations that best meet their needs and provide outstanding service and value in the process. One way of anticipating and proactively meeting diverse consumer needs is to employ diverse talent capable of developing products, services and solutions to meet those needs. Although there are numerous other "business case" reasons for diversity, these help highlight some of the more commonly articulated ones. Beyond just giving lip service to diversity, however, organizations need to truly try to understand differences and promote inclusion among and between individuals and groups.

Understanding differences and promoting inclusion among and between individuals and groups

Critics of diversity initiatives often point out that people's personal lives do not belong in the workplace, so organizations need not bother addressing this issue. That naïve point of view readily assumes that people check their personal lives at the front door of the organization, a fact that simply is not true. Instead, people bring to work their own values, attitudes, needs, past experiences, expectations, problems and work styles, among other characteristics. The challenge for organizational leaders, therefore, is to understand and respect the differences among and between individuals, while simultaneously search for overarching similarities that serve to unite employees in pursuit of fulfilling the organization's mission. This is, of course, easier said than done.

Perhaps the most important philosophical and practical intervention an organization can make is the promotion of an inclusive culture. Inclusion moves beyond merely tolerating individuals and their differences. Instead, inclusive environments actively seek out, value and welcome points of view that are not held by the dominant culture. To do so permits individualized expression, while also unleashing creative potential that might otherwise be silenced or stifled. Inclusive practices require that organizations omit two potentially oppressive phrases from their vocabularies: "We've *never* done it that way before" and "We've *always* done it this way before." Intentionally being inclusive means leaders are willing—even desirous—to work with, listen to and provide opportunities for people different from themselves. As an old Asian proverb aptly reminds, "If both of us are similar, one of us is unnecessary."

Identifying the needs of and providing resources for a diverse workforce

One of the most important symbolic and practical things an organization can do is charging an individual or department with responsibility for promoting, managing and evaluating diversity initiatives within the company. Larger companies might have a dedicated department devoted to macro-level diversity issues involving employees, suppliers and communities. Small and midsized organizations may relegate diversity to the provinces of the HR department. It is vital that employees know which person or department can provide guidance and assistance on diversity matters.

Next, organizations should gather stakeholder input to determine what policies, practices, approaches and resources would best meet the needs of diverse employees. This can be accomplished through surveys, focus groups, suggestion systems, and formal and informal feedback from key informants within and outside the organization.

From there, specific programs or interventions that address diversity-related concerns or requirements can be created. These might include offering flex-time and telecommuting work options, expanding child-care and elder-care assistance, instituting domestic-partner benefits, making accommodations for religious practices, providing assistance to a differently abled employee or sponsoring social and support networks for like-minded individuals and groups (e.g., women; Hispanics; gay, lesbian, bisexual and transgendered employees). In some instances, partnering with community organizations, vendors and consultants or subject-matter experts to assist with diversity issues is needed.

Auditing, evaluating and improving workplace climates for diversity

Like so many complicated and ever-changing phenomena in organizations, diversity must be viewed and treated as an ongoing process. Therefore, regularly seeking feedback from employees, customers, business partners and community members, among others, on how well the organization is doing relative to diversity is needed. Closely related is the need to review diversity-related initiatives of other organizations, including competitors and benchmarking practices against best-in-class companies. This information is useful in providing comparative data, but the goal should not be to merely be "better" than others; instead, the organization should seek to optimize its capacity and capabilities related to diversity performance indicators.

Finally, to ultimately improve the organizational climate for diversity, leaders need to keep track of changing demographics, preferences and trends in the internal and external labor forces. Knowing how and why people are attracted to, stay with and leave the organization, from a diversity perspective, is key to increasing retention, promoting satisfaction and enhancing engagement. Regularly taking stock of, improving and communicating relevant changes to the workforce can go a long way toward signaling the organization's commitment to diversity and inclusion.

How Can Safe Work Environments be Provided?

Providing Safe Work Environments Involves:

- Understanding causes and preventions of organizational safety-, health- and security-related accidents

- Identifying, documenting and describing safety, health and security hazards associated with work

- Developing programs and approaches that emphasize safety, health and security

- Fostering a climate free from fear, intimidation and harassment

- Ensuring that the workplace is regularly monitored and improved for enhanced safety, health and security practices.

Understanding causes and preventions of organizational safety-, health- and security-related accidents

Safety, health and security are important ingredients in providing workers a comfortable, enjoyable and productive workplace experience. Safety involves setting up work conditions free from personal harm for the employee. Health promotes personal well-being by eradicating or minimizing conditions under which illness, disease or discomfort occur. Security ensures that the organization's property, intellectual assets and employees are protected from damage, theft, sabotage or destruction. There are many causes for safety, health and security lapses in organizations.

Carelessness on the part of an employee performing his or her job is, perhaps, one of the biggest reasons for workplace safety infractions. Working too fast, performing duties while tired or distracted, not following standard operating procedures, failing to use personal protective equipment and merely forgetting safety-related steps in a process are all examples of how employees can unintentionally make unsafe mistakes at work. Beyond these direct causes, there are a number of other ways safety is minimized or undervalued. The lack of proper training, failure to supply workers with proper protective gear, pressure to step up production, cluttered or wet floors and high levels of stress can all contribute to workplace accidents and injuries.

The Occupational Safety and Health Administration (www.osha.gov) is the federal agency charged with interpreting, enforcing and giving guidance on the Occupational Safety and Health Act of 1970. Nearly all nongovernment organizations must comply with this act. OSHA provides numerous rights and responsibilities for employers and employees, all with the intent of making workplaces—and the work itself—safer for the employee. One way to do this is through identifying, documenting and describing safety, health and security hazards associated with work.

Identifying, documenting and describing safety, health and security hazards associated with work

To understand the nature of work, including equipment used and conditions under which work must be performed, a job analysis should be conducted. Job analysis involves collecting extensive data about jobs, typically through a combination of direct observations, interviews with job incumbents and supervisors, analysis of workflow (inputs, throughputs and outputs), and review and validation by subject-matter experts. A job analysis identifies the physical, mental, emotional and other conditions under which employees work. It can also provide evidence of how and why certain procedures must be used to accomplish the job and the resources needed to perform the job. Thus, a job analysis is the first step in assessing safety, health and security hazards associated with work.

Beyond the job analysis, an assessment of work procedures, tools used, worker behaviors, ergonomic requirements of workstations and other sources of potential hazard must be an ongoing activity. OSHA also requires that employees be told—explicitly and in writing—aspects of the harmful materials regularly used to perform work. Material Safety Data Sheets (MSDS), as these documents are known, provide information to employees about items such as ingredients, fire and explosion potential, ways to protect the person and the environment and other special precautions that need to be taken relative to the use of the specific material described.

While MSDS provides the documentation required by OSHA, companies that place a premium on their employees' well-being do not stop there. Instead, extensive training and communication is provided to employees to minimize unsafe practices in the workplace. Managers and supervisors also play a critical role in ensuring that safe working conditions and procedures are not shortchanged in favor of increased productivity. These organizations recognize the necessity of developing programs and approaches that emphasize safety, health and security.

Developing programs and approaches that emphasize safety, health and security

Making safety a part of the organization's culture and, indeed, a requirement of everyone's job, is necessary if unsafe activities are to be minimized or avoided. However, while safety might be everyone's responsibility, its authority and accountability, like that of diversity, should be situated with a clearly identified person or department. Many organizations employ safety professionals as part of senior leadership teams (e.g., chief safety officer). Some medium and large organizations have safety departments, while in other organizations, safety is assumed under the jurisdiction of HR departments. Finally, some organizations identify an individual-contributor employee as a safety expert and permit that person to be the internal champion for safe working conditions. Whatever the approach, the person or department must be well trained about preventative measures related to safety, health and security issues.

Conducting formal training programs on preventative measures related to unsafe practices and procedures can go a long way toward reducing these types of incidents in the workplace. Closely related to training, of course, is the acquisition and distribution of personal protective equipment and other safeguards that individuals should use in performing hazardous or potentially harmful duties. Again, the job analysis, in part, is one source for determining the extent to which such equipment or gear is needed to safely perform the work.

Finally, appropriate tracking and reporting of safety, health and security violations must be ensured. OSHA requires that organizations record and, in many cases, report work-related injuries or illnesses that result in, among other things, death, medical treatment, loss of consciousness, limited work and transfers to another job. In addition to tracking safety occurrences for OSHA purposes, smart organizations also integrate safety performance measures as part of a larger quality initiative. The goal in these instances is to continually improve and track progress related to improvements. Some organizations go so far as to benchmark their safety effectiveness with others in their industry and to offer safety incentives to employees based on some predetermined measure of effectiveness (e.g., number of days without an "OSHA recordable" injury or accident). While all of these activities are designed to reduce or eliminate conditions that cause employees physical harm, there are several other factors that must be addressed to minimize emotional or psychological harm or discomfort for employees.

Fostering a climate free from fear, intimidation and harassment

For some employees, coming to work represents an escape from a home life filled with stresses and distractions. For these employees, work is viewed as a stable, secure anchor in an otherwise hectic life. For other employees, however, coming to work can be a dreaded experience, but not necessarily because of the work. Rather, the stress level associated with dealing with arrogant, abrasive or abusive co-workers or bosses can make coming to work intolerable. Thus, it is important for organizations to create a climate that is free from fear, intimidation and harassment.

Fear involves not knowing what to expect from a given situation and the thought that harm may occur as a result. Not knowing the daily mood of a boss or colleague and being subjected to wild shifts in personalities as a result is an example of fear at work. Intimidation occurs when people use their position, their physical being, their knowledge or their personality in such a way as to belittle or make subservient others in the workplace. Harassment involves two things: creating a hostile work environment and/or the unwelcome sexual advances from someone in a position of authority or power, often with the subtle or explicit condition that failure to comply will result in an unfavorable outcome, such as loss of job or compensation. To minimize or avoid a climate of fear, intimidation and harassment, organizations need strict and ongoing policies and approaches.

One of the most important things an organization can to do minimize fear, intimidation and harassment is to speak out against these things. Having a clear, consistent and concise policy statement that such actions will not be tolerated is the first step. Next, it is important to train managers and employees on what constitutes fear, intimidation and harassment and the organizational resources available to discourage these practices. Finally, continually assessing the climate, evaluating data (e.g., number, type and sources of sexual harassment claims filed) and making adjustments are all ways to make the workplace more enjoyable and productive for all employees. This type of activity is not limited to just fear, intimidation and harassment issues, however, but should be part of a larger effort to monitor and improve safety, health and security within the organization.

Ensuring that the workplace is regularly monitored and improved for enhanced safety, health and security practices

Safe, healthy and secure practices in the workplace are not the result of a one-shot intervention. Instead, organizations that succeed in these areas regularly take stock of their performance and ways to improve their efforts. One way this occurs is through audits for safety compliance. These audits, typically conducted internally by the person or department charged with safety-related oversight, determine the extent to which approved policies, practices and procedures are being followed. They are also used to determine if the organization is complying with OSHA and other laws, rules, standards or regulations. Results from these audits are aimed at improving practices, not necessarily in punishing individuals.

In addition to internal audits, many organizations routinely invite outside investigators to inspect safety practices within the organization. Whether these are consultants or OSHA officials, third-party evaluation and validation can be useful in uncovering issues that might otherwise go unnoticed within the organization. When initiated by the organization, the results of these outside audits can be the basis for voluntary improvements. In some instances, OSHA (or another party) initiates third-party investigations, in which case the outcomes of the investigation results in fines or other sanctions of varying degrees. Continuous monitoring and improvement efforts on the part of the organization, however, should go a long way toward avoiding the need for OSHA-initiated inspections.

Summary

As this chapter highlighted, doing the right thing is more than just happenstance. Instead, a focus on ethics, diversity and safety requires serious commitment from senior leaders and the articulation and execution of specific strategies to encourage its widespread adoption by organizational members. While each of these concepts, by itself, requires specific approaches, there are some overarching requirements for all three. These include understanding and acceptance by employees on why and how these initiatives are important and the capacity and infrastructure internally to support ethics, diversity and safety as well as ongoing monitoring, reporting, learning and improvement efforts. Ethical decision-making, specifically, requires attending to personal and organizational values, creating an environment conducive to honest, transparent interactions and control mechanisms to root out or avoid problems. Diversity and inclusion can facilitate talent attraction, retention and motivation. To manage diversity effectively, organizations need to understand their own "business case" for diversity, assess current practices and continuously meet the needs of and provide resources for a diverse workforce. Finally, safe work environments can be realized by understanding causes for unsafe conditions; identifying, disclosing and preventing harmful work conditions; and regularly auditing and monitoring the workplace for hazards related to safety, health and security.

Focusing on ethics, diversity and safety is important, and not only because they are, indeed, the right things to do. As data from the Workforce Engagement National Benchmarks highlighted, these matters are very important, to employees. In fact, there can be significant performance and productivity gains when employees feel like the organization has created an honest, safe environment that treats people with dignity and respect. Unfortunately, as the case study *"Inch By Inch"* illuminates, there can be serious consequences when lapses, however unintentional, are permitted to happen.

Case Study:
Ethics, Diversity and Safety and Workforce Engagement
'Inch By Inch, Row By Row'

"Inch by inch, row by row
Gonna make this garden grow
All it takes is a rake and a hoe
And a piece of fertile ground"

The conference room was bathed in sunlight, and its corner location provided spectacular views of a pale blue, cloudless sky. But, for the six people seated around the table, they might have been in an underground and windowless chamber. Each one seemed determined not to look at any of the others. There was total silence, no small talk, no group conversations, nothing. To look at them, they might have been relatives of someone in critical condition in a hospital, waiting. This was a group that expected bad news.

The double doors opened and a tall, muscular man strode in. He was almost to the head of the table when someone standing in the doorway said, "Excuse me, General …" He went back toward the entrance, had a whispered conversation, shook his head sadly and returned to the head of the table. No one said a word. He looked at each of them intently, as if trying to assess how much complicity and responsibility each of them would bear for what had happened.

For several minutes, he held the gaze of his protégé and friend, the vice president for quality assurance and safety. Finally he spoke, his jaw trembling: "What happened? What have you done?"

Chamber Point Power Generation Facility was the largest power-producing facility in Georgia and among the 20 largest facilities in the United States. Chamber Point began its operations in 1984 and was one of the new generation of nuclear power plants built after the Three Mile Island "incident." As such, it had state-of-the-art technology to monitor any breaches in its safety and containment protocols and mandatory training, certification and recertification programs for employees who worked in proximity to anything potentially hazardous. Because nuclear power plants in the United States offered the potential of relatively low-cost energy, sustaining them in people's minds as safe and reliable was a national priority. Scrutiny and oversight were cumbersome, duplicative and expensive but, for the most part, were accepted as one of the costs of doing business.

Chamber Point, like all nuclear plans, was regulated and inspected by a host of federal, state and local agencies. For example, Chamber Point submitted annual reports to 16 different federal agencies, and nine of those agencies were required to complete on-site inspections each year.

Because the facility had potential hazards from three different—and highly toxic—sources, the ability to respond quickly to breaches in safety was an ongoing concern. The toxic hazards were as follows:

1. **"Spent" radioactive water**, heated by the plutonium core. It could cause serious burns on the skin and lead to potentially fatal radiation poisoning if an individual was in proximity to the "hot" water without wearing protective outer clothing.

2. **Airborne lead particles**, released from the lead sheathing around the containment vessels when the vessels were heated to temperatures in excess of 800 degrees F. The airborne particles were known to be carcinogenic even after moderate exposure.

3. **Toxic fumes** from pressurized chlorine solvents, used to clean and decontaminate the water tanks and rod casings.

Each of these hazards required different protocols, and federal and state regulations mandated that personnel certified in each area be present at all times. The regulations prohibited having the same person "on call" for more than one potential hazard. This meant that nine certified workers had to be present each 24-hour period, three for each eight-hour shift. **Exhibit 2** (on page 110) provides a summary of oversight regulations for two of the three hazards.

All of these compliance issues were the responsibility of Chris Schiffler, the vice president for quality assurance. An engineer by training and a retired U.S. Army colonel, Schiffler was an experienced manager who had a reputation as "a guy who gets things done." He faced particular challenges at Chamber Point because there were so many regulations, so many procedural "safeguards" and so many compliance activities which, together, actually reduced the facility's productivity.

For example, if the procedures for monitoring the radioactivity of the spent water were followed precisely, the facility would need to be "powered down" every week for about eight hours. Over time, Schiffler accepted certain "shortcuts" which he considered to be within a comfort zone of low risk. He had confidence in his senior staff, knew they were professional and committed and accepted the lapses in procedures as necessary and expedient. He knows what each of them did—and did not do—in considerable detail. Each of them cut corners, but in different ways.

Certification: Hays Bedford

Hays Bedford was responsible for certification at Chamber Point. He was experienced and knowledgeable and occasionally taught courses and workshops for those seeking certification in various areas. His expertise was in airborne contamination, but he was very familiar with the certification needs for all those who worked at the facility. A strong advocate of initial certification, Bedford was often frustrated by the procedural complexities of recertification, which required detailed logs of time spent in instruction and numerous forms detailing activities in the workplace during the past year. Shift supervisors constantly complained about how time consuming the recertification procedures were.

To deal with this problem, Bedford held a meeting every six or eight weeks for *everyone* who needed to be recertified, rather than having *separate* meetings for each category of recertification. He knew this was a shortcut, but there were just so many hours in the day, and he believed there was little risk of recertifying someone who was not qualified because, after all, they were being observed and monitored on the daily job performance. He was just bypassing some cumbersome procedures, not undermining safety.

Inspection: David Ranelli

The inspection procedures called for a certified supervisor to be present when measurements for toxicity were taken. This was cumbersome, at best, because the quality assurance offices were in a different building than the power plant, and the times when the measurements were taken sometimes conflicted with activities in the quality assurance department. Occasionally, David Ranelli conferred by phone with the two-person inspection team, received its report orally and then signed the inspection reports indicating that he had been "present" during the inspection. Ranelli told Schiffler that he "ducked under the wire" every so often, and Schiffler acknowledged that actions like that were sometimes necessary.

Similarly, the "containment rods," the primary safety devices protecting the nuclear core, were to be tested daily for pressure tolerance in the presence of a certified inspector. At one time, Ranelli had an employee assigned to this task, but the testing was normally done at change of shift at midnight, which was costly because it was the only task the inspector had to do. Ranelli encouraged the 4 p.m. to midnight and midnight to 8 a.m. shift supervisors to seek certification; when that did not work, he devised a form to be filled out each night with the requisite information, and the next day he entered the information of the proper form and signed it. "No big deal," he thought.

Compliance: Alice-Ann Brewster

Alice-Ann Brewster had to manage the complex area of keeping facility operations and employee safety procedures in compliance with federal, state and local ordinances (as well as United Nations' treaties to which the United States was a signatory). Approximately 20 percent of all Chamber Point employees worked within the perimeter where testing for lead contamination was required by OSHA. This involved a blood test every 90 days. Some of those within the perimeter worked there only occasionally, and others were never in proximity to the nuclear operations. As a practical matter, Brewster approved a "waiver from blood testing" for some employees and permitted others to be tested twice a year instead. Although she knew that this was not "full compliance," she also knew that attempting to be in full compliance would be expensive and time consuming.

Another compliance procedure concerned employees who worked in the "hot room" where the nuclear reactors were situated. These employees were required to wear "glow patches." The "patches" detected increased levels of radioactivity by changing color from white to blue. Any employee with a blue patch had to undergo extensive testing for radioactive poisoning. Technically, each employee was to turn in her/his "patch" every month and be issued a new one. The old "patches" were to be stored *by employee name*, for record-keeping purposes. In practice, employees simply tossed their old "patches" in a big cardboard box and took a new one from another box. Most employees were not even aware that each "patch" had its own identifying serial number, and no match of employee to serial number was maintained.

Chamber Point had an admirable safety record, and reports from the mandatory "unannounced" federal-state inspection teams mentioned only small problems in operating procedures and compliance. Schiffler thought the facility's track record was very good, but he was aware that a pattern of incremental shortcuts had developed. He rationalized this by thinking, "no harm, no foul." That is, although there were shortcuts, the facility operated very safely.

Until. Until one day when everyone at Chamber Point heard some bad news. Like everyone else, Schiffler first heard that Ned Fowler, a senior radiation specialist, had been in a serious car crash. More details emerged over the next few hours. He was in critical condition, but his wife and one of his children had been killed. He had been driving, but suddenly lost control of the car, "probably because he had a heart attack or stroke," people said. Further reports were grim: it was touch and go, and he might not survive.

The next day, with no change in his condition, people tried to get back to work. Around noon, Schiffler got a call from Hank Hamilton, the executive vice president. Hamilton asked him to come to his office immediately. When he arrived, Hamilton wasted no time: "This is an unbelievable tragedy for the Fowler family. And for us. Listen, Chris, Ned Fowler didn't crash because he had a stroke or heart attack. He lost consciousness as a result of massive radiation poisoning. The radiation levels in his body were so high that there were trace elements in everyone in his family, including the dog. His house, his car, his locker here, everything is showing dangerous levels of radioactive toxicity."

Schiffler sat down, dazed. "What should we do?" he said. Hamilton replied, "We have a lot of explaining to do, to the press, to the public, to the NRC, to our workers and to the Fowler family. But first, we need to go upstairs and talk to the general."

Exhibit 1: Organization Chart for Chamber Point Power Generation Facility

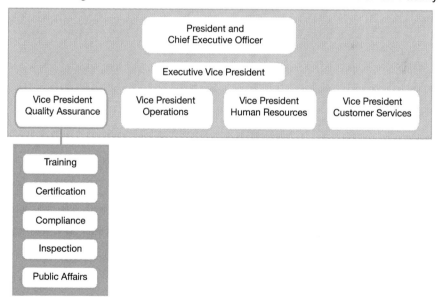

Exhibit 2: Summary of Oversight Regulations for Major Environmental Hazards

| Hazard | Requirements for | | Mandated On-Site Oversight |
	Certification	Recertification	
"Spent" radioactive water	32 hours of instruction; online exam	Six hours of instruction annually; submission of previous year's log	Certified supervisor must be present at all times while water flows through activator rods
Airborne lead particles	Satisfactory completion of EPA-approved online or "real time" program	Online exam or attendance at EPA workshop	Certified employee must confirm air quality readings every six hours

Questions for Consideration and Discussion
'Inch By Inch, Row By Row'

1. What are the personal and organizational consequences of actions associated with the events that unfolded at Chamber Point Power Generation Facility? How could these events have been avoided?

2. Suppose you were hired as a consultant to Chamber Point in the wake of this incident. What would you suggest the organization do to avoid a repeat of this circumstance and why? What specific strategies should be adopted?

3. Unethical issues and unsafe practices typically start small and then pick up speed on a slippery slope of carelessness and apathy. What are some control mechanisms or other approaches that can be established or implemented to monitor ethical decision-making and compliance with safe standards? How would an organization such as Chamber Point know if it were successful in these endeavors?

4. In what ways—large or small—do the events at Chamber Point remind you of circumstances in which you have been involved? What was the outcome of the situation? What did you learn from the experience? What would you do differently next time, if faced with a similar circumstance?

CHAPTER 5:
Stakeholder Input

Introduction: What do We Mean By 'Stakeholder Input'?

Stakeholder input involves the ability of organizational leaders to seek regular feedback from customers, business partners and others; benchmark with other organizations on effective practices; measure employee perceptions; and improve work and other organizational experiences. The stakeholder input component of workforce engagement reflects the extent to which employees perceive the company requests and use stakeholder input for product and process improvement. This includes seeking input from customers and employees, putting ideas into practice and involving employees in organizational change.

Highlights from the 2004-2005 National Benchmark Study on Workforce Engagement

A late-1990s study of senior management conducted for *Management Review* showed that nearly nine in 10 senior managers highly valued customer satisfaction information, and two-thirds highly valued employee performance data. However, when the researchers asked these same senior managers if they would be willing to bet their jobs on the quality of the customer satisfaction information they received, only three in 10 senior managers answered affirmatively, and only two in 10 were willing to risk their jobs on the quality of the employee performance data.

It is no surprise that the *pan* study showed only half of all employees worked for organizations that regularly sought input from customers, employees and business partners to improve their business practices, products and services. Health services employees were the most likely to work for companies that collect this stakeholder information, although many health-care organizations have to collect customer-satisfaction data for accreditation purposes. State/local government employees were least likely to work for organizations that regularly surveyed their stakeholders, with less than four in 10 giving a positive response. Interestingly, companies with less than 500 employees or more than 2,500 employees were significantly more likely to have a formal method of collecting stakeholder data.

Only half of all employees agree that their company makes an effort to get their input when decisions are made that impact them. Employees in information services, health services and financial services were most likely to agree (53 percent agreeing in each industry segment), with state/local government employees being least positive (41 percent agree).

Nonunion employees are more likely to be asked for their input than union employees, while workers in companies with less than 500 employees feel their input is important to collect before changes are made. Not surprisingly, senior executives are nearly twice as likely to be asked their input as are individual contributors. Although only half of all employees felt that their input was requested before changes were made, a slightly lower percentage felt that their ideas were actually put into practice (48 percent). Of interest, employees who received work-related training and education were 50 percent more likely to feel their ideas were put into practice, leading to an improved workforce engagement for these employees.

Finally, only four in 10 employees in the *pan* benchmark believe their organization includes employees when planning changes, while one in three disagrees. Although financial services, health services and information services are the most likely to include employees in changes, just half of employees in these industries indicated they were included in the planning. And as seen with other workforce components, nearly twice as many state/local government employees disagreed that they were included in planning changes than agreed (47 percent versus 27 percent).

Front-line employees are often the best internal resource when going through product-and process-improvement efforts. These *individual contributors* have the majority of customer contact and have significantly more interaction with their day-to-day processes and those of other business units and departments than do supervisors, middle managers and senior executives. So why is it that only one in three of these "worker bees" agrees they are involved in planning changes, while the same number disagrees? Employees need to feel that their supervisor is open to and listens to their suggestions and that their suggestions for improvement are recognized by others.

Every suggestion an employee provides does not need to be acted upon, however it is incumbent on management to thank employees for their ideas and provide feedback. Employers would be well served to include these employees in the planning and execution of improvements in business practices.

Highlights from the 2006-2007 National Benchmark Study on Workforce Engagement

A new driver in 2006-2007, the performance of *stakeholder* input, the strongest of the secondary drivers of engagement, follows a familiar trend: performance dropped from 51-percent positive in 2004-2005 to 46-percent positive in 2006-2007, another significant decrease.

Less than half of all employees (45 percent) agreed their ideas *are put into practice* in their organization, while more than a quarter disagree (26 percent). As the size of the company increases, the likelihood the employee feels ideas are put into practice declines. In addition, individual contributors are the least likely to agree with this statement (41 percent), while senior executives are the most likely to agree (72 percent).

Nearly as many employees agree their *organization involves employees in planning changes* as disagree (38 percent versus 34 percent). Given the majority of changes made in an organization impact the individual contributors the most, it is worrisome that more of these employees disagree with the statement than agree (36 percent disagree while 34 percent agree). Eighty-five percent of the communication between your organization and your customers comes through the individual contributors in your company. Whether a customer service representative, pediatric nurse, member of a technical support staff or in-store salesperson, these employees and their supervisors have the most knowledge of how the process works and should be counted on most when developing process-and product-improvement initiatives.

As noted in other workforce engagement components, participation in a company-sponsored social event and being provided work-based education or training showed the largest impact on this secondary driver:

- 52 percent who received training or education agree their ideas are *put into practice*, versus 39 percent of those who did not receive training
- 48 percent who received training or education agree the *organization involves employees in planning changes,* versus 29 percent of employees who did not receive training or education
- 51 percent of those employees who participated in a company-sponsored social event feel *an effort is made to get my input when decisions are made that impact me*, versus 37 percent who had not participated
- 53 percent of those who participated in a company-sponsored social event agree employee ideas are put into practice, versus 36 percent of employees who did not.

Why is Stakeholder Input Important?

Broadly defined, stakeholder input involves seeking regular, relevant and reliable input from key individuals or groups who benefit from or depend upon the organization for some purpose. Measuring, evaluating and improving the organization's effectiveness in a number of areas is an important component that contributes to workforce engagement. Employees, in general, want to work for a company that commits itself to growth and adaptation; few employees seek stale and stagnant work environments.

In the past three decades, in particular, considerable attention has been placed on total quality management, continuous improvement, customer-focused policies and practices, and external accreditation and validation of internal business processes (e.g., Malcolm Baldrige National Quality Award; ISO certifications). All of these endeavors require regular feedback from customers, business partners and employees, among others.

Common business sense should compel leaders to regularly take the organization's temperature, even when outside entities do not require the organization to gather input from stakeholders. Too often, however, such feedback is not effectively coordinated, collected, analyzed and used in ways that seek to add value to business processes or organizational relationships, internally or externally. Thus, stakeholder input should be part of a larger relationship management strategy that seeks, values and welcomes input from others on an ongoing basis.

Stakeholder Input is Important Because It Helps Organizations:

- Identify people who work for, do business with, depend on and buy from the organization.
- Involve those impacted by decisions in the decision-making process.
- Signal the organization's commitment to quality, learning and change.
- Foster improved relationships between the organization and its stakeholders.
- Use experiences and perceptions of stakeholders to gauge organizational responsiveness.

Identify people who work for, do business with, depend on and buy from the organization

To meet their needs effectively, companies first need to identify individuals and groups who work for, do business with, depend on and buy from the organization. These stakeholders rely on the organization to provide product, service, solution or opportunity. Employees, customers, investors, business partners, community members and industry/trade professionals all have a stake in the organization's ongoing viability.

In some instances, an organization may have stakeholders with vastly different needs, priorities and expectations. For example, a college or university's scope of stakeholders typically includes diverse groups such as students, alumni, faculty, staff, governing boards, accreditation agencies, industry representatives, community members, researchers at other universities, state and federal government agencies, fans of collegiate athletics and prospective students. Each of these groups relies on the institution for a different purpose, and each group potentially experiences the college or university in vastly different ways. Thus, understanding who stakeholders are, what they need and how they can contribute gives the organization the ability to involve them—in varying degrees—in providing input during the decision-making process.

Involve those impacted by decisions in the decision-making process

One fundamental concept in change-management approaches is the notion that individuals and groups are more likely to support the outcome of a decision if they were involved in the creation of that outcome. This is true for organizational stakeholders, many of whom must adapt to changes initiated by the company's leaders. A change in a company's strategic direction, for example, potentially impacts the level of investor risk, the nature of employee work, resources needed from suppliers and either growth or decline in the organization's physical presence in a community. Thus, the ability to seek advice or guidance from relevant stakeholders on matters associated with the new strategic direction is one way to facilitate buy-in from each group. Not all decisions require widespread involvement by and consultation with stakeholders. A savvy leader understands the "high stakes" conditions, such as a change in strategy, under which to involve them. Beyond facilitating improved decision-making, however, stakeholder input also signals the organization's commitment to quality, learning and change.

Signal the organization's commitment to quality, learning and change

Regardless of whether the organization manufactures a product, is engaged in knowledge-based work or provides a service to customers or communities, it must continually adapt to changing marketplace realities. As a result, the focus on quality, individual and organizational learning and change has increased exponentially in the past two decades. Regularly involving stakeholders in providing feedback facilitates these processes and signals to others the organization's commitment to continuous improvement.

General Electric provides an excellent example of how stakeholder input is used in quality, learning and change initiatives. The "GE WorkOut" process, as this approach is known, actively involves employees from all levels of the organization in setting goals, identifying and solving problems, and fostering and creating innovation. Programs like GE's WorkOut tend to use a diagonal slice of the organization—that is, intentional and active involvement of employees from all levels and areas of the enterprise—in improvement endeavors. Although this approach is useful for generating ideas and solutions, perhaps equally important is the message such explicit actions send about the organization's culture of involvement and how relationships with stakeholders (in GE's case, employees) can be used to provide a sustainable competitive advantage.

Foster improved relationships between the organization and its stakeholders

Simply listening to stakeholders can go a long way toward enhancing or improving relationships with them. This is especially true when various stakeholder groups hold different perspectives on issues important to the organization. It is important for organizational leaders to understand the positions or viewpoints held by stakeholders and to see ways that collaboration, compromise and consensus can occur. Seeking regular and specific input from stakeholders can go a long way toward reaching those goals.

An example of fostering improved relationships with stakeholders comes from Proctor and Gamble's Western European division, P&G Beauty. In 2004, P&G Beauty hosted a series of "Inside Out" meetings that invited and involved wide stakeholder input. Top-level representatives from the European Union, industry and consumer associations, Non-Governmental Organizations (NGOs), retailers, academics and other experts discussed the opportunities and challenges facing the beauty industry across three areas: the industry's potential for growth; the ethics of beauty; and future trends and innovations. By inviting diverse groups with convergent interests together, P&G Beauty used the "Inside Out" meetings to seek input while simultaneously enhancing relationships with its various stakeholders.

Use experiences and perceptions of stakeholders to gauge organizational responsiveness

Healthy organizations regularly take their temperature to determine the extent to which they meet the needs of their stakeholders, especially customers and employees. This is accomplished, in part, through surveys, formal and informal feedback from customers and employees and tracking performance on measures related to customer and employee satisfaction.

A large, multilocation health-care organization recently sought to improve the overall satisfaction and experience of outpatients, mainly those individuals who are recipients of same-day-surgery services. To determine how they experienced the organization, patients and their families were surveyed by members of the patient services and advocacy department (PSAD). Specifically, PSAD asked them to describe their experiences in dealing with the organization, its staff and the ease with which the same-day-surgery service was provided. PSAD representatives also took photographs and video of the physical appearances of buildings, including parking lots, admissions areas, waiting rooms, dining rooms and recovery lounges. Then, every step in the process from admissions through recovery and discharge for same-day surgeries was listed. When PSAD staff analyzed the survey results, viewed the photographs and videotapes and identified the complexities and redundancies involved in business processes, they realized that patients and their families experienced the organization in a vastly different way than employees intended. By using the experiences and perceptions of stakeholders—and by seeing the organization through their lens—improvements to business processes and physical surroundings were initiated, and overall responsiveness to patients improved.

From Whom is Stakeholder Input Sought?

Stakeholder Input Is Typically Sought From:

- Employees
- Customers
- Investors
- Vendors, Suppliers and Business Partners
- Community Members.

Employees

Employees are probably one of the most important constituencies from whom to seek candid, ongoing feedback. After all, they are the ones who most know the customers, the work requirements, the business processes, the breakdowns in those processes, and the formal and informal relationships that exist within and outside of the organization. If employees cannot give feedback without fear of reprisal (getting called a troublemaker, getting fired, being held back from promotion/transfer, willingness of manager to recommend them for another job), then the employees will likely do what is best for them: not share their honest feelings with their manager. Thus, managers have the responsibility to cultivate an environment that fosters open, candid communication. Employees must feel comfortable being honest with the manager, even when providing less than favorable information. Failure to value employee input might cause the company to lose the benefit of what could be important feedback from an individual contributor.

Customers

No company would contradict the importance of getting feedback from customers. In one way or another, customer feedback is sought to improve the quality of products and services and to assist the organization in differentiating itself in an increasingly competitive and crowded marketplace. There are a variety of measures an organization can use to gauge its effectiveness in meeting customer needs. Typical customer queries might include perceptions and experiences of the quality of products or services offered; the depth and breadth of the product line; how easy or difficult it is for the customer to buy from and interact with the business; and the value of the product or service offered. In many companies, customer satisfaction is measured at regular intervals (e.g., the same time every year) or constantly, in which every touchpoint or transaction tries to obtain some type of customer feedback. The process should yield useful, actionable data for improvement purposes, regardless of when, why and how organizations seek input from customers. Such improvements should go a long way toward enhancing the firm's competitiveness and impacting its bottom line.

Investors

As sources of capital for and owners of the organization, investors play a crucial role in the organization's ability to survive and thrive. "Maximizing shareholder wealth" is the rallying cry in most private-sector, publicly traded organizations. Because investors contribute funds to a business, they are entitled by law to receive quarterly and annual reports of the financial and operational performance of the organization. Savvy investment-relations professionals actively seek input from key individual and institutional investors on what measures are useful in evaluating the firm's performance. Investors might seek to enhance their knowledge and understanding of the organization's future direction, planned products or services, growth or acquisition strategies, selected accomplishments and leadership capabilities. Knowing what information, beyond just financial performance, matters to investors can help organizational leaders report on progress in areas of importance.

Vendors, Suppliers and Business Partners

More and more companies are discovering the value of vendor-, supplier- and business-partner feedback in their stakeholder-input processes. Just-in-time inventory delivery, in which parts, products or services are coordinated to arrive at a prescribed location at a key time in the business process, require increased coordination, communication and collaboration. Additionally, the ability to bundle products and services and to realize greater efficiencies through the supply chain requires that regular feedback is sought. In most organizations, formal measurement of vendor, supplier or business partner relationships occur yearly or, at the very least, prior to contract renegotiation or renewal. The type of measures used to assess these relationships might include ease of doing business with organization; the benefits associated with and derived from doing business with the organization; fairness and equity of the business relationship; and an evaluation of the overall manner in which business needs are being met.

Community Members

Because of the positive or negative impact government and/or community relations can have on the success of a business, receiving input from community leaders, other business executives and members of local government is also critical to management. Typically, input from these constituencies is sought every year or two, or as crises or negative events occur, such as layoffs, scandals or poor financial performance. How the organization is viewed in the community, how it is perceived as a corporate citizen and how the organization is known for treating customers, employees and business partners are some of the measures used to determine how community members feel about the organization.

Organizations that are major employers in a geographic area provide tremendous direct and indirect financial and other benefits to the communities in which they are located. They contribute through the "economic multiplier" effect, their community involvement and the philanthropic endeavors they support. Thus, as part of both business-improvement processes and reputation management activities, seeking input from community stakeholders should be an ongoing priority for these types of organizations.

The stakeholders described in this section are representative of the types of individuals and groups from which an organization should seek regular input. There are, of course, other stakeholders than those previously identified. Union officials, industry or trade groups, policymakers and others might be involved in providing information for organizational decision-making purposes. Beyond simply identifying stakeholders, however, companies need to engage in a logical, thoughtful process for seeking stakeholder input.

What Does the Stakeholder input Process Entail?

A Typical Stakeholder Input Process Entails:

- Identifying information to be sought
- Determining sources of information
- Collecting information from stakeholders
- Analyzing and interpreting information received from stakeholders
- Developing action plans as a result of information received
- Implementing, monitoring and evaluating action plans
- Seeking additional information from stakeholders as necessary.

Identifying information to be sought

The first step in a stakeholder input process involves identifying what information is being sought. This includes determining the categories (customer, employee, community, etc.) and sub-categories (spending habits, satisfaction with benefits, reputation held in the community) of the desired information. In general, the more narrow, explicit and specific the framing of the issue(s) to be addressed, the greater likelihood that targeted sources of accurate information can be identified.

Determining sources of information

In some instances, the sources of information will be readily apparent. For example, if seeking feedback from civic leaders on the organization's perceived reputation, obvious choices include the mayor, chamber of commerce officials and other easily identifiable community leaders. When seeking input from customers or employees, however, it is often useful to define *which type* of customer or employee would be best suited to provide useful information. Customers are typically organized around specific demographic, market or relationship characteristics. It is quite common for organizations to identify their most valuable customers (those from whom the organization derives the most significant source of revenue), most growable customers (those loyal customers who hold the promise of even greater revenue maximization) and even below-cost customers (those customers for whom the transaction costs exceed generated revenue). Determining the specific type of information sought from a specific type of customer is needed to effectively collect information from stakeholders.

Collecting information from stakeholders

After identifying the information needed and determining the most appropriate source(s) for supplying the information, the next step is the actual collection of information. There are a variety of ways to gather data from stakeholders, each of which will be explained later in this chapter: interactions and transactions; meetings; surveys, interviews, focus groups; observations; content analysis; and benchmarking. Each of these methods used alone or in combination with each other provides information that can be analyzed and interpreted to yield insights into stakeholder perceptions, behaviors, expectations or experiences.

Analyzing and interpreting information received from stakeholders

Several questions emerge in the analysis and interpretation of information received from stakeholders. For example, what are the facts (what do you know for certain)? What are the categories of data that emerge (e.g., people issues, product or service issues, technology issues)? What do the results of surveys, interviews, observations, etc. mean to you? What are the underlying themes, patterns and connections that can be made from your interpretation of the data? What are the overall conclusions and implications that can be drawn? Accurately answering these types of questions helps in developing specific action plans.

Developing action plans as a result of information received

Specific action plans can be developed as a result of information collected and analyzed from stakeholders. Such plans typically include a breakdown of tasks and duties; identification of resource requirements needed (physical, financial, human, technological, etc.); timeline associated with activities; and responsibility (at the individual or department level) for each task, duty, resource or activity. Once the action plan is developed and approved, implementation can occur.

Implementing, monitoring and evaluating action plans

The ultimate goal of stakeholder input is the ability to affect changes that are meaningful for and valued by the individuals or groups who provided information to the organization. Thus, implementing the action plan is the outcome of the preceding steps in the process. As such, continual monitoring and evaluation of the plan's intended verses actual impact is needed. Organizations that have committed themselves to continuous improvement will likely seek additional information from stakeholders even after the implementation of an action plan.

Seeking additional information from stakeholders as necessary

The "steps" previously outlined are representative of a typical stakeholder input process. Hopefully, many organizations will make regular information gathering a normal part of doing business and create a culture with an ongoing, stakeholder-involved, evidence-based approach decision-making. To make this process a reality, however, there are a number of specific methods that can be used to gather stakeholder input. The next section defines more common methods used.

What Methods are Used to Gather Stakeholder Input?

Methods Used to Gather Stakeholder Input:

- Interactions and Transactions
- Meetings
- Surveys
- Interviews
- Focus Groups
- Observations
- Content Analysis
- Benchmarking.

Interactions and Transactions

One of the most frequent and continual means of gathering stakeholder input is through the regular interactions and transactions that occur in organizational life. These interactions and transactions can occur among and between numerous stakeholder groups. Employees who sell to, serve or are otherwise involved with customers have several opportunities to seek feedback from this important constituency. Greeting customers by name, asking how the employee can help and providing a timely and useful solution to customer needs is one example of stakeholder input in action. Other ways to elicit feedback from customer interactions and transactions include formal complaints or compliments received, input from the customer provided at point of sale (e.g., name, address, preferred brand or style), clickstream analyses of Web site activity, tracking of prompts used in an automated call-distribution system and use of formal customer-relationship management systems.

Beyond customers, organizational interactions and transactions also extend to employees. Managers can gauge how employees feel by simply interacting with them regularly ("managing by walking around"). These informal relationships can yield input useful for improved efficiencies and effectiveness. Other transactions that provide useful information from employees include time and attendance-tracking measures, use of knowledge-sharing tools (e.g., Lotus Notes), use of employee self-service capabilities via a corporate intranet and use of certain services either inside or outside the organization.

Meetings

Although most individuals tend to espouse a dislike for meetings, they are a useful venue for giving and receiving information. Meetings can range from the highly structured and formal (e.g., annual shareholders meeting) to the ad hoc, unstructured and informal type, where employees "huddle" around the proverbial water cooler to share stories, work related or otherwise. Effective managers regularly meet with their direct reports in one-on-one meetings, in which employee performance is discussed, goals and plans are made and other information is shared. Like managers, effective teams and departments regularly meet to identify common issues or problems, provide updates on team/departmental activities and initiatives and evaluate progress on key projects or assignments. In some organizations, it is feasible to have organizationwide meetings, in which all employees from every area of the enterprise can gather to hear common information and updates on the business.

To maximize meeting effectiveness, especially as it relates to stakeholder input, many organizations use an approach known as open-book management during meetings with employees. Open-book management, as the name implies, shares financial and operational information with employees and trains them to use this type of information in their jobs. Meetings are often a primary way of introducing this type of information to employees and providing subsequent, ongoing updates on the firm's performance.

Surveys

Surveys can provide a formal, consistent means of gathering specific information from customers and employees. Surveys can be conducted by paper-and-pencil methods, online or by phone. These surveys tend to work best when small goals are identified and a few focused, well-chosen questions are asked. Customers can be surveyed at the point of sale, a short time after a sale or transaction has been completed (e.g., one to two weeks), as part of an annual update of customer records or on an ad-hoc basis when the need for customer input arises. Formal employee surveys tend to be administered annually or every two years, depending on the size and scope of the organization and the nature of and need for employee input. Informal surveys of employees may occur on a more frequent basis.

By surveying customers and employees, it tells them that you value their input, but can also be viewed as a timewaster if not properly designed, introduced and structured. As such, surveys should anticipate likely customer or employee responses in advance and have predetermined "categories" for such responses. Surveys sometimes capture demographic data and may also allow for the inclusion of verbatim comments. Regardless of how a survey is designed, it is important to ensure confidentiality (if, in fact, that is a goal) and, especially for employees, to explain who will see the results, when the results will be tabulated and how the results will be used. To elicit a more holistic point of view that may not always be afforded through survey research, organizations may augment this approach with follow-up interviews and/or focus groups.

Interviews

While most people think of interviews as one of the first steps in the hiring process, in this context they are used as part of a stakeholder-input process. Interviews with key informants, including customers and employees, can yield significant information that effectively expands upon, explains or enhances data contained in surveys. Interviewing customers about preferences, needs, expectations, experiences and plans can provide useful information for developing solutions to better serve them. These types of interviews work best when they are structured and use open-ended questions designed to elicit rich, detailed responses from customers.

Along the same lines, interviews can assist employers in finding out what employees need, want and value from their work experiences and how well the organization is presently meeting those needs. "Exit interviews" with departing employees are another source of useful information that might not otherwise be captured. Finding out why employees are attracted to the organization, why they stay and why they leave can permit the creation or improvement of policies, practices and procedures that enhance employee loyalty and engagement. In some instances, "skip-level interviews" with current employees are conducted. These permit employees to talk to their manager's boss; hence, they are "skipping over" their superior and providing direct feedback to a higher-level manager. These interviews permit the rooting out of problems, issues or concerns that might not otherwise be heard. In addition to interviews, focus groups are also often used to gather information from several customers or employees.

Focus Groups

When multiple points of view are needed to holistically solve a problem or provide information in an efficient manner, a focus group might be more appropriate than individual interviews. Focus groups can be used for customers and employees and, as the name implies, require a group of individuals who are willing to share their insights during a moderated discussion forum.

For customers, focus groups are often used as part of a marketing and customer-relationship management strategy. Present and potential products, services, solutions and other customer-centric issues are introduced by the focus-group leader, and participant comments are recorded for subsequent analysis. The composition of the focus group has a direct bearing on the quality, robustness and usefulness of information obtained. Thus, it is important to ensure that customers participating in a focus group are, indeed, representative of the population or segment of customers from whom input is sought.

Like customers, employees, too, can be involved in focus-group research. Typically, employees are asked about their perceptions of particular organizational practices and may be queried for suggestions or advice on how to improve a function, process or approach. One variation on focus groups for employees is the organization development intervention known as *Appreciative Inquiry* (AI), developed by David L. Cooperrider and Suresh Srivastva. Using AI, a facilitator asks focus-group participants to focus on what works especially well in organizational settings, versus the usual focus on problems and their causes. While not ignoring the utility of organizational problem solving, AI seeks to bring out innovation, creativity and a focus on striving for best practices rather than simply correcting deficiencies. Whatever the ultimate approach or philosophy behind focus-group research with employees, it is one useful tool to enhance stakeholder-input efforts. Another equally useful source of information occurs through the direct or indirect observations of employees, customers and even competitors.

Observations

To understand the dynamic phenomena that occur in organizational settings, regular observation of participants (managers, employees, customers, visitors, etc.)

in that setting is needed. Identifying the work-flow patterns, customer behaviors and sequences in retail environment; exchanges between employees and customers in person or over the phone; or correspondence sent or received by employees and customers in an electronic environment all rely on direct or indirect observations. These observations can provide managers and other decision makers with input that might not normally be captured through self-reporting methods such as surveys or interviews.

One common observation tool that is widely used in retail and service-oriented establishments is mystery shopping. Mystery shopping is used to gauge an organization's interaction with its customers. It also views the organization through the lens of how a customer experiences interactions with people, business processes, merchandise, technologies and other touchpoints. Some organizations hire outside firms to conduct mystery-shopping research, while others use their own employees. Whatever the approach, a typical mystery-shopping process involves planning for the mystery-shopping experience; conducting the mystery-shopping experience; analyzing mystery-shopping results; communicating the results to managers and employees; and developing recommendations, interventions and evaluative measures. Often, mystery-shopping observations provide evidence of the reality of organizational experiences, rather than the espoused experiences touted by leaders and in marketing and advertising campaigns.

Content Analysis

While observations provide evidence of the dynamic phenomena that occurs in organizational settings, content analysis yields information from a variety of written, electronic and other sources. Customer-centric content analysis examines items such as brochures, sales literature and signage; correspondence from customers, including complaints and commendations; suggestions received from customers and data from customer-relationship management systems, such as credit card balances, spending habits, types of coupons or offers redeemed; and demographic profiles. Such information is useful in analyzing customer behaviors and in positioning products or services to better meet customer needs.

For employees, content analysis is useful in revealing trends, issues or areas of concerns related to the workforce. HR audits identify the extent to which the organization is compliant with federal, state and local laws; grievances and complaints from employees can uncover sources of frustration or dissatisfaction among particular employee groups or locations; and suggestions received from employees can yield significant savings, innovations, improvements or sources of untapped revenue.

Finally, content analysis can also be applied to an organization's competitive intelligence-gathering endeavors. Examining the product and service descriptions, warranties and catalogs of competitors; their Web sites and e-mail solicitations; and annual reports, public quarterly financial filings, and articles and items in business, trade and professional literature can provide useful input for decision-making purposes.

Benchmarking

Benchmarking is the art and science of making comparisons between an organization and a "comparison other" on select measures. Organizations chosen as a "comparison other" are typically viewed as either a leader in their industry or are widely acknowledged as using best practices in a particular area (e.g., customer service). Benchmarking permits an organization to improve its performance by analyzing the specific practices and processes of other organizations. Data collection and analysis is followed by the determination of gaps between present and benchmarked practices. Organizations then develop plans and methods to improve their practices or processes in an effort to meet or exceed the benchmarked organization's standard.

Summary

All of the methods described in this section are important tools to assist in measuring, evaluating and improving organizational effectiveness. Indeed, organizations in the true pursuit of excellence realize that stakeholder input works best when integrated into a larger, multifaceted relationship management strategy. What does such a strategy include?

First, stakeholder input as part of relationship management involves a commitment from everyone in the organization. This includes not only senior leadership but also employees at all levels. Commitment goes beyond lip service and extends to policies, practices and approaches that permit the organization to truly deepen relationships with its stakeholders. Second, it recognizes and incorporates regular feedback from customers, employees, business partners and others. Employee surveys, meetings, "management by walking around" and customer-relationship management systems, among other techniques, all facilitate communication. Third, relationship management naturally includes competitive intelligence, benchmarking and continuous improvement efforts. Finally, it should not be viewed as a flavor-of-the-month management fad. Rather, it requires serious commitment, discipline and dedication to competitively differentiate the retailer in an ever-crowded marketplace. Thus, stakeholder input is a key ingredient in an organization's ability to manage its reputation, improve its processes, serve its customers and engage its employees.

The case study that follows, *The Silence is Deafening*, examines efforts at seeking feedback from employees as part of an overall improvement process. This case highlights the inherent challenges, opportunities and mistakes made when attempting to seek stakeholder input.

Case Study:
Stakeholder Input
and Workforce Engagement
'The Silence Is Deafening'

The annual managers' meeting was not even half over and Tony Anterra was bored. Really bored. The briefings from people at corporate headquarters were tedious. The team-building activities with other managers were silly and irrelevant. The motivational workshop was trite and repetitious. But the session Anterra disliked the most was the one he was getting ready to attend. It was the annual "review of feedback" session at which senior executives would provide an analysis of information gathered about company operations, including customer and employee satisfaction, industry surveys of quality, and media comments and assessments.

Although there were occasional suggestions made which were helpful, for the most part this session went over material familiar to experienced managers. What was especially disheartening was the lack of corporate responsiveness to new ideas and suggestions for improvement. It was as if talking about these things was a substitute for doing anything about them.

Anterra was an experienced manager and believed that he was receptive to change. That made him even more frustrated when, year after year, the talk never turned to action. He moved toward the entrance of the room where the session was about to begin. "Here we go again," he thought.

SALSA! was the fastest-growing fast-food restaurant chain in the United States. Its southwestern decor and menu were distinctive, appealing to a broad spectrum of customers, from the health conscious seeking an alternative to "burgers, burgers, burgers" to teens and young adults who enjoyed ethnic cuisines. Unlike some national fast-food chains, SALSA! did not franchise its restaurants and operated with a highly centralized structure. Managers like Anterra did not interact much with other managers in his local area, or even in the state. He reported to one of six regional vice presidents in the national office in Phoenix. Managers and the vice presidents to whom they reported did not meet face to face more than once each quarter, but maintained a steady flow of e-mails, sometimes daily.

Despite the emphasis on centralization and top-down decision-making, managers like Anterra had a certain amount of autonomy that was a real plus in what could be an overregulated job. For example, store managers received an allocation for advertising, and as long as they stay within their budgets, they could choose where and when to advertise. Similarly, each manager was permitted to offer a certain number of special promotions each quarter, but the specifics were left to managers. Anterra thought he could probably operate more effectively if he had greater autonomy, but he was basically happy in his job.

One of the few things that really bothered Anterra was the corporation's commitment to obtaining information about how people felt, what people enjoyed, what went wrong and how things could be improved. Anterra thought this was more than a strategy; it was almost an obsession. He was expected to have each employee complete an Employee Satisfaction and Suggestion Form twice a year, and departing employees were expected to complete one as part of the separation process.

In addition to soliciting information, opinions and suggestions from employees, the corporate office expected Anterra to have 5 percent of customers complete Customer Satisfaction and Suggestion Forms, even if he had to offer incentives (such as a complimentary dessert or beverage) to reach the monthly quota. As a SALSA! manager, Anterra had to submit a detailed quarterly report to corporate headquarters answering items such as: *What are the three changes you would make to improve service and customer satisfaction? What improvements would you like to make in the hiring process? Provide one new idea for the corporation's Suggestion Box.*

Despite the emphasis SALSA!'s executives placed on information gathering, few reports describing and explaining the information obtained were distributed, and there was little evidence of change or innovation based on survey results. When talking with other managers, Anterra found many of them were skeptical about whether or not senior management took the input from employees, customers and managers seriously or if they were simply "going through the motions."

Anterra believed that asking for so much information and then not using it was bad for morale, and he occasionally heard some of his employees making jokes about filling out surveys that nobody read and nobody cared about. Two years before, he even raised the issue at the annual managers' meeting, but received only a bland and noncommittal response from the vice president for strategic planning who was leading the session.

The meeting was well way under, introductions were made, pleasantries were exchanged and the vice president moved to the lectern to begin his PowerPoint presentation. "We have received many exciting and innovative ideas this year, and I want to give you an overview of the information we received," he said. "You, the managers, along with our employees and customers, have spoken to us in a loud and clear voice about what they would like to see happen at SALSA!" Anterra thought that people may have spoken in a "loud and clear voice" but if they were waiting for a response, the silence is deafening.

Questions for Consideration and Discussion
'The Silence Is Deafening'

1. Tony Anterra perceives that the leadership at Salsa! is not acting on information received from various stakeholders. To what extent do you agree with his assessment? What suggestions might you make to Salsa's leadership?

2. Suppose you were hired to evaluate the feedback programs (both employee and customer) at Salsa! How might you go about evaluating the process and outcomes of these feedback programs? With whom would you consult? What would you ask? How would you determine the program's effectiveness?

3. What are specific strategies that organizations can undertake to receive feedback from customers and employees? How often, and in what ways, should feedback be sought? In what ways can and should feedback be used to make improvements and changes?

4. Under what conditions should the feedback received from stakeholders be shared with managers and employees? Under what conditions should the feedback received from stakeholders be withheld from managers and employees? What are the likely benefits and consequences of sharing and/or withholding information received from stakeholders?

PART III

Core HR Processes in Workforce Engagement

Workforce Selection

Organizational Orientation

Training and Development

Rewards and Recognition

Work-Life Balance

CHAPTER 6:
Workforce Selection

Introduction: What do we Mean by 'Workforce Selection'?

Workforce selection involves the ability of HR professionals to assist the organization by designing meaningful job and work experiences; outlining hiring criteria and competencies; developing effective recruitment methods; and implementing appropriate selection processes. The workforce selection component of workforce engagement reflects the extent to which employees agree the company hires the right people, with the right skills, at the right time.

Highlights from the 2004-2005 National Benchmark Study on Workforce Engagement

Organizational success depends on having the right employees with the right competencies at the right time. Workforce planning provides managers the means of identifying the competencies needed in the workforce, not only in the present but also in the future, and then selecting and developing that workforce.

With roughly half of companies not employing rigorous testing or assessment in their selection process beyond a simple training and experience point method on an application, is it any wonder that according to *pan*'s 2004-2005 Workforce Engagement Assessment, less than half of all employees believe their organization does a good job hiring the right people, while one in four disagrees? Not surprisingly, the employees with the most positive perceptions of their organization's selection practices are new hires; nearly two-thirds of those employees with less than one year of experience feel their organization does a good job hiring the right people, dropping to half of those with their organization one to five years and four in 10 of those with their companies six or more years.

HR professionals know that they should "never hire a sure fire." Ensuring that they avoid bringing on a new employee who does not have the necessary skills and abilities is much easier than "helping them graduate out of the company" once they have already been hired and one of the reasons workforce selection is critical to the 4 R's (recruit, retrain, reward and retain). However, good workforce selection starts at the recruiting phase of the selection process. Great applicants want to work for great companies. It is one of the reasons that the 100 companies on the most recent *Fortune* "Best Companies to Work For" list have an average of 70 applicants for every job opening. The top five companies on the list have significantly more.

One reason there is a significant drop in workforce engagement and an increase in "disengagement" after an employee's first year with an organization may lie in the fact that less than two-thirds of all employees believe that the duties and responsibilities of their job were accurately explained during the interview process.

As most hiring/recruiting managers are rated on "time to fill" (the amount of time between when the job is "open" and when the opening is filled), it is not surprising that some HR professionals may feel pressured to oversell the importance of the job or undersell the high-stress nature of the organization in order to quickly replace the position. This might fill a short-term need, but the **pan** survey data foretells a longer-term problem.

Interestingly, part-time workers are much more likely than full-time workers to feel the duties and responsibilities of their job were accurately explained, perhaps because their duties were more limited than those of full-time employees.

The **pan** study also found that those employees who were given a pre-employment test (other than a drug test) during the hiring process were more positive about the workforce selection processes of their organization. In fact, employees that were given a pre-employment test or assessment are:

- More likely to be *fully* engaged and significantly less likely to be *unengaged* than employees who were not given a pre-employment test or assessment during the selection process
- Significantly more likely to remain in their jobs, even if offered a similar job at slightly higher pay
- Significantly more positive in how they felt their job compared to similar jobs at other companies in the areas of:
  - Pay and benefits
  - Training and development
  - Advancement opportunities
  - Work-life balance
- Much more positive in their feelings about their organization in all the drivers of workforce engagement
- Much more positive about issues related to fairness, communications and

their relationship with their supervisor.

Some have hypothesized that companies that understand the benefits of pre-employment testing and assessment in an overall continuous talent-management strategy would correspondingly have better HR strategies and improved worker engagement. Experts at **pan** have coined the phrase the "Fraternity Effect" to offer an alternative supposition: the harder you make it for someone to join a club (your company), the more hurdles you give them to overcome, the tougher you make the vetting process, the more likely they will be if they are invited to join the club (be hired by your company) to stay longer, work harder and recommend the club (your company) as a great place to be. Whatever the reason, there is a clear correlation between employees who were given a test or assessment during the selection process and higher levels of engagement and the associated behaviors.

Is there a business case for a better selection process, including the testing and assessment of applicants? Yes, starting with legal defensibility in hiring, firing and promotions. According to a 1998 white paper from the Society of Human Resource Management (SHRM), 60 percent of firms have been defendants in employment practices or wrongful terminations lawsuits since 1993. The legal notion of "due diligence" in hiring and promotion is based on a myriad of laws and guidelines including:

- Title VII of the Civil Rights Act of 1964
- Age Discrimination in Employment Act
- Uniform Guideline on Employee Selection Procedures
- Title I of the Civil Rights Act of 1991
- Americans with Disabilities Act (ADA)
- EEOC Guidelines.

These laws and guidelines require that hiring decisions are valid, fair and job related, and having a consistent process that uses more than just the training and experience point method to decide who will be the next new hire helps ensure these guidelines are met. Improving the selection procedures would also tie directly to the overall job performance of the employee. According to the *Psychological Bulletin, Journal of Applied Psychology*, the selection procedures with the strongest predictors of overall job performance are:

- Work sample test (validity score of .54)
- Structured employment interview (.51)
- General mental ability test (.51)
- Training and experience behavioral consistency method (.45)
- Integrity test (.41)
- Unstructured employment interview (.38)

- Assessment center (.37)
- Biodata measures (.35)
- Situational judgment test (.34)
- Reference checks (.26)
- Training and experience point method (validity score of .11).

Clearly, if companies are worried about their employees providing the highest levels of customer service, tightening up the selection process is the quickest way to get there.

Not only does an organization need to recruit top talent, it also needs to ensure that these new hires can perform acceptable work with a minimum of training and supervision. This is not to say that employees should be expected to excel at all the functions of the job without the need for any training, but new employees are expected to do their fair share of the work once they start the job. However, less than half of all employees in the **pan** study agree that their organization hires employees who hit the ground running, while more than one in five disagrees.

As would be expected, senior managers have a much more positive perception of their hiring practices than the individual contributors. In fact, in the area of workforce selection, senior managers rate their company performance an average of 20 points higher than the individual contributors do. This may be because individual contributors are closer to the majority of new hires than are the organization's senior leaders.

Disappointingly, less than two thirds of all employees believe their job provides the right amount of challenge. Nearly one in six newly hired employees disagreed, another sign that employers are not matching the skills and abilities of their (new) employees and the duties and responsibilities of their job during the hiring process. Whether hiring managers are not adequately explaining the duties and responsibilities of the job, or the organization is not continually training and developing its talent, lack of challenge can quickly lead to an unengaged worker.

Finally, according to the **pan** survey results, less than two-thirds of all employees agree that their organization is interested in hiring a diverse workforce. Larger organizations (those with more than 2,500 employees) are perceived as doing better in the area of diversity, as is the federal government, while those in state and local government rate their employers more negatively than any other industry classification. One in seven employees who work in sales/client development disagrees, and given the ever more diverse customers today's businesses service, this is a potential danger spot for today's employers.

Highlights from the 2006-2007 National Benchmark Study on Workforce Engagement

As was the case in 2004-2005, slightly more than four in 10 employees (43 percent) in 2006-2007 agree their organization does a good job hiring the right people, while one in four disagrees (25 percent):

- Employees in retail trade (32 percent agree) and state government (33 percent) were least positive, while leisure/hospitality (62 percent agree) and information services (57 percent) were most positive.

- Employees in the East South-Central (Kentucky, Alabama, Tennessee and Mississippi) are most positive (53 percent), while New England employees were most negative (31 percent).

- Employees who had a positive perception of the job interview were three times more positive in their assessment than those that had a negative view of the job interview process (53-percent versus 18 percent).

- Part-time workers are significantly more positive in their assessment than are full-time workers (56 percent positive versus 41-percent positive).

- As the employee's tenure increases, positive perceptions of workforce selection decrease, a continuing trend seen elsewhere in the benchmark results.

Current employees recognize the importance of hiring the right people, because when organizations do not, more work falls to them. However, less than half of all employees agree the company *hires employees who can hit the ground running*, while more than one in five disagrees (47 percent versus 22 percent). Not surprisingly, three-quarters of all senior executives agreed with the statement. However, the group with the lowest ratings are those employees most responsible for working with new employees and supervisors, where only four in 10 agree with the statement.

It is critical that applicants understand the job and its requirements before committing their time and energy to a new job. However, only six in 10 employees felt the *duties and responsibilities of my job were accurately explained to me during the interview process*. A successful job orientation and onboarding does not start after the employee has been hired, it happens during the selection process. More than eight in 10 fully engaged employees agree their responsibilities were accurately explained, while only half that number of unengaged employees believed the same (81 percent versus 40 percent).

The first of the Four R's of Workforce Engagement—recruit—is critical to a successful relationship with employees, and employers have a long way to go.

Why is Workforce Selection Important?

One of the most daunting tasks confronting any organization is finding the right person, for the right job, at the right time. Recruiting and selecting talent is, indeed, a challenge, especially given the relatively tight labor markets for highly skilled, hard-working, experienced and ambitious employees. Because employees represent the intellectual capital of an organization and are often the first (and only) face of the business to customers, considerable attention should be given to workforce selection.

Too often, however, hiring managers face the pressures of daily operations and are thus tempted to make shortcuts, sacrifices and trade-offs in selecting employees. Finding any person versus finding the right person demonstrates the tension between wanting the best and settling for mediocrity. As a result, many fast hiring decisions often result in substandard performance or improper fit. No wonder, then, that many subsequent employee problems could have been avoided had greater care been provided in the workforce planning, recruiting and selecting process.

As a component of workforce engagement, workforce selection is necessary to equip the workplace with the most appropriate talent for the job, the working conditions and the organizational context. In many organizations, employees represent the single greatest expense, and the cost of replacing workers ranges from six to 18 months of pay or longer. Thus, the ability to attract and select the best talent represents a financial and operational imperative that requires the attention of leaders, managers, HR professionals and individual-contributor employees.

Workforce selection involves more than simply choosing the best candidate. To find the right person for the right job at the right time, it is necessary for organizations to take a strategic view of their employment practices. This entails thorough planning, which considers the organization's strategy, its demand for future products and the availability of talent in relevant labor markets. After planning, recruiting is necessary. This involves articulating an employment philosophy, identifying the sources of potential talent and actively marketing to and attracting those candidates into the organization. Finally, selecting involves the series of activities designed to find the "right fit" employee. These include interviews and other supplemental activities, background checks and employment offers.

What is Involved in Workforce Planning?

Workforce Planning Considers the Following:

- Current versus future demand for products, services or solutions

- Organizational strategy

- Job analysis and job descriptions

- Anticipated labor needs and labor market issues

- Legal issues in workforce planning, recruitment and selection.

Current versus future demand for products, services or solutions

One of the most important determinants of the need for talent is the anticipated increase in sustainable demand of products, services or solutions provided by an organization. This means that the organization's customers value what it offers, and their purchase behaviors indicate a long-term desire to continue doing business with the enterprise. Companies in such positions, therefore, must take proactive and continuous measures to ensure the availability of employees to serve their customers on an ongoing basis.

In addition to demand, changes to the nature of how products, services or solutions are produced, provided or delivered impacts the structure and nature of the workforce. Re-engineering the workflow within an organization often results in changes in the internal labor force. Automation, redesigned business processes and the deployment of customer or employee self-service capabilities all serve to redefine how work is performed. As airline passengers increasingly use electronic tickets and self-service check in, for example, the role of the airport ticket counter agent has been changed and, in many cases, has forced a reduction in the number of agents needed. Thus, continued consumer demand and the nature of how that demand is fulfilled directly impacts workforce selection and utilization.

Organizational strategy

The organization's position in its life cycle has an impact on staffing. Is the organization starting up, growing, maturing, declining, retrenching or ceasing operations (in part or in whole)? It stands to reason that firms that are starting up, growing and maturing will likely be in need of talent, while those that are retrenching or ceasing operations will need less staff. In some cases, however, organizations experiencing a reduction in force are hiring staff simultaneously. Even organizations engaged in "downsizing" continue to have unmet, specialized labor needs that require finding and keeping talent.

Mergers and acquisitions can impact workforce staffing issues, as redundancies are identified, consolidated and eliminated. In recent years, the numbers of mergers and acquisitions skyrocketed, requiring many companies to deal with the impact that integration issues have on their workforce. With some mergers and acquisitions, seniority of employees determines who is retained, whereas in other merged or acquired organizations, staffing issues are determined by business needs, the past performance of employees, or both.

Finally, changes in the nature of organizational strategy necessarily impact organizational structure. Reporting relationships, type of work performed, type of product/service/solution provided, type of customer served, etc., all have implications for staffing issues. When Westin Hotels decided to make service excellence more explicit in its strategy, it restructured a very important role at each property: the hotel operator. With the new strategy, Westin wanted guests to have a one-stop-shopping experience. Thus, the hotel operator position was redesigned to provide guests everything they needed at the touch of literally one button. Now, hotel operators at Westin do more than connect phone calls—they handle any and all guest requests and relay that information to the appropriate person or department. Thus, a change in strategy had a profound impact on the structure of this one position, and it resulted in a change to how candidates are recruited and selected for that position.

Job analysis and job descriptions

To aid in workforce planning endeavors, job analysis and job descriptions provide useful information to hiring managers. Job analysis involves identifying certain conditions of work for each job and then determining the various duties and requirements for the job. Job analysis has a direct impact on many work-related aspects, including recruitment and selection; training and development; performance management; compensation; and tools and technology used.

There are several ways to conduct a job analysis. Interviews, observations and work logs of job incumbents are most common, as are interviews with supervisors, peers and other subject-matter experts. Regardless of the approach, a job analysis seeks to answer questions pertaining to the following: how work is performed; physical, mental, emotional and other stress involved in work; potential hazards involved in work; machines, technologies and resources used to perform work; types, severity and impacts of errors potentially made in performing work; how assignments are received and reviewed; employees supervised; and specialized knowledge, skill, or ability used to perform work.

For workforce staffing purposes, information from the job analysis can be used to develop written job descriptions. Job descriptions translate information from the job analysis into language about a job that is easily reviewed and understood by recruiters and candidates. Job descriptions are often the basis against which employment advertisements are created and, in some cases, interview questions and other selection methods are developed. The job description is one tool used to assist in determining expectations that organizations have for candidates and can be useful in helping to explicitly document criteria and competencies for laborforce selection.

Anticipated labor needs and labor market issues

Anticipated labor needs require an understanding of the workforce's current profile, while identifying the likely future workforce requirements of the organization. A current workforce profile typically includes headcount information, specific knowledge or skills possessed by employees, candidates for promotion and lateral moves and an analysis of the extent to which the internal labor force mirrors the external labor force found in the Metropolitan Statistical Area (MSA) in which the organization operates. Future labor needs are then constructed around these matrices, and an identification of the type of position—including specific knowledge, skills, abilities and experiences needed—emerges.

The external labor market composition has a direct bearing on the ability of an organization to select the talent it needs to be successful. The presence or absence of talent in the local labor market dramatically influences recruitment approaches. If an overabundance of talent exists (common for lower-skilled/low-wage jobs), organizations can be choosier when it comes to recruitment and selection. However, highly skilled workers tend to be in short supply in nearly every labor market, making the "war for talent" for these individuals quite fierce. This also leads to recruitment platforms that extend beyond the local environment and, increasingly, results in importing talent from other countries to meet organizational needs.

Legal issues in workforce planning, recruitment and selection

It is important to note that workforce planning, recruitment and selection—like so many of the core HR processes—reside under the auspices of numerous federal laws and regulations. Most notably, Title VII of the Civil Rights Act of 1964 prohibits employers from discriminating on basis of race, color, religion, sex or national origin. Additionally, employers cannot limit, segregate or classify employees on the basis of race, color, religion, sex or national origin. Title I of the Civil Rights Act of 1991 amended the Civil Rights Act of 1964 by allowing for compensatory (pain, suffering, loss of income, etc.) and punitive damages (meant to discourage illegal employment practices by fining employers beyond just compensatory damages).

Other laws that impact workforce selection include the Age Discrimination in Employment Act (ADEA), Americans with Disabilities Act (ADA) and the Equal Pay Act (EPA). The ADEA prohibits discrimination of individuals older than age 40, while the ADA prohibits discrimination against individuals with disabilities. Under the ADA, employers must make "reasonable accommodation" so long as it does not cause "undue hardship" to the organization. The EPA reads that men and women performing similar work must be paid equally. Similar work involves comparable skill, effort, responsibility and working conditions.

The Equal Employment Opportunity Commission is the federal entity charged with interpreting, enforcing and investigating complaints concerning the Civil Rights Act (Title VII), ADEA, ADA and EPA. The commission also issues uniform guidelines on employee selection procedures that serve as a resource for employers in their workforce planning, recruitment and selection endeavors.

What is Involved in Workforce Recruitment?

Workforce Recruitment Includes:

- Employment philosophy and branding
- Internal recruitment methods
- External recruitment methods
- Applicant tracking.

Employment philosophy and branding

An employment philosophy is the widely held assumptions and beliefs held by an organization about its relationship with employees, and directly supports efforts by the organization to find, keep and motivate employees. If, for example, an organization desires to be a true leader in its labor market(s), the alignment of selection, compensation, training and development and other interventions geared toward finding top talent is necessary. Employment philosophies also allow current and potential employees to know what they can expect, as employees, from the organization. The organization's commitment to and policies for employees are often acknowledged and discussed as part of the employment philosophy.

Branding, in this context, involves creating a consistent look, feel and approach to employment matters by enhancing the organization's reputation in the marketplace. This involves determining how a firm wants potential applicants, competitors, current and former employees, staffing agencies, college career centers and others to feel about the organization as an employer. Some branding approaches have resulted in an organization's actively seeking and subsequently promoting external accreditation, awards or evidence of their employment practices. Appearing in ranking or lists of "best companies" for employees is one example of how branding can be used in workforce selection endeavors.

Internal recruitment methods

There are several internal recruitment methods that can be used to find, keep and advance top talent within the organization. Most successful companies tend to promote from within, and there are numerous advantages to this approach. First, existing employees are already familiar with the firm's products, services, solutions, customers and industry. Second, they are also familiar with the organization's culture, values, decision-making styles, business processes, formal and informal networks and sources of knowledge. Third, existing employees can be groomed for advancement through effective mentoring, coaching and training, thus permitting the employee to prepare for upward or lateral moves and giving the organization a chance to determine the employee's capabilities and initiatives. All of these reasons permit an existing employee to "hit the ground running" with his or her new position and to make immediate, significant contributions that might otherwise not be as immediately felt with an external candidate.

While promotions from within are generally organization initiated, employees who respond to job postings that announce position vacancies elsewhere in the organization are typically doing so by their own initiative. Thus, when an existing employee expresses a desire for a new position, the organization must handle such requests with care. First, many organizations restrict the time frame by which an employee may "post" for a new position (e.g., six months). This is done to discourage frequent moves that wreak havoc on the enterprise's daily operations. Second, organizations may seek to determine the availability of talent within the organization first, before searching externally. In cases where internal talent is insufficient due to a lack of knowledge, skill, ability, experience or a host of other factors, the organization must communicate this reason delicately and explicitly to internal candidates. Finally, when employees initiate an internal job search, they are expressing their desire for a change. The specific conditions that warrant the change may be positive (wanting to advance in a career) or negative (wanting to escape an abusive boss or co-worker). Regardless of the reason, managers must be sensitive to the employees' desire to advance or make a lateral move. When this cannot happen, they must give the employees an honest reason.

Employee development opportunities are one way to equip internal employees with the knowledge, skills, abilities and experiences necessary for them to be primed for internal advancement. Training, development, job experiences, project work, ad-hoc assignments and exposure to other jobs or departments are ways to facilitate an employee's development. During the manufacturing-oriented economy heyday of yesteryear, in which employees typically spent their entire employment relationship with one employer, heavy emphasis was placed on career development. Career-development systems stressed a variety of personal and organizational factors that led to advancements within the organization. The organization almost always initiated and managed the control for career development. This is not the case anymore. Today, employees are expected to manage their own careers, with some help and guidance from their employers. This puts the burden for participation in training, formal schooling, continuing education, and professional networking and affiliation on the shoulders of individuals. The strength of this new philosophy is that it permits greater individual control and accountability over one's career. Meanwhile a weakness is that organizations send the message—intentionally or unintentionally—that they do not necessarily value their employees' long-term loyalty.

The advantages of internal recruitment methods were previously noted. There are, however, some disadvantages of relying on talent from within the organization to fill position vacancies. First, the lack of diverse people, thoughts, perspectives and experiences is potentially exacerbated by relying on internal candidates. What these candidates make up for in internal knowledge is sometimes offset by an inability to see new perspectives, challenge old assumptions and infuse a sense of energy and creativity into the organization. Second, an over-reliance on internal candidates may inadvertently create a paternalistic culture of employee dependence. This exists when individuals feel as if the organization will always take care of them and that if they bide their time long enough, a promotion will occur. Finally and perhaps most importantly, relying on existing employees to fill positions potentially deprives the organization of the truly best talent available in the marketplace. While every company likes to brag that its employees are the best, this is simply a faulty statement. Often, excellent talent— the type of talent to take the organization to the "next level" in products, financially or in strategy—is found elsewhere. Thus, to maximize the recruitment process, smart companies employ a mixture of internal and external recruitment methods.

External recruitment methods

Employee referrals are one effective method of externally recruiting talent. Current employees are often an excellent source for new employees. Because they work in the organization, current employees are best equipped to understand the real challenges, pressures, working conditions, reporting relationships, extent of supervision, etc. that form conditions under which individuals are expected to work. Thus, when current employees refer candidates, the potential employees have already been informed about many of the nuances of organizational life. Armed with this knowledge, they are initiating their candidacy for employment. Many companies understand the value of employee referrals and regularly pay a stipend or incentive for each successfully hired candidate an employee refers. A drawback to employee referrals is that employees tend to refer people just like them. As a result, organizations interested in increasing workplace diversity—in all its many forms—might find that an overreliance on employee referrals runs counter to that goal.

Rehiring former employees is another way to secure talent externally. Even better than employee referrals, these candidates have first-hand experience with the organization. Often, individuals leave an organization (or boss) to advance their careers elsewhere. In some instances, the "grass is always greener" phenomenon does not exist, and these employees desire to return to their original employer. These "retread" employees, as they are known, are often advantageous hires for the organization because they can typically make contributions sooner than other candidates. The experience or perspectives gained while working elsewhere might serve to provide a value-added component to their hiring dynamic. Of course, rehiring a former employee assumes that the employee left on good terms, was a satisfactory or better employee, is willing and able to return to the organization without causing hard feelings among existing, retained employees and is truly the best fit for the job.

Newspaper advertisements and direct communication to potential candidates are more common methods to attract external talent. Placing position announcements in newspapers is efficient and can be cost-effective, yielding a significant number of candidates in the applicant pool. The downside of newspaper advertisements is the sheer number of people who apply for a position who are unqualified based on their knowledge, skills, abilities and experiences. To be effective, newspaper advertisements must provide a significant yield ratio—that is, the number of qualified candidates who apply for the position and advance to the selection process. In some instances, newspaper advertisements increase the amount of work required to fill a position due to the inability of some applicants to self-select out of applying for the job. Many organizations have found it useful to simply post "help wanted" or "now hiring" signs or other announcements at their establishments. This attempts to attract customers and visitors who already frequent the business and, presumably, reside in an area of close proximity to the business. Like newspaper advertisements, this can be an efficient method, but can also yield unqualified applicants (though on a typically much smaller scale than via newspaper advertising).

In the past several years, great strides in employment recruiting have occurred via the Internet. Typically, employers post job openings either on their corporate Web site or use an outside source such as Monster.com. When recruiting on their Web site, organizations have the ability to provide tremendous information about the organization, and candidates can get a better understanding of the corporation's mission, products, leaders, history, etc. Additionally, many organizations provide information about benefits, their diversity commitment, testimonials from existing employees, descriptions of a "day in the life" of the organization, photos and other information to assist candidates in making informed decisions. The strength of recruiting using a corporate Web site is that candidates are searching for positions available exclusively at that organization. External sites, such as Monster.com, vastly extend the reach of the organization by exposing the job availability to many more job seekers, yet the job opportunity is also frequently presented with jobs from other employers as well. While the Internet has made posting and applying for jobs and managing the recruitment process easier and efficient, there are some drawbacks. Like the low-tech newspaper advertisements, individuals applying for positions online may not sufficiently self-select out of the process, thus yielding a tremendous amount of unqualified and underqualified candidates. Again, analyzing the yield ratio is one way to determine the costs and benefits of using external online-recruiting resources.

Staffing agencies, professional recruiters and professional associations are also useful in assisting organizations in finding talent externally. Staffing agencies serve as an intermediary in finding talent and, in many cases, deploying that talent for use in organizations on a temporary or project basis. In some instances, temporary or contingent employees recruited through a staffing agency may ultimately be hired by the organization. This typically involves a waiting period and/or fee payment to the staffing agency.

Like staffing agencies, professional recruiters serve as the intermediary between the organization and external talent, with one noticeable difference. Whereas staffing agencies tend to focus on short-term or contingent employment assignments, professional recruiters often seek to match organizational needs with talent resources for more permanent employment arrangements. Organizations typically pay fees, ranging from a few thousand dollars to one year's salary, for the services of professional recruiters. These resources are especially useful when the organization is seeking specialized or senior talent and requires a more customized, strategic approach to recruiting these positions.

Professional associations are useful in providing leads for job seekers and employers. Most professional associations sponsor job-search functions and Web sites and, in many instances, these associations provide the level of networking opportunities unmatched by others in locating specific sources of talent.

Finally, colleges, universities and community resources are additional ways to locate external sources of talent. Organizations frequently reach out to colleges and universities as a way of securing talent, especially employees who possess the most recent knowledge or skill in a given field. Many employers work with career-center professionals in institutions of higher education. Career centers typically assist students with assessing their career interests, résumé-writing workshops, mock-interview practice sessions, business etiquette, job fairs and other career-preparation services. The level of outreach to colleges and universities by employers largely depends on the organization's needs. Some companies are in a continuous hiring cycle and are thus recruiting annually on campus. For others, recruiting on campus makes sense only when an ad-hoc increase in position availability occurs. Additionally, the nature of on-campus recruiting varies, from local to national, general to specific, all based on the needs of businesses seeking talent.

In addition to colleges and universities, many organizations use community-based resources, including not-for-profit organizations, churches, synagogues, schools and neighborhood centers as a means of attracting talent. Regardless of which external approaches are used, the goal of recruitment is to populate a candidate pool with qualified and diverse applicants. Applicant-tracking systems are often used to assist hiring managers and others in the recruitment and selection process.

Applicant tracking

Candidates typically indicate their interest in a position vacancy through the submission of a résumé or application for employment. Organizations need to establish a system to track applicants from one phase of the recruitment/selection process to another (this is required by the Office of Federal Contract Compliance Procedures for organizations doing business with the U.S. government). Increasingly, applicant-tracking software provides users with a database of applicant and job information. This information is useful for finding matches between openings and applicants. Typical automated applicant-tracking systems permit letter-generation capabilities to applicants, have the ability to schedule and track interviews, include job description information and can generate a variety of internal and external reports (e.g., EEO reports).

What is Involved in Workforce Selection?

Workforce Selection Involves:

- Interviews
- Supplements to the interview
- Reference checks and other background checks
- Extending employment offers.

Interviews

Interviews are one of the most common ways to select employees. The purposes of interviews are to determine if candidates can perform the job as envisioned by the organization, are able to behave in ways that are consistent with the organization's value system and are, in general, a good fit for the job, department and organization. Successful interviews begin with the interview's thorough preparation. This includes having an up-to-date job description and a good understanding of the nature of the position, including knowledge, skills and abilities needed and duties and responsibilities expected of the job incumbent. Additionally, it is necessary to set up an appropriate, comfortable and professional environment in which the interview will occur. Finally, interview preparation occurs by reviewing the candidates' résumés or applications. Typical "red flags" or warning signs include conflicting or overlapping dates, periods of unaccounted time, unusual reasons for leaving prior jobs ("my former boss was an idiot"), lack of specificity in job responsibilities and job instability.

Successful interviews tend to follow an approach known as REAP: Rapport, Experience, Attitude and Potential. Interviewers should seek to establish *rapport* with candidates by opening the interview on a cordial note, typically with small talk about nonevaluative issues (such as the weather). Establishing rapport also involves telling the candidate a little about the organization, the job and the interview process, all with the purpose of putting the candidate at ease. Next, the interview shifts to a focus on the candidate's *experience*. In this context, experience includes past jobs, education, specialized courses of study, apprenticeship or internship opportunities and other skills that a candidate has that are relevant to the job. The purpose is to see if the candidate has the competencies necessary to succeed in the job. Identifying a candidate's *attitude* is also an important component to the interview process. The purpose is to see if the candidate will "fit in" with the work environment and if the candidate will match the organization's values and business practices. Finally, all good interviews should determine the candidate's *potential*. The purpose is to identify any strengths or challenges a candidate has and whether the candidate has potential in the job, in the organization or in both.

Interviews inherently involve asking a series of questions and making judgments about the answers provided by candidates. Interviewers can maximize the quality of answers received by asking the right types of questions. The following are types of open-ended questions designed to elicit detailed responses from candidates:

- "Explain how/why..."
- "Describe when/how/why/what..."
- "What did you like best/least..."
- "Tell me about..."
- "Give me more information on..."
- "What role did you play in..."
- "Why did you propose..."
- "Why have you applied for this position?"

Interviews are, of course, subject to legal guidelines. As a result, it is best to ask questions that are explicitly and specifically job related in nature. Thus, the job description is a useful resource in providing a basis for interview questions. The following are representative of subjects that are illegal, improper, unethical and/or typically unnecessary for interviews:

- Family status
- Arrest record
- Height and/or weight
- Sexual orientation

- Race
- Sex
- Religion
- Age
- Veteran status
- Nationality
- Pregnancy
- Disability.

To avoid legal troubles in interviewing, consider several safeguards. First, do not ask illegal or nonjob-related questions. Second, to ensure standardization of the interview process, it is also wise to ask each candidate the same series of questions. Third, consider having two or more individuals within the organization interview candidates (either as a panel interview or separately). This permits multiple perspectives and potentially reduces interviewer bias. Another safeguard is to ask candidates to sign a form indicating the interview questions they were asked. It is also wise to consult legal counsel for advice and guidance on interviews and other potentially treacherous legal territories. Finally and perhaps most saliently, consider using a more holistic approach to selection beyond just interview.

Supplements to the interview

In addition to interviews, there are numerous employment tests and assessments designed to determine the fit between an individual candidate and the requirements of a job. To ensure legal defensibility, employment tests and assessments must be job related and must have high degrees of validity (does the test/assessment measure what it purports to measure?) and reliability (does the test/assessment yield consistent results over time?). Additionally, employment tests and assessments must not provide adverse impact on minority populations. Adverse impact occurs when fewer than four-fifths (80 percent) of the minority group pass an employment test or assessment. Because of the proliferation of employment tests and assessments, it is wise to consult legal counsel and/or test and assessment publishers to determine validity, reliability and job-relatedness aspects of such tests and assessments. Closely related to employment tests and assessments are work-sample tests. Such tests require employees to actually demonstrate their competence and capabilities by performing a simulated aspect of the work required for successful performance on the job.

Beyond tests, assessments and work samples, another supplemental activity involves asking candidates to develop a written statement about some sort of work-related philosophy (e.g., teamwork, leadership styles, customer service). Such a statement is typically obtained as part of the application process and reviewed prior to the interview. It reveals organization, written communication patterns and how a candidate feels about the particular subject. In some instances, interview questions can subsequently be based, in part, on what was written in the philosophy statement. This exercise is typically used for managerial- or professional-level candidates.

Another supplemental activity includes a situational exercise. In this context, a candidate is given a case study of a likely workplace scenario (e.g., conducting a performance appraisal, dealing with an angry customer/client). The interviewer allows candidates time to formulate their response, including making recommendations about how they would solve the problem. Again, their responses can be used as a basis for follow-up questions.

Regardless of selection methods chosen, it is vital to ensure that each method is related to the content of the job and is executed in a legally compliant, consistent manner with all candidates.

Reference checks and other background checks

In spite of sound interviewing and supplemental activities, it is still vital that employers perform reference checks on prospective employees. Thus, interviewers (or employment applications) should always ask for professional references. While many prior employers may not provide references, hiring organizations should, nonetheless, make the effort. This helps show due diligence on the part of the hiring organization and can serve, in part, as a legally defensible measure against a charge of negligent hiring. When checking references, it is common to verify dates of employment, job title, responsibilities and other attributes about the candidate. Many companies have also instituted other forms of background checks, including drug testing, a criminal background check and a credit check (if financial matters are a routine part of the job). Again, it is wise to ensure job relatedness of these background checks and to consult legal counsel with questions or to seek advice.

Extending employment offers

After undertaking a thorough planning, recruitment and selection process that has, presumably, yielded a top candidate, the time comes to extend the offer of employment. In medium and large organizations, this is typically done through the HR department, whereas in smaller organizations the offer may be extended by the manager to whom the position reports. When extending employment offers, it is necessary to provide information about the company, the importance of the job to the company and how the applicant's background meshes with the job and the organization. Also important to highlight are the professional development and advancement opportunities available, the nature of the person's supervisor and co-workers, the compensation and benefits packages and other perks or important information, such as relocation expenses and procedures, if applicable. While offers of employment should not necessarily be construed as an employment contract, they are often made in writing. Candidates should be afforded respect in their decision-making process, and the goal of extending the offer of employment is to provide a positive foundation for a successful relationship between the organization and the new employee.

Summary

The ability to find the right person, for the right job, at the right time is a critical indicator of an organization's effectiveness in workforce planning, recruitment and selection. To maximize the intellectual capacity of the organization, a systemic approach to sourcing talent is necessary. Due to the increasing diversity of the workforce and the myriad of laws and regulations governing the employer-employee relationship, it is necessary to allocate sufficient resources—including the appropriate amount of time—to workforce-selection matters. The case study that follows, "*Being Sorry Isn't Enough. You've Lost A Customer,*" highlights what can happen when workforce selection matters are left unattended.

Case Study:
Workforce Selection
and Workforce Engagement
'Being Sorry Isn't Enough. You've Lost a Customer'

"Yes, I understand that you waited a long time," he said. "She is a new employee and this is only her second week. She may have misunderstood you or perhaps she could not find what you asked for. I am very sorry about what happened. We try to live by our motto," he said, pointing to a large banner hanging on the wall: "GOOD SERVICE & EVEN BETTER PRICES!"

The woman looked at his name tag, looked at her watch and then slowly said to him, "Mr. Valdez, as the manager of this store, you should make sure your employees know what to do and know where to find things. Thank you for the apology, but being sorry isn't enough. You've lost a customer."

As she walked out the door, Roberto Valdez thought to himself that things certainly weren't getting better. That woman wasn't the first customer to walk out angry, and he was pretty sure she wouldn't be the last.

Valdez was the general manager of Choose Your Shoes, a national chain of outlet stores selling women's shoes. The store had an excellent location midway between two large shopping malls and a national reputation of offering "deep discounts." In nine years as the store's general manager, Valdez had seen sales and profits rise and then stabilize. There were no major problems, and Valdez spent a good deal of his time working with his advertising department, looking to expand existing markets or create new ones.

The one nagging problem Valdez faced was the high turnover among the "floor staff" at the store. Over time, he had been able to outsource many of the key operations. Purchasing, accounting, payroll and inventory control were automated through Choose Your Shoes' central office in Missouri. Two other functions, cashiers and security patrols, were handled through contracts with local companies.

Both companies provided adequate—but not outstanding—personnel to cover the store's needs. Valdez liked the hassle-free service they provided. He avoided tasks he did not enjoy—interviewing, background or reference checks and "awkward" performance reviews.

Valdez was responsible for hiring about 120 employees, about 10 of whom were supervisors. The rest were stock-room and inventory clerks, custodians, sales staff, shipping and packing staff and a few people to file papers, answer phones, etc. These were entry-level jobs, requiring minimal skills, and there were few opportunities for advancement. Turnover was high, approaching 20 percent for the last year, and so was absenteeism. Only a handful of these employees had worked for Choose Your Shoes for five years or longer.

Valdez felt he could live with high turnover and even with absenteeism, but he was troubled and frustrated by how frequently customers complained about the staff. Sales staff, whose major tasks involved helping customers find the right size shoe, or checking in the stockroom to see if particular shoes and sizes were available, were often indifferent in dealing with customers, or were very slow in meeting requests. On many occasions, Valdez heard staff members say, "You better check up front."

When he thought about these staffing issues, he realized that there were three problems.

First, the pool of potential workers was small, not because particular skills were required, but rather because there were many other jobs for those with minimal skills.

Second, Choose Your Shoes had no training program for new workers. At best, someone who already worked at the store would take an hour or two to show new workers "the ropes." Some well-intentioned workers failed simply because no one ever taught them how to do things, find things or deal with customers.

Third, there were no tangible rewards for good work or length of service. With no formal performance-appraisal system, good workers were known to Valdez only by word of mouth. Salaries were increased across-the-board by the same percent each January. After five years, employees received an additional week of vacation and three more days of paid sick leave each year, but so few people were there long enough to earn the benefit that it was virtually nonexistent, unknown to most employees.

The company was also hindered by its policies regarding part-time employees, who received the same hourly wage as full-time workers, but received no benefits. Valdez speculated that providing health benefits to part timers might increase the pool of potential workers. However, he had no proof of that, and he found it hard it justify the added costs based on a "hunch."

Any change would involve additional expenses, but he was willing to make that commitment if he could feel confident that things would improve. His dilemma was in trying to figure out what to do: More selective hiring practices? Instituting a training program? Creating a more attractive reward system? Each potential plan had its own strengths and weaknesses.

Valdez was frustrated. He had been having this debate with himself for months and still could not decide on a plan of action. To do nothing was foolish because these employee problems were having an effect on customer satisfaction and "the bottom line." But what should he do?

The phone rang. He answered and heard one of the cashiers say, "Mr. Valdez, could you come to the front of the store? There is a lady here who is very angry and insists on talk to you personally."

Questions for Consideration and Discussion
'Being Sorry Isn't Enough. You've Lost a Customer.'

1. Has Valdez correctly assessed the problems causing high employee turnover at Choose Your Shoes? Why or why not? What are other potential problems that would lead to employee dissatisfaction and turnover?

2. Valdez faces short- and long-term problems with workers at Choose Your Shoes. What are some of his immediate concerns, and what are larger, more systemic issues that must be addressed? What tactics should he use in approaching each of these problems?

3. Prepare a list of three to four specific actions Valdez should undertake during the next few weeks. What measurable outcomes should Valdez utilize to determine the effectiveness of each of the approaches he is considering?

4. To what extent is attracting, retaining and motivating minimally skilled workers a problem for organizations today? Are there specific things that managers can do to make entry-level jobs more appealing? How might entry-level workers be best selected to perform these jobs?

CHAPTER 7:
Organizational Orientation

Introduction: What do We Mean By 'Organizational Orientation'?

Organizational orientation involves the ability of HR professionals to assist the organization by developing processes for effective employee integration; educating employees about organizational values and business practices; and developing relevant orientation, mentoring and coaching programs. The organizational orientation component of workforce engagement reflects the extent to which employees perceive the company that provides them with the knowledge they need to adequately perform their job. Unlike job-specific training, this component measures how well the organization teaches the mission, vision and values of the organization during the onboarding process.

Highlights from the 2004-2005 National Benchmark Study on Workforce Engagement

According to a January 2003 survey of nearly 5,700 workers conducted in the United Kingdom, 4 percent of the "new starters" had such a disastrous first day that they never went back (Reed Executive/Press Office). A report by the American Hotel and Lodging Association found it takes 90 days for a new employee to reach the level of productivity of an existing worker. If new hires do not receive proper training and support during orientation, 47 percent leave their jobs within the first six months. Finally, according to the Studer Group, 25 percent of employees in the health-care field leave within the first 90 days.

Organizational orientation, or onboarding as it is increasingly referred to by HR experts, is a critical component of workforce engagement. In fact, it is a "key driver" of engagement based on the *pan* 2004-2005 workforce engagement national benchmark. The goal of onboarding is simple: *create bonds with new employees that are strong and meaningful and that encourage a strong commitment and engagement with the organization.*

Seventy-five percent of employees in the *pan* 2004-2005 Workforce Engagement

Benchmark Study indicated they received a *clear understanding of the company's mission, vision, values and the objectives and the role I play in them.* This was the highest-rated workforce engagement component in the **pan** study. In fact, there was no demographic group analyzed where less than two-thirds of the employees felt their organization did a good job in orientation.

What is most important to employees? Being informed as to how their job fits in with the total company. Remember, all employees can fit into two groups: those that work directly with customers and those who support those employees that do. Once you accept this premise, it shouldn't be difficult to help employees better understand the impact their job has on customer satisfaction and company success.

Less tenured and younger workers perceive their employers more favorably with regard to understanding their job fit, indicating that "onboarding" is not a process that should ever end; employees need to have continual reinforcement as to the importance of their job as it relates to the entire company. In fact, as employees increase their tenure and their job responsibilities, it may be more important to make sure employees know the critical requirements of their job and those duties and responsibilities that can be offloaded to others.

The importance of proper ethical conduct is one of the most critical factors to employees as it relates to onboarding and organizational orientation. Less than three in four employees agree that the importance of ethical business conduct has been communicated to them throughout their employment, while more than one in 10 disagrees. The importance of providing an ethical culture was previously discussed in the "Ethics, Diversity and Safety" chapter; however, laying an ethical foundation for employees and continually reinforcing good behavior is critical to engagement. Responses from employees in different industries show the linkage between employees who receive this constant feedback related to ethics and their perceptions of the ethical fitness of their organization and the integrity of senior leadership.

Of concern, two in 10 senior executives could not agree the importance of ethical conduct has been communicated to them effectively and that ethics is a "top down," not a "bottom's up," process. If 20 percent of senior executives are not continually communicated to about the importance of ethical business practices, is it any wonder that companies continue to struggle with the effects of having a "less than ethical" culture? This is one area where communication needs to be continuous and intentional. Corporate priorities change, but the importance of ethical decision-making cannot.

Also important to a successful orientation is ensuring the new hire understands the requirements and responsibilities of the job. In fact, this is a critical step during the workforce selection process, as well. Although it might be seen as advantageous to a hiring manager not to tell applicants the "entire truth" to get them to accept a job offer, the negative impact on engagement and the corresponding job behaviors and actions *after* employees fully understand the requirements and responsibilities makes this a short-term gain with a long-term consequence.

Not surprisingly, HR employees are most positive about this issue, with more than eight in 10 having positive perceptions about their employer, compared to just seven in 10 from the overall *pan* results. Nearly one in five MIS/IT employees actively disagrees that their job responsibilities are well defined.

Finally, employees must be informed early in their orientation of their performance expectations and how they will be measured on those expectations. No performance-review feedback should be a surprise to an employee, either related to his or her performance on the job or what he or she is being rated on. Although seven in 10 employees agree that the performance expectations of their job have been explained by their manager, three in 10 employees do not feel the same way. Employees in health services rate their employers the highest, those in information services, the lowest.

This feedback related to individual performance expectations is important throughout the entire career of employees with their organization, as witnessed by the drop in perceived company performance from employees with their organization for more than 10 years. Interestingly, middle managers and individual contributors rate their employers equally in this area; only senior management rates the company performance in this area stronger than the other groups. Finally, employees who received a prehire test or assessment were significantly more positive in their perceptions than those who were not given an assessment. Ensuring that your new employees are successfully onboarded and oriented to the organization guarantees that the significant investment you make in recruiting is paid back by employees who stay longer, work harder and guarantee customer satisfaction.

Highlights from the 2006-2007 National Benchmark Study on Workforce Engagement

Although organizational orientation made the least impact of all workforce engagement drivers in 2006-07 (just as it was in 2004-2005), it is still important that today's employers perform well in the organizational orientation of its employees. As with all other workforce engagement drivers, the perceptions of employees regarding their onboarding weakened since the last benchmark in 2004-2005. Although it's the only key driver that is considered a strength to leverage (more than 70 percent of employees feeling positively), the 2004-2005 results were 75-percent positive. Other results include:

- Nonunion employees are significantly more positive about their overall orientation than are union employees (72 percent versus 61 percent).
- Those participating in a social event are significantly more positive than those who didn't participate (73 percent versus 66 percent).
- Leisure/hospitality, health services and education are most positive (84 percent, 82 percent and 81 percent), while information services and manufacturing were least positive (60 percent each).
- Women feel more positively than men regarding their orientation (73 percent versus 67 percent).
- Those who had a positive rating of the entire job-interview process and who felt the interviewers were fair and impartial were significantly more positive than employees who did not feel the same way.
- Nine in 10 fully engaged employees felt positively, versus less than half of unengaged employees (88 percent versus 48 percent).

Again, the importance of ethics is shown to be critical to workforce engagement. Less than seven in 10 employees (69 percent) believe *the importance of ethical business conduct has been communicated throughout their employment,* while one in nine disagree (11 percent). Employees in the East South-Central region are significantly more positive in their assessment than employees in any other geographic region, while health services and financial services (both compliance-based industries) are most positive of any industry, and manufacturing and retail trade are the least positive.

Finally, only six in 10 employees feel they are *given the information they need to make good decisions.* Interestingly, part-time workers are significantly more likely to agree with that statement than are full-time workers (71 percent versus 60 percent). Positive perceptions drop as the tenure of the employee increases, a trend seen in nearly every engagement factor, and nonunion employees are significantly more likely to feel positively (64 percent) than are union employees.

The adage "you only have one chance to make a first impression" works in the workplace, too.

Why is Organizational Orientation Important?

Organizational orientation, or onboarding, is a series of planned activities designed to welcome employees to the company and to equip them with the knowledge and resources to settle in and become productive in their job. The importance of orientation cannot be underestimated. For example, a study at Corning Glass found new employees who went through a positive employee orientation program were 69 percent more likely to be with the company three years later than those who did not. A similar study at Texas Instruments concluded that employees who had been carefully oriented to the company and their jobs reached full productivity two months sooner than those who had not. Thus, beyond just making employees feel welcomed, orientation programs can contribute to enhanced performance, reduced turnover and improved satisfaction with the workplace.

While responsibility for orientation may rest with a single person or department (e.g., HR), significant involvement from others in the organization is needed if orientation is to be successful. Senior leaders must recognize the importance of aligning new employees with values and business practices of the organization. Managers and supervisors are in a unique position, as they will likely directly supervise the new employee. Thus, they should ensure that new hires are properly supported from day one by allocating resources, setting expectations, providing ongoing support and feedback and facilitating the settling-in process. Finally, individual-contributor employees—those individuals who form the peer group of the new employee—play a unique role in orientation, too. Peer-group members need to recognize that their actions, intentional or unintentional, go a long way toward creating a welcoming environment or, conversely, an environment that a new employee might find intimidating or closed to outsiders. Thus, given the costs associated with recruitment and selection, it is vital for all members of the organization to assist in ensuring a positive orientation experience for new employees.

Organizational orientation is necessary to give new employees a firm foundation for a successful job experience in the organization. To design programs and processes that effectively onboard employees, it is first necessary to understand the reasons for orientation. Welcoming employees, ensuring that they are knowledgeable about business practices and explicitly outlining performance expectations and behaviors ensures that employees are provided with sufficient information to begin their work. There are several approaches to orientation, including training programs, introductions to the supervisor and peer-group members, formal and informal networking and other resources. Additional considerations in orientation include proper planning for the new hire's arrival, setting up workspaces and determining any unique or unusual conditions under which the employee will be expected to work.

What is the Purpose of Organizational Orientation?

> **Organizational Orientation Is Necessary Because:**
>
> - First impressions can positively reinforce that the employee made the right employment decision.
>
> - Organizational values and business practices need to be understood.
>
> - Orientation costs are far cheaper than turnover costs.
>
> - Clear expectations for employee performance and behavior need to be communicated.

First impressions can positively reinforce that the employee made the right employment decision

While seemingly an obvious statement, new employees need to be explicitly and appropriately welcomed to the organization. This is important because employees form long-lasting impressions based on their initial encounters with companies. Like customers, employees are consumers; they make "purchase" decisions based on how they are treated by organizations. In this case, the new employee is a consumer of the work experience and seeks to have the decision to work for the organization positively reinforced during organizational orientation. Too often, what results from a poorly planned and executed orientation and onboarding process is a case of "buyer's remorse," in which new employees question their decision to align themselves with the company. Thus, the goal of orientation is to positively reinforce that employees made the right decision to work for the organization, that they are truly valued and welcomed by their colleagues and that they will be effectively supported as they carry out their job assignments.

Organizational values and business practices need to be understood

One of the most important opportunities that organizations can take advantage of during orientation activities is the imparting of their values to new employees. Every organization operates under a series of espoused values, such as quality, service, teamwork, diversity, innovation, etc. It is necessary to identify, describe and instill these values in new employees, so that they will better understand the organization and how the values impact approaches to work. Additionally, it is important to ensure that new employees understand the organization's commitment to ethical conduct and decision-making. Issues concerning conflicts of interest, decision-making approaches, internal whistleblowing and ways to report suspect behaviors should be explicitly addressed. Finally, new employees should be introduced to the specific businesses practices and processes that are unique to the organization. They should understand how and why the organization is competitively differentiated and the ways in which the organization adds value to its products, services and solutions.

Orientation costs are far cheaper than turnover costs

The ability to find, keep and motivate talented, productive employees is a goal of every employer. It might seem odd to mention retention in the context of orientation, yet the reality is that it is far cheaper to invest in orientation (and ongoing training, among other things) than it is to deal with the high costs of turnover. A recent Hay Group study put the costs of replacing workers at 18 months for salaried employees and six months of pay for hourly workers. The "soft costs" of turnover include lack of production during predeparture, lost productivity of the vacant position, lower morale of remaining employees, lower productivity of a new hire and additional supervision time for new hire. Some of the "hard costs" of turnover include separation processing, co-worker burdens (e.g., overtime, added shifts), recruitment, selection, orientation and training. Many employees leave their jobs within the first few weeks or months because they are dissatisfied with the nature of their work. Thus, a modest investment in finding the right person to ensure a proper fit and equipping that person with sound orientation to the job and workplace can help reduce the likelihood of turnover.

Clear expectations for employee performance and behavior need to be communicated

New employees want and need to know the specifics about their work. Although certain information is presented to candidates throughout the selection process, orientation is the time to make explicit the exact nature of the job. This includes detailed information about how and why work should be performed in a certain way, and performance expectations held by the manager or supervisor. New employees should be informed how, when and by whom they will receive feedback about their job performance and the sources of data that will be used to evaluate that performance. Additional considerations also include how the employee should behave at work, the type of dress code and other regulations with which to comply and the ways organizational members are expected to interact with external stakeholders, such as customers or business partners.

What are Approaches to Organizational Orientation?

Organizational Orientation Approaches Include:

- Training programs
- Supervisor and peer-group responsibilities
- Formal and informal networking
- Resources for settling in and becoming productive.

Training programs

Training programs are perhaps the most widely used form of orienting a new employee to an organization. There are several options for new-employee orientation training programs. First, classroom training is a common way of indoctrinating employees into the company. Such training can last as short as one to two hours, or as long as three to four days, depending on the scope of material to be covered, level of sophistication of the training provided and resources allocated to orientation endeavors. Classroom training is often augmented by computer-based training (CBT). When CBT is used, it is often done to expound upon concepts introduced in class. In some cases, CBT is used in place of classroom training, in which new employees use CBT programs to learn about the organization without interaction with other employees or a formal orientation facilitator. Some orientation training programs also use self-study materials to aid in the new employee's acquisition of organization knowledge. The new employee's direct supervisor may also be part of orientation training, usually to ensure that relevant organizational information is cascaded down to and contextualized within the scope of the individual department and job. Finally, many successful orientation programs use a blended approach—classroom-based training, CBT, self-study and supervisor involvement—in introducing the organization to the new employee.

Regardless of delivery method, successful orientation programs have some common characteristics when it comes to the content presented to new employees. The organization's mission, vision and values are identified and communicated. Closely related to this is background information about the products, services and solutions the company provides and the nature and type of customers it serves. Additionally, the history and future directions of the organization are also highlighted to provide information to the new employee about past accomplishments and promising opportunities. Policies, practices and procedures for operating within the organizational environment or performing specific job-related duties are also usually part of new-employee training programs. Finally, information concerning employee-employer relationships, grievance and dispute-resolution procedures, benefit information and other employee resources are also presented. The discussion of specific benefits packages, programs and options, however, may take place later when an employee becomes eligible for benefits. Training programs are one way to introduce an employee to the organization, and the information contained in these programs is best reinforced through specific supervisor and peer-group responsibilities.

Supervisor and peer-group responsibilities

The supervisor and members of the new employee's peer group have specific responsibilities that can aid in the orientation and satisfaction of the new hire. Supervisors should take the lead in facilitating introductions between the new employee and his or her peer group. Such introductions need to highlight the work-flow and interdependent nature of jobs, as well as special issues in communication, reporting relationships and peers who can serve as a resource for the new employee. Next, supervisors need to review the job description and nature of job assignments and duties with the employee. Closely related to this, of course, is having the supervisor outline explicit expectations for employee performance. Finally, supervisors should discuss their management style, including how they assign and review work, the frequency of meetings, communication requirements and any other information that will provide the new employee with information to fully maximize and enjoy the supervisor-employee relationship.

While the supervisor has many responsibilities to ensure that the new employee begins on the right foot, so, too, do members of the new hire's peer group. One obvious, but sometimes overlooked, responsibility of peer-group members is to introduce themselves to the new employee and welcome him or her to the organization or department. Although this should be facilitated by the supervisor, it is wise for peers to redouble their efforts at making their new colleague feel welcome. Additionally, peer-group members should provide information and resources to the new employee and assist that person's settling in by answering questions, offering advice and assisting with understanding the job and organization. Finally, peers should be patient with the new employee when mistakes are made, errors are uncovered or organization-specific experience is lacking. Great efforts should be made to avoid embarrassing the new hire, something not always explicitly practiced.

Formal and informal networking

In addition to training programs and supervisor and peer-group responsibilities, organizational orientation also occurs through formal and informal networking opportunities. Formal networking approaches include company tours, in which a new hire is walked around the organization, introduced to people and departments with whom that person will have frequent contact and made aware of the location of key organizational functions and resources. The establishment of a "buddy system" with a peer, either in the new employee's department or elsewhere in the organization, is another formal networking mechanism used in orientation. "Buddy systems" assign the new hires to a more experienced employee for the purposes of navigating through organizational policies and providing a friendly resource. "Buddy system" relationships can last for as long as necessary, though typically these fade after the first 90-120 days. Finally, other formal networking opportunities, such as affinity groups, are ways to further integrate a new employee into the organization. Affinity groups are organizationally sponsored groups comprised of individuals with a common goal of promoting understanding, awareness and resources about a particular issue (e.g., working mothers; gay, lesbian, bisexual or transgendered individuals; African Americans).

In addition to formal networking, there are several informal networking approaches. Daily communications and interactions with a variety of employees, business partners, customers and outside constituents provide ways to further orient a new employee and to make that person's bond to the organization even stronger. Meetings with the boss, the peer group or with others inside and outside the organization are another way to inform a new hire about current issues facing the organization and the new employee's job. Additionally, invitations to attend company-sponsored events, such as a bowling team or task force, can also go a long way toward making the new employee feel welcome. Regardless of the formal or informal networking approaches in organizations, it is important to remember that relationships that bind an employee to a company are often formed outside of the strict limitations of the organizational chart.

Resources for settling in and becoming productive

All of the well-intentioned training, relationship building and networking can be undermined if a new employee lacks the proper resources to aid in settling in and becoming a productive member of the organization. Thus, successful orientation programs ensure that employees are given the necessary tools and technologies to perform their work. Policy manuals, company regulations, the organizational chart, standard operating procedures and access to training opportunities are all part of the resources a new employee needs to be successful. Where applicable, access to the company's intranet (and, in some cases, the Internet) should be provided. Too often, the appropriate resources are allocated after the fact, when a new employee has already begun his or her job. The lack of preparation potentially signals to the employee that he or she may not be truly valued, or that the company is disorganized and not prepared for his or her arrival. Thus, there are several important additional considerations that are needed as part of successful organizational orientation endeavors.

What Additional Considerations are Involved in Organizational Orientation?

Additional Organizational Orientation Considerations Include:

- Planning for the new employee's arrival

- Preparing the new employee's workspace

- Determining unique conditions under which an employee will work

- Evaluating the effectiveness of orientation activities.

Planning for the new employee's arrival

The saying "the devil's in the details" is an accurate descriptor for planning a new employee's arrival. After recruiting and selecting talent and after the offer of employment is extended and accepted by the chosen candidate, it is necessary to arrange the specific details concerning the new hire's arrival. One of the first things to coordinate between the organization and the new employee is the start date for the job. After this has been determined, HR (or the hiring manager, or both) should arrange for new-employee orientation activities to occur. Additionally, a new-hire packet containing all of the relevant forms, policies and information should be assembled. It is also important to ensure that the new employee's direct supervisor and members of the new employee's peer group know when the new hire is scheduled to start.

Preparing the new employee's workspace

Another aspect of planning for a new employee involves preparing the specific workspace in which the employee will perform his or her job. As simple as this might sound, there are some instances of newly hired employees reporting to work on their first day and having literally no place to work due to lack of preparation on the organization's part. Thus, it is necessary to allocate space for the employee; order relevant supplies; ensure that passwords, parking permits, business cards, and other tools and resources are available; and determine the nature of supervisory and peer-group responsibilities for welcoming the new employee. During this preparation phase, it is also necessary to determine in which additional orientation activities, beyond new-employee orientation, the new hire will participate.

Determining unique conditions under which an employee will work

Some jobs have unique conditions under which an employee will be expected to work. While these issues should have likely been addressed at the recruitment and selection phase, it is wise to review specific issues during the orientation period. Some unique conditions that might impact a new hire include the following:

- *Flex time*, in which an employee may have latitude in arriving and departing within a range of time, so long as he or she works the minimum number of core hours each day and week
- *Telecommuting*, in which an employee may work from a remote location, typically home, to accomplish a portion of duties via remote access
- *Different shifts of work*, in which an employee may be scheduled to work varying or rotating periods of time, including nights, weekends and holidays
- *Varying locations of work*, in which employee work assignments might take employees to remote organization or client sites
- *Exposure to hazards*, in which an employee's job duties and responsibilities create potentially hazardous, challenging or stressful conditions
- *Travel issues*, in which an employee is expected to plan and manage work-related travel arrangements that take that person away from home
- *International assignments*, in which an employee is assigned to work in a foreign country, for varying lengths of duration, as part of that person's job duties and responsibilities

Those unique conditions are representative of the types of specific issues that must be addressed during orientation, or whenever they begin to impact an employee's position. Having a firm understanding of what is expected and what organizational resources can assist goes a long way toward alleviating stress and anxiety associated with unique working conditions.

Evaluating the effectiveness of orientation activities

Successful orientation programs and onboarding processes do not just happen.

They involve planning, implementation and, most importantly, evaluation. There are several ways to evaluate the utility and effectiveness of organizational orientation activities. First, regularly seek feedback from new employees about their experiences with and first impressions of the organization. Ask how they were treated during the interview/selection process, the nature and extent of effective, timely communication between the organization and the candidate, and how they enjoyed and experienced orientation activities. It is also important to follow up with new employees to ensure they are supported by supervisors and peers. In managing orientation programs, there is a need to continually update orientation materials to keep abreast of and current with organizational changes. As a result, modifications to orientation activities, programs, content, sequencing, etc. should be made based on organizational changes and feedback from new employees.

Summary

Equipping new employees with an understanding of the organization and their job is necessary to ensure success. The purpose of orientation is to welcome employees and to indoctrinate them into the company. Included in this is an explicit understanding of the values and ethical approaches to business conduct. Orientation approaches can range from training to mentoring to other networking activities. While several individuals and departments from around the organization might be involved in orientation activities, significant responsibility for orientation matters falls to the manager or supervisor of the new employee, as well as members of the new hire's peer group. Proper planning, implementation and evaluation of orientation activities can yield effective programs that start employees on the pathway to success in the organization. The case study that follows, *"Painting the Golden Gate Bridge,"* highlights a well-intentioned, yet resisted, orientation approach.

Case Study:
Organizational Orientation and Workforce Engagement
'Painting the Golden Gate Bridge'

Although they exchanged pleasantries and were having coffee together facing each other in the seating area of the well-appointed office, there was tension in the air. Saria Hopewell cleared her throat and said, "Dr. Guthrie, I was concerned about your note to me. Our orientation program for new employees is outstanding and has done well for us since it was introduced over four years ago. I have been planning to do a thorough evaluation in a year and half. I don't understand what you mean."

Eric Guthrie, the recently appointed president of University Hospital and Medical Center (UHMC), looked at the vice president for HR and said, "Saria, please don't become defensive. I said that I had some questions and concerns about the orientation program and that I wanted to discuss with you the possibility of making some changes in our procedures. This is the same type of meeting and discussion I have been having with all of the vice presidents."

Hopewell said, "Well, naturally, I would like to explain how the overall program works. I have been asked to give presentations about the program at several professional meetings, and I am very proud of what we have put in place here."

UHMC was one of the largest employers in the city, with more than 4,000 full-time and 6,000 part-time employees working in hundreds of professional, technical, support and clerical positions. The employment classification system at UHMC was complex, with many highly skilled professionals working part time or full time and some even moving back and forth between full time and part time depending on research priorities, strategic needs within the organization and program priorities. UHMC was less than 15 years old, a consolidation of five public and private hospitals, an extended-care facility, a nursing school, and numerous outpatient diagnostic and treatment centers. Establishing standardized personnel policies, consolidating records, guaranteeing specific "vested" benefits from the merged organizations, simplifying procedures and creating uniform operating systems had been a complex and time-consuming process.

When Hopewell became UHMC's vice president for human resources six years earlier from a position in the Department of Health and Human Services, she embarked on an ambitious program of making the existing disparate human resources systems compatible, producing training and procedures manuals for key hospital and organizational functions and developing a comprehensive orientation and training program. Within three years, more than two dozen training manuals had been published by her office, and she developed a comprehensive orientation.

Hopewell believed that organizational effectiveness could be maximized by the consistent and systematic application of procedures and by ensuring that certain "baseline information" about how the organization functioned was shared by all employees. These beliefs were manifested in the detailed manuals her office produced and by an orientation program that was comprehensive, specific and—ultimately—time consuming.

Initially, Hopewell's detailed and methodical approach was favorably received by veteran and new staff members. People said it made them feel "involved" to have so much information available to them. Hourly, support and nonprofessional staff applauded what Hopewell described as the "vertical approach" to orientation: whether you were in an entry-level or executive position, you were required to attend the same sessions and hear the same information.

There were several indicators that Hopewell's ambitious orientation modules were having positive results. Attendance was high and there were few requests for exceptions to participation; the number of employees electing benefits and the range of benefits requested increased; procedural mishaps, such as redundancy of operations, decreased; and "incident reports" pertaining to compliance were submitted in timely fashion.

After it had been in place for three years, with changes and modifications made each year, the four modules that form the orientation program totaled almost 14 hours *per employee*. With a "new hire" rate of 10 percent for full-time and 15 percent for part-time employees, approximately 15,400 hours (2,800 hours for full time and 12,600 hours for part time) were committed to orientation activities. Some departments and units, especially those devoted to patient care, actually had to pay overtime to "cover" for new staff taking the modules.

When Hopewell announced that she was implementing a mandatory three-hour "update" module annually, people complained that orientation took up too much time, and there were some things that people could learn just as well "on the job." A group of supervisors met with Hopewell to voice its concerns. Hopewell said that she was planning an evaluation of the orientation modules in the future and that she wanted to see those results before making any changes. She ended the meeting with this statement: "Let me assure you that the more knowledgeable the people in an organization are about that organization, the more effectively it will operate."

In the first year of implementing the "update modules," only 60 percent of *all* employees and 25 percent of professional employees attended the session. In the same year, the number of requests for waivers or exceptions tripled. The majority of these requests were not from the new employees, but from their supervisors whose basic message was "I can't spare the time for this person to be away from her or his job."

When Guthrie arrived at UHMC, he almost immediately heard the complaints about how time consuming the modules were. He was impressed by the way in which people could separate their frustration with the modules from their assessment of Hopewell. The consensus appeared to be that although she was unwilling to consider change and was too invested in the "everyone should know everything" approach, she was diligent and thorough and could shorten and improve the modules if she set her mind to that task.

Guthrie felt that he needed to speak to Hopewell and that changes in the modules were needed, even if she resisted those changes initially.

The moment was at hand. Guthrie said, "Let me tell you what I have been hearing, not from one or two disgruntled people, but from men and women throughout UHMC who are very committed to their work and to UHMC's success. These modules go on for too long, and by the time you finally finish learning everything, you have to start all over again with an 'update' session. It never ends. Someone said to me that it was like painting the Golden Gate Bridge. By the time you finish painting one side, it is time to repaint the other side."

He stood up, signaling that the meeting was coming to an end. "I am counting on you," he said, "to come up with a plan that will address the concerns I have described. The only problem is we need to act quickly."

Questions for Consideration and Discussion
'Painting the Golden Gate Bridge'

1. To what extent does the orientation program at University Hospital and Medical Center presently meet the needs of the organization? What are the

strengths and challenges facing the program? What needs to change?

2. In what ways can Saria Hopewell leverage the support of managers and supervisors elsewhere in the organization to "buy into" the orientation program? What specific advice would you give her to obtain this support?

3. Suppose you have been hired as the consultant to evaluate the orientation program. Describe how you would go about evaluating its effectiveness. With whom would you consult? What would you ask? How would you determine the program's effectiveness?

4. With whom does responsibility for orienting new employees lie? What role do newly hired employees, managers, peers, HR/training departments and senior leaders play in orientation activities?

5. What types of information should be provided in orientation programs? How can an organization avoid providing "information overload" to new employees, while still equipping new hires with the knowledge and resources needed for success?

CHAPTER 8:
Training and Development

Introduction: What do We Mean By 'Training and Development'?

Training and development involves the ability of HR professionals to assist the organization by assessing needs and establishing priorities for training; designing appropriate performance-improvement approaches; and implementing and evaluating training and development activities. The training and development component of workforce engagement reflects the extent to which employees perceive that the company adequately prepares them for their current job and is interested in providing them career-development opportunities for the future.

Highlights from the 2004-2005 National Benchmark Study on Workforce Engagement

The importance of training and development as it relates to employee satisfaction, engagement and commitment has been well documented, and the 2004-2005 *pan* study shows that employers have a long way to go.

Six in 10 employees reported they believe they received sufficient training to perform their job to the best of their ability, while one in six disagree. In one of the few cases where a significant gender difference exists, women are significantly more likely to feel positively than men. Other findings are that employees who are 18-24 years of age are significantly more positive than any other age group, and in a recurring pattern in the *pan* study, senior executives are significantly more positive about working to their highest potential than are individual contributors.

Critical to the positive impression of training and development is giving employees the opportunity to learn new skills. The highest-rated item in the training and development section of the *pan* benchmark was two-thirds of all employees felt they were given the chance to acquire new skills and abilities, while only one in seven disagreed. Naturally, this item corresponds strongly to the number of promotions an employee has had in the last three years, with 90 percent of those with three or more promotions feeling they were given the chance to acquire new skills. Also, employees who travel internationally for work are significantly more likely to learn new skills, perhaps because of the need to learn new languages and understand other cultures to be successful.

More than 70 percent of employees working in financial services and HR felt positively about learning new skills, while employees in research and development and operations were least positive, with only six in 10 agreeing. The data related to the research and development function is very concerning, as these are the groups of professionals that companies count on to ensure they are on the leading edge of technology and innovation.

Showing that employers do not understand the true value of training and developing their employees, according to the *pan* study, only 47 percent of all employees regularly attend training programs or courses related to their job. HR employees were significantly more positive, with nearly six in 10 updating their skills on a regular basis, perhaps due to certification and continuing-education requirements. Interestingly, in two of the most technologically advanced jobs, engineering and MIS/IT, only four in 10 employees attend training programs, especially surprising given the speed of change in technology and the impact technology has on company success. Even the senior leaders voice concern in this area, providing one of their lowest ratings to this measure on the *pan* survey.

Six in 10 of health-services and education-industry employees attend training programs regularly, some due to training and certification requirements that may be necessary for their job and organization. Hospitals that have invested heavily in training and developing their professional staff have seen decreases in employee turnover (especially in nursing) and corresponding improvements in patient satisfaction and patient outcomes. Although nurses are going to leave anyway, providing training and development opportunities for nurses (and other employees) will impact their engagement level and their likelihood to stay longer, work harder and recommend the company as a great place to work.

Given the hospitality industry's competitive nature and the need to differentiate their company offerings by the service and support personnel they provide to their customers, it is surprising that the leisure and hospitality industry is the weakest of all industries. Managers in the hospitality industry may be misunderstanding the cause and effect of turnover in their industry. They may feel that their turnover is systemic, so training and development initiatives would never provide an adequate return on investment. However, the *pan* data clearly indicates that training and development is a key driver of engagement, a *cause of* engagement, and therefore leads to the kinds of behaviors employees need to exhibit.

As mentioned before, employees link training and advancement opportunities, fully expecting to use their new skills and talents for their organization and, if not, at another organization. It is very important for companies to help employees achieve their long-term career objectives, even if this means that the employer may be an "exporter of talent" sometime in the future. The average employee will have seven jobs by the time they are 30, however, if planned successfully, these jobs can be with the same company. According to Richard Judy, co-author of *Workforce 2020*, *"Every employee is CEO of one organization and that one organization is themselves."* If employees do not feel that their organization provides them an opportunity to advance, they will take their talents elsewhere.

In the *pan* study, only 42 percent of employees believe their organization is interested in helping them achieve their long-term career objectives, while 29 percent disagree. Of serious concern, these employee perceptions drop quickly as the job and company tenure of the employee increases. Also, these results correspond strongly with the age of the employee, which shows an identical pattern as the age of the employee increases.

Another interesting *pan* study trend in the area of training and development relates to the size of the company. In all aspects of training and development, perceptions of companies with 1,000-2,499 employees were weaker than companies having less than 1,000 employees or those having more than 2,500. Perhaps these companies are "too small to be big and too big to be small" and are feeling financial pressure to hold back costs.

Employees who receive work-related training are significantly more likely to feel positively about their long-term career objectives with their company than employees with no work-related training (50-percent positive versus 31-percent positive) and are significantly more positive across all the dimensions of training and development than those employees who did not receive work-related training in the past year.

More important, employees in the *pan* benchmark who received job-related training or education in the past year were significantly more likely to stay with their employer, even if they were offered slightly more money to leave. They were also significantly more *fully* engaged and significantly less *unengaged*, guaranteeing the kinds of attitudes that organizations need to rely on as they continually improve their product-and service-delivery systems.

Highlights from the 2006-2007 National Benchmark Study on Workforce Engagement

With regard to training and development, a new secondary driver of workforce engagement, the 2006-07 national benchmark results are weaker than they were in 2004-2005. Only 49 percent of all employees believe *their organization provides training and development that supports short- and long-term career objectives*, slipping from 53 percent in 2004-2005:

- Employees who were given a pre-employment test or assessment were significantly more likely to feel positively about training and development than those who were not given a pre-employment test (55 percent versus 46 percent).

- As the number of promotions increased, so did an employee's positive perceptions of training and development.

- Perceptions of training and development decrease as the tenure of employees increases, a trend seen elsewhere in the survey.

- 72 percent of fully engaged employees feel positively about training and development, while just 26 percent of unengaged feel the same way.

One of the most disappointing results from the 2006-07 study relates to the significant drop in the number of employees who regularly attend training programs/courses related to their job. In 2004-2005, 47 percent of all employees attended training programs; this dropped to just 39 percent of all employees in the 2006-07 benchmark study. Clearly, employers do not realize that training is an investment in their company's success.

Also surprising, just more than half of all employees feel the quality of orientation and training received for their current job was satisfactory, meaning just less than half of employees couldn't agree with the statement. Not only are employees dissatisfied with gaining skills to improve their future, they are less than satisfied with training to do their current job. The linkage to customer dissatisfaction cannot be overstated:

- 70 percent of all East South-Central employees felt positively about the orientation and training they received for their current job, versus just 41 percent of all California employees.

- One of the industries with the highest turnover also has the strongest employee perceptions in this area. 71 percent of leisure/hospitality employees feel positively about the training they received for their current job, while just 45 percent of manufacturing employees feel the same.

- Nonunion employees feel more positively than union employees (55 percent versus 50 percent).

- Part-time workers are significantly more positive than full-time workers (64-percent positive for part-time workers versus 52 percent for full-time workers).
- Middle management had the lowest level of agreement (43 percent) and the highest level of disagreement (25 percent) of any position in the company.

Training has a direct bearing on workforce engagement and the likelihood of employees to go the extra mile for customers.

Why is Training and Development Important?

Training and development encompasses all aspects of formal and informal learning that occurs in the workplace and, in some instances, away from work. Individuals, work teams and organizations rely on continuous learning to maximize performance, achieve results, manage change and innovate business processes. From a workforce engagement standpoint, training and development represents a tangible, specific series of activities an organization initiates for its employees. Access to training, development and other performance-improvement interventions goes a long way toward enhancing the workplace experience.

In the United States, more money is spent on training and development than all of the expenditures for K-12 and higher education combined. Thus, the sheer amount of money spent on training warrants its attention as a component of workforce engagement. Many companies mistakenly classify training as a cost, rather than as an investment. When one considers that payroll costs can account for up to 70 percent of total expenses in some companies and that training, as a percentage of payroll, rarely tops 4 percent, it would appear that many companies are not properly nurturing their investment.

To be fair, the direct and indirect costs of training employees are expensive. That is why it is important that organizationwide commitment to continuous learning—in all its many forms—be embraced, championed and effectively managed. The ability to find, keep and motivate top talent depends, in large measure, on the types of continued investments employers make in their employees. Training and development, therefore, is one of the most important investments necessary for workforce engagement.

Training and development opportunities seek to equip employees with the knowledge, skills, abilities and experiences so that they can be continuously engaged in performing meaningful work that adds value to the organization. To accomplish this, training involves assessing needs, designing programs and approaches, developing instructional materials, implementing training and evaluating the outcomes of training. Employee development focuses on other specialized educational programs and affiliations for employees, coaching and mentoring, job experiences, and delegation and special assignments. Finally, additional performance-improvement interventions might include workflow and business-process improvements; other HR enhancements; leadership-development experiences; and team-building, communication and change-management strategies.

What is Involved in Training?

Training Involves the Following Components:

- Assessing learner and organizational needs
- Designing training programs
- Developing materials for use in training
- Implementing training programs
- Evaluating the results of training.

Assessing learner and organizational needs

The first component of effective training is assessing learner and organizational needs. This is done to ensure that training is needed and that an evidence-based approach is used in planning training initiatives. Typically, a needs assessment identifies gaps between current and desired performance and helps to prescribe the specific training (and other) strategies to close the gap.

There are several sources that can inform the needs assessment. First, employee testing can determine what employees already know and can do. Second, individual employee-performance appraisals can identify individual employee needs and common organizational needs. Third, operational data, such as customer feedback, safety records, quality reports, etc., can provide information about problems and opportunities confronting the organization. Fourth, advisory committees, or a group of experts from inside or outside the firm, can provide advice on key skills necessary for doing the job. Fifth, job analysis identifies specific elements of the job and may reveal training needs in areas such as processes, procedures, technology and communication skills. Sixth, evaluation data from previous training sessions also serves as a useful form of needs assessment. Finally, the strategic directions of the organization, including future knowledge, skills and abilities required by employees, should also be considered. If properly conducted, the needs assessment should inform training design, instructional development, implementation and evaluation.

Designing training programs

The second component of effective training entails designing the specific training program based on the specific learner and organizational needs identified during a needs assessment. To design training programs, there are several things that must be considered. First, an explicit identification of the overall goals of the training program must be articulated. A specific timeline and milestones leading up to implementation must be developed, as must a description of the training program that can be used to market the program or inform trainees, supervisors and others about program content.

A specific training outline must then be constructed. This outline should include the learning domains to be addressed, including concepts, information, skills, attitudes and values that should be learned, practiced, reinforced or enhanced as a result of participation in training. From there, SMART (Specific, Measurable, Action-Oriented, Reasonable and Timely) learning objectives can be developed, and specific training topics and activities can be sequenced.

In designing training programs, there are a multitude of instructional strategies that can be used to impart learning and improve overall performance. Some common techniques include:

- Prework/assignments
- Lecture
- Group discussion
- Demonstrations
- Practice
- Q&A opportunities
- Role plays
- Simulations
- Games
- Work/assignments between training sessions
- Video and audio
- Self-directed/self-paced learning
- Team/group-learning projects
- On-the-job training
- Computer-based training (including Internet based)
- Post work/assignments.

Developing materials for use in training

After needs have been assessed and identified and after the overall training program has been designed and sequenced, it is necessary to develop specific materials for use in training. Some training programs are developed in house by the organization, while others are purchased from an outside vendor or supplier ("off the shelf"). Regardless of the source of training, most training programs have some sort of participant manual that can be used by learners throughout the program. Closely related to the participant manual, of course, are relevant handouts that serve to expand upon training topics or that serve as a reference for use after training is completed.

Effective visual aids, in the form of PowerPoint slides, multimedia presentations, posters, flip charts and other objects for demonstration purposes, must be located or created. Technological resources, used either during training or as pre- or post-work for learners, must also be developed or launched. Relevant job aids that can be referenced after training is completed must be identified and prepared. Finally, any additional supporting materials, including supplies, equipment, refreshments, door prizes/rewards, etc., must be sourced in advance of the training program.

Implementing training programs

The fourth component of effective training is the implementation of the training program. Here, the specific delivery systems (classroom, computer-based training, on-the-job training, etc.) must be managed. Specific facility and equipment needs should be coordinated and arranged, as should the specific trainers or facilitators. Finally, the specific schedule of training, including the lengths of the training program and the specific learning sequences as part of the program, must be continuously managed and tweaked.

Evaluating the results of training

The final component of effective training is evaluation, which involves determining the extent to which the training met its intended objectives. Some reasons why training should be evaluated include justifying to senior leaders (and others) the importance of training, making improvements to the contents of training and deciding whether to continue or discontinue a particular training program. There are several types of questions that can and should be asked as part of training-program evaluation, including the following:

- To what extent does the subject content meet the needs of those attending?
- Is the trainer or facilitator the one best qualified to teach?
- Does the trainer or facilitator use the most effective methods?
- Are the facilities satisfactory?
- Is the schedule appropriate for the participants?
- Are the aids effective in improving communication and maintaining interest?
- Was the coordination of the training program satisfactory?
- What else can be done to improve the training?

Many training evaluations employ Donald Kirkpatrick's "4 Levels of Evaluation"—reaction, learning, behavior and results. *Reaction* seeks feedback about how well learners liked the training, typically in the form of end-of-training sheets that capture the general level of satisfaction and enjoyment with the trainer, the facilities, the activities, etc. It can provide trainers with information about how to improve their performance and can serve as a benchmark for measuring their future performance. *Learning* determines what knowledge was learned, what skills were developed or improved and what attitudes were changed on the part of learners as a result of participating in training. *Behavior* determines the extent to which a change in behavior was realized on the learner's part and also the extent to which transfer of the learned behavior back to the job setting was evident. Finally, *results* determine what final outcomes occurred because of attendance and participation in a training program, including the training program's impact on people, performance, productivity and, in some cases, profitability. Training programs are, indeed, an important ingredient in workforce engagement. Beyond formal learning opportunities, however, there are numerous other employee-development and performance-improvement interventions that the organization should consider.

What are Additional Development and Performance-Improvement Interventions?

Additional Development and Performance-Improvement Interventions Include:

- Participation in formal, specialized education programs and affiliations

- Workflow and business-process improvements

- Other HR enhancements

- Team-building, communication and change-management strategies.

Participation in formal, specialized education programs and affiliations

The training programs described in the section above are all predicated around the notion that training largely exists to enhance current job-performance capabilities. Thus, to provide opportunities for employees to learn the knowledge and skills necessary for mobility elsewhere in the organization (and, in some cases, to positions at other organizations), formal, specialized education programs and affiliations are made available to employees.

College and university programs are one common approach to formal, specialized education. These can range from continuing-education classes and seminars to degree-completion programs to executive-development experiences. The focus is on providing a specific set of learning outcomes and credentials that enhance career and skill development and promotion possibilities.

Another type of formal, specialized education program offered to employees might be a professional certification or licensure offered by a specific industry, trade or professional association. Many occupations and professions have such credentialing programs, and these programs often provide a means of validating knowledge and experience in a very specialized field and demonstrating and documenting currency in a field. Involvement in industry, trade or professional associations, including attending conferences and educational events sponsored by these groups, is an additional way to strengthen education and affiliation opportunities, thus further enhancing an employee's development.

Workflow and business-process improvements

The goal of training and development is to improve individual and organizational performance. However, there are other performance-improvement interventions. Often, when a performance deficiency is realized, there is a temptation to "throw" training at the problem in an effort to provide a speedy resolution. While training may be necessary, it is also useful to consider other, holistic issues that might also be inhibiting performance.

One of the first areas to investigate when performance problems are noted is the nature of workflow and business-process issues. How an employee interfaces with other employees, customers, outside entities (e.g., vendors, suppliers and business partners) and technologies may serve to inhibit performance. These techno-structural issues may be a contributing factor to performance deficiencies. When ignored or not considered in favor of employee training, the ultimate impact of the training program will likely be minimized. Thus, to maximize performance potential, workflow and business-process improvements should be investigated and considered concurrent to employee training brought about to solve a performance problem.

Other HR enhancements

Rarely does a performance problem require training and development in isolation to aid in solving the problem. Instead, other HR enhancements should be considered as part of the performance-improvement process. As an example, many organizations send employees to "team building" training in the hopes of having employees work together more efficiently and harmoniously. "Team building" alone might be an enjoyable learning opportunity. However, without knowing how the organization recruits, selects, orients, evaluates, rewards, recognizes and promotes individuals, "team-building" training will likely not have significant, sustainable impacts on improving performance. Thus, when performance problems are identified and training is one of the prescribed solutions, it is also necessary to determine which other human resources issues, policies or practices will likely be impacted by the ripple effect of such training. Aligning all of these issues, policies or practices will go a long way toward ensuring that performance improvement occurs.

Team-building, communication and change-management strategies

Team-building, communication and change-management strategies are often used to enhance performance in work teams, in departments and throughout the organization. Team building focuses on building a commitment to a common, shared goal. It also provides opportunities to develop mutual trust with colleagues, to achieve higher levels of productivity, to increase employee satisfaction and motivation and to expand job skills through cross training and work interdependence. Improving communication can provide strategies to assist managers, supervisors and employees in relating to one another and to help teams work together more effectively. Finally, change results from a variety of internal and external factors. Managing change requires that leaders involve the people affected by change to gain their support. It also ensures that everyone understands why change is necessary, shows people how things will be better as a result of the change and provides resources (including tools, technologies, training, etc) to assist in preparing for, dealing with and embracing the change.

Summary

Training, development and performance-improvement interventions work in harmony to create and enhance organizational environments that place a premium on learning. Employees want to work for organizations that invest in them. By having a well-planned and well–integrated series of learning opportunities for employees, organizations can further strengthen their intellectual assets. Indeed, true competitive advantage lies less in the features of products and more in the ability for employees to create new solutions, engage in long-term relationships with customers, improve business processes, and embrace and lead change. These endeavors, among others, require continual access to learning opportunities. The case study that follows, *"This Call May Be Monitored or Recorded ..."*, examines the dynamic nature of learning and change in organizational settings.

Case Study:
Training and Development and Workforce Engagement
'This Call May Be Monitored Or Recorded …'

"I don't think you understand that the program we have addresses only one part of the problem. It's good, but incomplete." Andy Ward, the executive vice president of Northern National Airlines, looked tired and harried as he spoke to Doug Fairwell, the company's vice president for training and development. Fairwell said, "I know it's been a long day for you, and the satisfaction numbers haven't moved very much since the new program was implemented, but hell, Andy, it's a great training program, and sooner or later it will pay off."

"It better be sooner. The board thinks the numbers are lousy and they wonder why we spent so much money developing a new training program and got so little in return for it," Ward said. Fairwell looked defensive, but he spoke calmly. "I am certain that we now have the best customer-service representative training program in the industry. Our people know how to get the information and get it quickly. The complaints we get now are from people who complain about everything, people who are never satisfied."

"Doug," Ward said, "the only thing that matters right now is figuring out how to raise the satisfaction ratio. Just focus on that."

Northern National (NN) is the fifth-largest air carrier in the United States, serving more than 150 cities across the northern tier of the United States. One of the first airlines to utilize a "hub system," NN had a niche market among "second tier" cities, where it was often the major carrier. Because of the hub system, however, 60 percent of passengers taking flights of more than 500 miles had to change planes. This created a particular problem for NN because it had the highest rate of lost luggage in the industry.

The high rate of lost luggage was annoying to passengers and costly to the airline and, despite numerous attempts to create better monitoring systems for tracking luggage, lost luggage was an enduring problem that seemed impervious to all efforts to improve the overall track record. One of the problems created by lost luggage was passenger dissatisfaction, and a litany of questions were inevitably asked: *Why* was the luggage lost? Where was the luggage *now*? *When* would it be returned? Can it be returned *faster*? Where was the person "*in charge*"?

Even while NN struggled to reduce the lost luggage rate, the airline also sought to improve how to deal with those whose luggage was lost. Ward put it succinctly several years earlier: "We can't make them happy that we've lost their possessions, but we should do our best to make them *less unhappy*." The proposed solution was to develop a training program for the customer-service representatives who fielded the calls, obtained the necessary information and served as liaisons to those whose luggage had been lost. Overall responsibility for creating an "efficient, user-friendly" system was assigned to Fairwell, whose expertise in employee training and development had enabled NN to make a very successful transition from paper tickets to e-tickets.

Fairwell's approach to the "lost luggage" problem was based on two principles:

First, lost luggage problems were self-correcting, and most luggage would "turn up" even if passengers provided no information to the customer-service representatives.

Second, the most effective stance to take with stressed passengers is to be low keyed and businesslike, not overly friendly or overly optimistic.

During a period of several months, Fairwell and his staff developed a training program for customer-service representatives that consisted of three "scripts" to be followed when talking to passengers with lost luggage. Fairwell wanted the representatives to use *only* the first script whenever possible. The second and third scripts were to be employed *when necessary* if there were unusual circumstances. The first script enabled customer-service representatives to verify basic information, give the passenger a tracking number and phone number to obtain information and then—politely but expeditiously—end the conversation.

Another component of the training program was to "teach" the customer-service representatives how to "stay focused" on the script and not be drawn into discussions (or arguments) with callers. Customer-service representatives had 15 hours of classroom instruction before answering any calls. Even after their initial training, all customer-service representatives had three hours of supplementary training each month to ensure that they were effective in their interactions. Finally, as was the practice in many business organizations relying on consumer/service representative interactions, calls were routinely monitored or recorded so that Fairwell's staff could evaluate individual performance.

A third component of the customer-service representatives' training was the average interaction time for each incoming call. While the HR staff never set specific goals (such as a four-minute average for each call), the training did emphasize the importance of brief conversations. The training manual stated: "The longer the conversation, the greater the likelihood that the passenger will raise other issues, or be repetitious, or ask questions you don't want to answer."

Fairwell thought that 80 percent of all calls should be handled with the first script; another 15 percent could be handled by the second script (which was, in essence, an attempt to determine if there were *really* extenuating circumstances requiring action by NN). Only 5 percent, he thought, needed to be handled by the third script, which involved direct action by the airline.

The training program was pilot tested with favorable results, and some small changes were made in the scripts. The training for the initial group of customer-service representatives was doubled, with hours of simulated conversations, to make certain they were ready for "implementation."

No one believed that this program would have any effect on the amount of luggage that was lost, and no effect was seen. After 90 days of operation, a survey was sent to everyone who called a customer-service representative, asking for comments about the services provided. Overwhelmingly, respondents criticized the fact that the luggage had been lost and few gave anything more than a cursory comment that the customer-service representative was "adequate."

Anxious to see if the problem was being addressed, Ward told Fairwell to commission focus groups to get more information. Fairwell objected, arguing that it was "too soon," but Ward overruled him. The results provided by the focus groups were very informative. People felt that they had been treated politely and that the customer-service representatives were "well organized."

In their criticisms, however, focus group participants described the process as "cold" and the representatives as not taking a personal interest in their situations. They felt that some of their questions were never answered.

Ward, whose background had been in industrial psychology, thought he knew what part of the problem was. He told Fairwell, "These people feel as if they have been injured, and as much as they want their luggage, they want us to understand what a terrible experience they have been through. They want us to find their luggage, but they want us to cluck and sigh, wring our hands and say how terrible this must be for them."

Fairwell disagreed. He thought most people really wanted to turn a frustrating personal experience into a purely business transaction. Ultimately, he thought that passengers would learn to call, provide the necessary information and then go about their activities until their luggage was found and returned. The focus-group results represented the remnants of "old thinking," which would eventually disappear. He told his staff that the best strategy was a very simple one: "Say hello, get the information, say goodbye."

Faced with Ward's challenge to raise the satisfaction level, Fairwell had to decide whether or not to change the scripts and abandon his "just the facts" approach, or if he could modify the existing scripts to appeal to needs Ward insisted were important. He also wondered if it would be beneficial to describe this problem during the training sessions and "brainstorm" new approaches. He knew that it was time to make decisions.

Questions for Consideration and Discussion
'This Call May Be Monitored Or Recorded …'

1. To what extent has the training program initiated by Northern National been effective in handling lost-luggage issues? What are the current strengths of the program, and what needs to be improved?

2. In what ways can and should employees be trained to have "empathy" for a customer, as is suggested in the case? To what extent can those skills be taught? How might such training take place?

3. Under what conditions is it necessary for employees to be trained to follow a specific script? Under what conditions might employees be best advised to handle each customer experience uniquely? What are the advantages and disadvantages of each approach?

4. How might the training program at Northern National be revised, based on initial experience, satisfaction scores and feedback from the focus-group members? What should be maintained, what should be changed and what should be improved?

5. To what extent is training the best intervention for the lost-luggage problem at Northern National? Beyond training, what other people, process or technology issues might need to be investigated and improved to minimize lost-luggage occurrences?

CHAPTER 9:
Rewards and Recognition

Introduction: What do We Mean by 'Rewards and Recognition'?

Rewards and recognition involves the HR professionals' ability to assist the organization by rewarding performance through a variety of approaches; recognizing employee contributions to organizational achievements; ensuring fair treatment in reward practices; and developing strategies for employee involvement. The rewards and recognition component of workforce engagement reflects the extent to which employees perceive the company fairly rewards and recognizes employees for their contributions to the company's success, including both cash and noncash incentives.

Highlights from the 2004-2005 National Benchmark Study on Workforce Engagement

Nothing can be more harmful to workforce engagement than the perception that hard work is not valued or respected inside the organization. When using rewards to instill a sense of achievement, it is important to frame them as an indication of excellence, not as a device to control employee behavior. Employees may be resentful if they perceive rewards for good work as merely an effort to manipulate them. On the other hand, if rewards are framed as recognizing accomplishment, employees will remain motivated to work hard for customers.

As the country's largest employer, state/local government employs one out of every seven people in the United States. Many government employees work in a "sealed environment." These employees know their salary and promotion schedule. Keeping the job once they have been hired is almost an afterthought. You do your 20 years, enjoy the great benefits, get your gold watch and pension and then move on—employees who work for the government like the stability of their job and the routine of their responsibilities. It is one of the reasons that state and local government employees stay in their job 60-percent longer than the average employee (6.4 years versus four years). Federal government employees enjoy the longest tenure of any industry, currently at 10.4 years and rising.

However, although pay and benefits might retain state employees in their job, it is the "intangibles" that move them to become engaged with their organization. These "intangibles" include feeling a sense of personal accomplishment, feeling valued as an employee, having managers that pay attention to how people feel at work and having the freedom to make their own decisions. And just like employees in other industries, state government employees want to be recognized and rewarded for their accomplishments (the third "R," *reward*).

According to the *pan* 2004-2005 study, less than one in four state/local government employees believes that people are fairly rewarded and recognized for their contributions to the company's success, the lowest (by far) of any industry and the lowest score for any demographic segment in the survey. In fact, nearly twice as many state/local government employees *disagree,* a whopping 43 percent of those surveyed, the highest negatives of any demographic segment in relation to reward and recognition.

Equally disturbing from the *pan* survey is that more than twice as many state/local government employees disagree that *excellent performance gets rewarded* at their organization than agree (46 disagree versus 22 percent). This takes on additional importance because this particular item is a top driver of the employees' overall perception of reward and recognition.

Remember, the definition of *reward*, the third of the "4 R's of Workforce Engagement," is "*recognizing individual, team and organizational achievement through cash, noncash and other performance-management approaches.*" In many cases, the intangibles are more important than the tangibles. How much weight does a simple "thank you" from a manager have on an employee, or recognizing the anniversary of an employee with a simple handwritten note, signed by a senior leader of the organization? Often times, these "intangible" acts have very tangible results on workers' engagement and their desire to stay longer, work harder for customers and recommend the organization as a great place to work and to buy from.

According to the *pan* study, only 40 percent of employees felt that excellent performance was rewarded at their organization, dropping to a pitiful 22 percent of state/local government workers. As stated, more than twice as many state and local government workers *disagree* that excellence is rewarded in their organizations than agree. As the strongest driver of the reward and recognition component, employers cannot afford a negative employee reaction to this ideal.

As with other data coming from the *pan* study, as the tenure of employees increases, the perception of whether or not their organization does more than "talk the talk" in regard to rewards decreases. In fact, while nearly six in 10 employees with less than one year of experience believe their organization rewards excellent performance, it drops to slightly more than one-third of employees who have been with their organization 10 to 19 years. More of these longer-tenured employees disagree with the statement than agree (44 percent disagree versus 36 percent who agree).

Employees who have received work-related training in the past year are significantly more positive and significantly less negative than employees who did not receive work-related training. It might be the training itself that is seen as a reward for excellent performance. Learning new skills is often coupled with taking on new and different responsibilities, or even promotions and advancement. Of little surprise, executives are twice as positive as individual contributors (71 percent versus 35 percent). However, individual contributors have the vast majority of customer contact. Not providing these rewards can have a real negative impact on engagement and the desire of employees to go the extra mile for customers.

Of interest, employees who are taking care of a family member (either a child or another loved one) are significantly more positive that excellent performance is rewarded than those employees who are not caring for a loved one. Of little surprise is that the number of promotions an employee has received over the last three years increases, so does his or her positive perception of rewards. Finally, employees working in operations are more negative than positive in receiving rewards for excellent performance, with 42 percent disagreeing (significantly higher that ever other department) and only 34 percent agreeing (significantly lower than every other department).

Employees want to feel a personal accomplishment in their work. That was important to 83 percent of employees in the 2004 SHRM/CNNfn Job Satisfaction Survey and 71 percent of employees in the *pan* study. As seen in other workforce engagement components, employees in health services and education were most positive, while government workers (federal and state/local) were least positive. All employees can be segmented into two groups: those employees who work directly with customers and employees who support those that do. Showing employees how their job fits in with the organization's goals and objectives and, ultimately, the customer's satisfaction and loyalty, is imperative if an organization wants an employee to feel a sense of pride in his or her work.

While nine in 10 senior leaders feel that personal accomplishment, only two-thirds of individual contributors feel the same. Unlike other data points, positive perceptions of the employees increase as their age increases. However, there is little change based on an employee's tenure. Perhaps as an employee gets older, he or she relies more on self-acknowledgment of a job well done than the acknowledgement of his or her bosses and peers. Not surprisingly, feelings of personal accomplishment decrease as the size of the company increases. Employees find it more difficult to link their performance to actual company outcome when they are one of more than 10,000 employees working for a company than when they are one of a couple hundred.

In the world of reward and recognition, there is always a constant struggle between doing what is *equitable* and doing what is *fair*, especially with those employees whose performance make the difference between barely meeting and exceeding customer requirements. Employees expect their excellent performance will be rewarded through cash, noncash and other performance-management approaches. However, only 40 percent of employees agree that their organization rewards excellent performance, while 33 percent disagree, according to the 2004-2005 **pan** National Workforce Engagement Assessment.

Only 41 percent of employees agree that employee loyalty is valued and *rewarded* at their company, while 34 percent disagree. Nearly as many workers disagree (35 percent) as agree (39 percent) that employees are viewed by senior managers as their most important asset. One in five employees do not agree that their organization treats employees well (20 percent), while nearly the same number do not believe they are valued as an employee (21 percent). One in seven does not feel that his or her managers understand the important of his or her personal or family life (15 percent).

Finally, slightly more than half of all employees agree that their organization carries out company policies in a fair and just manner, while nearly one in four disagrees. One out of six employees does not agree that his or her organization is highly ethical, while one in four disagrees that employees are treated with respect and appreciation.

Highlights from the 2006-2007 National Benchmark Study on Workforce Engagement

While the number of employees in 2006 who agreed people are fairly rewarded and recognized for their contributions to the company's success remained at 41 percent, the number of employees who disagreed inched up from 32 percent to 34 percent. The size of the company showed an interesting and yet unseen pattern in the numbers of employees who agreed with the statement:

- Less than 250 employees: 52 percent agree and 26 percent disagree
- 250 – 1,000 employees: 41 percent agree and 36 percent disagree
- 1,000 – 2,500 employees: 5 percent agree and 38 percent disagree
- 2,500 or more employees: 33 percent agree and 40 percent disagree

Clearly, as companies grow larger, employees are less satisfied that reward and recognition go to those who most deserve them. In fact, only four in 10 employees agree *Excellent performance gets rewarded,* while one-third of employees disagree. Interestingly, part-time employees are significantly more likely to agree excellence gets rewarded than full-time workers (48 percent versus 39 percent), and the impact of providing training and education to employees is witnessed in this area, as well.

Employees who receive training and development are significantly more satisfied with every aspect of reward and recognition than employees who had not received work-related training in the past year. Training and development are rewards for doing a good job, and employees recognize and appreciate it.

Weaker than the performance two years ago, less than four in 10 employees (37 percent) in 2006-20007 agree *My manager ensures that the best receive the greatest rewards and recognition,* while nearly one-third disagree (31 percent). Just as your organization treats its "best customers" better than ones that are not as critical to their success, the same should be done with your "best employees." Not surprisingly, 70 percent of executives agree with the statement; however, this drops to 40 percent of middle management and supervisors, and just 33 percent of individual contributors.

As seen in 2004-2005, there is only one question in 2006-07 in the reward and recognition workforce engagement component where union employees rate their employer at par with nonunion employees: *Compensation practices are administered consistently for all employees* (four in 10 of each of the two groups agreed with this statement). Otherwise, nonunion employees are significantly more satisfied in regard to rewards and recognition than are union employees.

Why are Rewards and Recognition Important?

One of the most significant costs in any organization is the payroll expenditure, which can range, in some companies, to upward of 70 percent of total organizational costs. When it comes to employee compensation, high costs are not necessarily a bad thing, so long as the organization is getting the appropriate results in areas such as productivity, revenue generation and profit to warrant the high cost. Thus, when one considers compensating employees, it neither implies "giving away the store," nor does it mean being the "cheapest ticket in town." Instead, effective reward and recognition approaches serve to assist the organization in finding, keeping and motivating productive, talented employees in pursuit of organizational goals.

Every organization wants the most talented employee it can find. Like so many things in life, the reality is that organizations get what they pay for. To be motivated to perform, employees do not necessarily have to be paid the most money in the marketplace. They do, however, have to be paid fairly for what they are expected to do. This is challenging, as perceptions often overshadow reality, and employees may seem to think they are under-rewarded compared to others in the marketplace. As a result, organizations must engage in explicit, honest discussions with employees about reward and recognition practices, and these practices must be tied to the overall strategic direction of the organization and performance-management systems designed to elicit certain behaviors and results from employees.

Broadly defined, rewards and recognition include compensation, benefits and other workplace conditions that serve to motivate employees. Organizational rewards are informed, in part, through sound compensation practices, pay approaches that influence performance, benefits that employees value and work environments that are satisfying and enjoyable for employees. There are many ways managers can recognize employee contributions to the workplace. This requires understanding what employees want and customizing recognition approaches accordingly, providing tangible and intangible rewards and ensuring fairness in recognizing employees.

How can Organizations Effectively Reward Employees?

Organizations Can Reward Employees Through:

- Sound compensation practices
- Pay approaches that influence performance
- Benefits that employees value
- Work environments that are satisfying and enjoyable.

Sound compensation practices

One of the most important aspects of reward and recognition involves an organization's commitment to and use of sound compensation practices. Total compensation includes cash, benefits, environmental considerations, work-life issues and other performance-management approaches, all with the objective of finding, keeping and motivating employees. To ensure that objective is met, compensation practices must be strategically oriented, evidence based and continually reviewed.

Strategically oriented compensation ties reward and recognition endeavors to the mission, vision, values and strategic directions of the organization. This means that compensation, benefits and other approaches are aligned with the broader purpose of the enterprise. This is important because employee behaviors need to be recognized and reinforced, as they contribute to the overall advancement of organizational capabilities. In some instances, however, reward systems are incongruent with the needs of the organization. Such misalignment leads to tensions between employees deciding to do what they are told versus what they know will be rewarded. Confronted with this dilemma, most employees tend to do what is rewarded, not espoused.

Evidence-based compensation ensures reward decisions are made, to the greatest extent possible, using objective criteria. While subjectivity and personal influences or biases are rarely fully removed from reward decisions, they should be minimized. Job analysis, the descriptive procedure to identify and document job content, is one way of using objective evidence in compensation practices. Job analysis typically yields information about compensable factors, which include skill, effort, responsibility and working conditions. Compensable factors are used to determine how much a position should be paid based on the nature and mix of factors present in a job.

Outcomes of job analysis and the determination of compensable factors for each job typically results in a job-worth hierarchy. As its name implies, a job-worth hierarchy seeks to establish the relative worth of each job in an organization, recognizing that some jobs are more heavily valued by the organization than others. For example, a hotel property's general manager is typically the job with the greatest degree of skill, effort and responsibility; thus, this position would likely be compensated the greatest. Entry-level hotel positions, such as groundspersons, housekeepers, bell-stand employees, etc., would likely be paid the least, compared to other jobs, based on the compensable factors present in each of these positions. Thus, each organization should establish its job-worthy hierarchy based on the nature of work (job analysis), how the organization values the job (job-worth hierarchy) and how the job ultimately contributes to the strategic directions of the organization. Other sources of evidence are market-based data, salary surveys and other indices of labor-market activity. All can be used, in conjunction with job analysis, to inform reward and recognition approaches.

Finally, sound compensation practices are continually reviewed. Inherent in this review is an understanding of the organization's overall compensation philosophy. This means a company has to determine what it is paying for talent, what it is getting in return for that pay and what type of talent it might attract if it increased or decreased pay for a particular type of position. Related to this is the organization's desire or strategy to pay at, above or below market rates of pay for positions. Not surprisingly, organizations seeking the best talent in a given field or occupation generally pay above-market pay rates. Continually reviewing compensation practices involves a regular review of market-based data, coupled with internal measures such as turnover statistics, employee-opinion survey results and public policies at the federal, state and local level that impact employee compensation.

Pay approaches that influence performance

To reward employees through cash compensation, there are a number of pay approaches, including seniority pay, merit pay, incentive pay, team-based pay, knowledge- or skill-based pay and outcomes-oriented pay. Each approach can contribute to performance, with varying degrees of effectiveness.

Seniority pay, as the name implies, increases cash compensation based on length of service in the organization, in the job, or both. Employees operating under seniority pay systems are rewarded for length of service as the main criterion. Under this approach, the organization rewards employee loyalty, not necessarily employee performance. A hallmark of union environments and the manufacturing-era economy, seniority pay has lost favor in recent years to other pay approaches that recognize the individual, meritorious contributions of employees.

Merit pay is one approach that identifies the performance-enhancing, value-added contribution an individual employee makes in carrying out his or her job duties and responsibilities. Employees who receive merit pay are likely rewarded based on how they worked, and this is typically more explicitly tied to performance management and appraisal than is seniority pay. Organizations using merit pay approaches distinguish between levels of performance and positively reward those individuals contributing to the performance the organization values most, regardless of length of service.

Related to merit pay, incentive pay provides employees with cash compensation based on the individual achievement of a broader work team, department or organizational goal. Incentive compensation is typically paid on an ad hoc basis, whereas merit pay is rolled into the base salary increase. Thus, incentive pay is context specific, situational and varying. It is possible for an employee to earn incentive pay in one time period, yet be ineligible for this pay in subsequent time periods based on performance

As more organizations structure jobs to work interdependently with others, team-based pay has increased. Under this pay approach, employees in a well-defined team receive all or a portion of their pay increases based on the overall performance of the team. This approach encourages collaboration and working together to accomplish team goals, yet can frustrate top performers who feel they may be pulling more weight on the team than "social loafer" employees. Thus, the ability for team members to rate each other's performance and to provide organizationally sanctioned "peer pressure" to underperforming colleagues, is necessary for team-based pay to be well received, especially by highly contributing employees.

Knowledge- and skill-based pay recognizes that, as individuals increase their overall capabilities and flexibility, the organization should reward their efforts. Common in fields where the acquisition and application of new knowledge or skill is valued, such as in information technology jobs, this pay approach explicitly and positively acknowledges the increase in intellectual capital in the organization. Knowledge- and skill-based pay works well when there are objective ways to measure new knowledge or skill use and when employees fully understand the benefits and consequences of this pay approach.

Finally, outcomes-oriented pay recognizes the ultimate impact that individuals or teams have on broader organizational goals. This pay approach recognizes results, not necessarily the processes used to achieve results. Profit-sharing, gain-sharing, and stock options and awards are often used to reward performance outcomes. Employees receiving outcomes-oriented pay must be made explicitly aware of the conditions under which the pay will be received. This approach is useful in motivating employees toward larger, more strategic organizational goals. The deferred nature of this pay approach may make sustained motivation toward goal accomplishment somewhat diminished.

The use of these approaches is dependent, in large part, on the organization's ability and willingness to pay. Potential consequences for not maintaining a fair and up-to-date reward system include employee dissatisfaction, lower productivity, increased absenteeism and, ultimately, higher turnover. While pay is an important component of reward and recognition, other, noncash elements are necessary, including a benefits program that employees value.

Benefits that employees value

It has sometimes been said that "you can't spend your benefits." This statement implies that the only motivating and rewarding aspect of work is pay and that an increase in pay will serve to provide additional satisfaction for employees. This is not necessarily true, as pay is a satisfier, not necessarily always a motivator. The addition of more pay may not necessarily lead to greater employee satisfaction, yet the removal of pay will likely contribute to greater employee dissatisfaction. Thus, as part of an overall reward system, employees value things beyond just pay. Benefits are one other way to provide overall reward and recognition to employees.

In most instances, U.S. organizations are not required to offer very many benefits. Instead, they do so to compete for talent and to provide the kinds of noncash rewards most sought and valued by employees. In general, there are three broad, legally required benefits that employers must provide: Social Security (old age, survivors and disability income insurance), worker's compensation (for job-related accidents and illnesses) and unemployment insurance (income replacement due to loss of job). All other benefits are offered voluntarily by employers as a means of attracting, retaining and motivating employees. The following list is representative of the types of benefits offered by most medium-to-large-sized organizations:

- Medical insurance
- Dental insurance
- Vision insurance
- Life insurance
- Personal accident insurance
- Retirement contributions
- Short- and long-term disability
- Legal assistance
- Pay for time not worked (e.g., vacations, holidays)
- Extended leave programs (e.g., sabbatical)
- Employee cafeteria/break room
- On-site conveniences (e.g., banking ATMs, postal services)
- Child-care/elder-care assistance
- Tuition assistance/reimbursement
- Company-sponsored events or social/sporting groups
- Matching gifts programs
- Employee discounts on goods and services
- Domestic partner benefits availability
- Flexible spending accounts.

While the above list is not an exhaustive review of all benefits an organization can make available to employees, it provides an indication that employees value, in general, protections against illness, financial safeguards, time off and other convenient services and solutions. Like cash compensation, benefits programs should be tied to the needs of employees, informed based on market data, and reviewed and updated on a regular basis.

Work environments that are satisfying and enjoyable

Pay and benefits are, of course, two important yet costly requirements for rewarding and recognizing employees. One far cheaper approach, one highly valued by employees, is a work environment that is satisfying and enjoyable. Because employees spend so many of their waking hours in the workplace, creating a welcoming environment is one vital way to increased employee motivation at work.

A good work environment is a plus because it aids in the retention of good employees, can boost morale and builds the reputation of the company as an attractive employer. When pay may not be as good as an organization (or its employees) may like, the company can meet other needs of employees by building a workplace that people want to join and remain in. This type of environment also helps make employees feel engaged and energized about their work.

Managers and supervisors play a large role in ensuring that the work environment is satisfying and enjoyable. That climate allows employees to feel a sense of personal achievement and feel that the job is challenging. Having access to the supervisor, receiving adequate recognition and feedback, experiencing professional development opportunities and having appropriate control over work are ways supervisors can create the kind of environment employees seek. Beyond pay, benefits and environment, there are additional ways that managers can recognize employee contributions in the workplace.

In What Ways Can Managers Recognize Employee Contributions?

Recognizing Employee Contributions Involves:

- Customizing recognition approaches to meet individual employee needs
- Providing both tangible and intangible rewards
- Ensuring fairness in reward, recognition and other approaches.

Customizing recognition approaches to meet individual employee needs

Employees want to be treated as individuals. As customers, employees are marketed to, sold to and served by companies that try to get to know their unique needs, wants and desires. This same "consumer" mentality applies at work, too: employees want managers to know what they seek, value and enjoy from work. This means that managers must really know their employees and understand what is meaningful to each individual. Thus, it means that recognizing employees cannot be approached as a one-size-fits-all intervention.

One of the best, yet often overlooked, aspects of customizing recognition approaches to individuals is to simply ask employees how they would like to be recognized. Many times, managers and compensation professionals work to develop intricate reward and recognition approaches—some of which are quite costly—when, in fact, employees might value something far simpler (and cheaper), yet this remains unknown because the employee was never consulted. In asking employees how they want to be recognized, it is useful to provide examples and parameters pertaining to feasibility of the recognition. While employees may often say "more money," savvy managers realize that money might be appropriate as an incentive to recognize a job well done, but it is not likely to be a sustainable motivator for the employee.

Providing tangible and intangible rewards

Recognizing employees with both tangible and intangible rewards can serve to improve their overall satisfaction at work. Tangible rewards include cash compensation, benefits, incentives, time off and other prizes. These are, of course, useful in recognizing outstanding performance. As part of an overall recognition strategy, tangible rewards can help to explicitly recognize the accomplishments of individuals, work teams and entire organizations.

Intangible rewards, those things that are harder to measure or quantify, are also highly valued by employees as part of recognition. Giving employees a piece of the action, in terms of greater responsibility, advancement potential or personal growth, is one intangible reward that can have longer-term impacts for employees. Another way to recognize good work is assigning employees to perform their favorite work or tasks. Freedom, autonomy and the ability to customize or personalize workspaces is another recognition approach. Additionally, infusing the work environment with fun and an innovative culture can unleash creativity and productivity while recognizing individual differences and approaches to work.

Finally, one of the most infuriating things any employee can experience is the phenomenon of having a manager take credit for the work of the employee. Good managers acknowledge and celebrate the ideas generated by their staff and are willing to share credit for good solutions, performance, productivity, etc. with their employees. By spreading the wealth of recognition through tangible and intangible rewards, including giving credit where credit is due, managers can go a long way toward increasing their employees' satisfaction and enjoyment in the workplace.

Ensuring fairness in reward, recognition and other approaches

Fairness in reward, recognition and other approaches means that managers treat different employees differently, especially as it relates to performance and results. This differs from equity, in which everyone is treated the same. One-size-fits-all pay plans tend to dilute good performers, inflate poor performers and encourage mediocre activity. Thus, managers who want to stretch their employees beyond the minimum expectations and requirements of the job should reward superstar employees differently than underperforming employees. Fairness, then, means that differentiated performance is rewarded and recognized, and managers can explain why and how employees are treated differently as a result.

Summary

The ultimate goal of reward and recognition approaches is to find, keep and motivate employees. This is accomplished, in part, through a variety of organizational interventions, including tangible and intangible rewards, cash compensation, benefits, recognition approaches, and employee involvement and motivation strategies. Rewards and recognition can go a long way toward engaging the workforce, if done correctly. Linking rewards and recognition to the strategic directions of the organization and insisting on evidence, as opposed to anecdote or opinion, in making reward and recognition decisions can go a long way toward objectivity. The case study that follows, *"All The Intangibles Went Up Like Smoke,"* examines reward and recognition in organizational settings. Instead of emphasizing cash compensation, however, the case deals with intangible and environmental considerations in overall reward and recognition approaches.

Case Study:
Rewards and Recognition and Workforce Engagement
'All the Intangibles Went Up Like Smoke'

With its long tradition of a "less is more" approach to government and its succession of fiscally conservative governors, the state of New Essex has long been viewed nationally as having a "government that worked." For more than two decades, New Essex had the lowest ratio of state employees to total population, as well as the lowest per-capita expenditure of any U.S. state for state government operations. As the governor said several years before at the annual Recognition of Merit luncheon for state employees who had worked for New Essex for at least 20 years, "Providing the quality of services that happen here every day is not a quirk and not part of the job description. It's a way of life. As a citizen, all I can say to each of you is 'thank you.' But, as your governor, I also want to say 'keep it up!'" In short, the effective operation of state government was a source of pride to everyone in the state.

Therefore, it came as a surprise when in Fall 2003 the Tipton Dispatch and Post, *the state's largest newspaper, published a series of articles detailing complaints about inefficiencies, errors and long delays in the Department of Automotive Affairs (DAA). At the end of the four-part series, the newspaper published an editorial entitled "Gridlock at the DAA: Something Must Be Done."*

A Reporter Searches for a Story

Shep Henderson, the journalist who wrote the articles about the DAA, had not intended to write an "expose" of the agency. He began spending time at the DAA to write a feature story about the impending retirement of the agency's director, Annette Foley, and her 30-year career in state government, 11 as the head of the DAA. When he interviewed her, he found her to be taciturn and not really willing to talk about her job, the agency or her future plans. "Let's just say it was the right time for me to leave. Things change. You come to expect that certain things will always be the same, and one day you wake up and see that the world is very different." Curious, Henderson talked to other employees.

He soon found that many of those he talked to repeated variations of what Foley said. There were changes at the agency that affected people's commitment to their jobs. This struck him as ironic because within the last three years, the DAA had moved from a rabbit-wren of dilapidated offices to a newly renovated single facility, and there had been major upgrades to equipment, including a state-of-the-art computer system. Henderson had a lengthy conversation with the DAA's director of human resources, Everett Hyde, in which Hyde acknowledged a morale problem. Like everyone else Henderson interviewed, Hyde was vague about what changed within the division. Henderson sensed that there was a story to pursue, but he felt that no one at the DAA was willing to tell him what happened.

Through a colleague at the newspaper, he was introduced to Katherine Burkett, the associate director of the state's Division of Highways and Bridges. Until a year ago, she was associate director of the DAA, an agency considerably larger than the Highways and Bridges operation. She made what could be generously described as a lateral move, and Henderson was certain that she could tell him about what had happened at the DAA. After several meetings, she opened up, and her thoughts and opinions emerged.

Burkett told Henderson that she wanted to "put things in perspective" for him. She said, "You need to understand that working as a state employee places you in a 'sealed environment.' You know what your annual salary increases will be, and you know how many years you must serve at one level before being promoted to the next level. You know how many weeks of vacation you will get and in what year vacation time will increase. You don't get rich working for the state and, believe me, there are no year-end bonuses.

"And, don't forget, in a state like New Essex it is even more constraining. State government is the second-largest employer in New Essex. People here don't have many options for jobs, and so when you get a good one, you stay put. So, most people get their satisfaction from day-to-day things at work, getting the job done, knowing what's expected, enjoying the established routine."

Henderson was impressed by what Burkett told him and by how well she seemed to understand the state bureaucracy and its workings. He asked her why she left the DAA. "It's simple. I was eligible for a director's job, but Annette Foley wasn't ready to retire, so I was stuck in that sealed environment if I stayed there. I left. Other people who felt they were stuck too reacted in different ways."

Henderson responded, "I don't understand what changed at DAA. It sounds like everyone knew the rules, the limitations, of working for the state. So, what happened? Ev Hyde told me there was a morale problem at the DAA, and I know from public records that there has been more attrition than in other state divisions. I think there's a story there. Was there a scandal? Is there some corruption going on?"

Burkett chuckled and then started to laugh. She laughed for a long time and then said, "So it's true! All reporters think that when something happens, there must be a scandal lurking somewhere! No, it's nothing like that. Look, everyone expects a paycheck and everyone wants some intangible rewards, satisfaction and recognition. That's what happened. All the intangibles went up like smoke. It may not interest your readers as much as a juicy embezzlement scandal, but that's the story."

The Reporter's Investigation

Within a few weeks, Henderson pieced together a montage of the circumstances and events that he thought changed the DAA. In his notes, he outlined three factors: changes in the workspace, new automated procedures for assigning work and changes in the perception of autonomy.

Changes in the Workplace

For nearly 60 years, DAA offices were on the third floor of the Capitol Office Building, but as the size and complexity of the state's operations increased, offices were reassigned, and in 1964, the DAA moved across the street to a small building that once housed a bank on the first floor and professional offices above. A decade later, the state purchased the adjacent building and connected the two buildings with an intricate series of half stairwells, rooms opening into other rooms and one office with four closets, two bathrooms and no windows. As the workload of the division increased, space needs grew as well. In 1996, about 40 people—15 percent of the DAA personnel—moved across the street to a building where space become available because other agencies were assigned other offices.

Finally, in late 2001, the DAA moved into a vacant factory that the state purchased. The facility was on one floor and was remodeled with flexible partitions. The floor plan was "logical," and it was easy for employees and visitors to navigate their way around the facility. With the entire DAA operation and staff in one location, a logical floor plan and standard-sized offices, the DAA for the first time had a professional and efficient "feel." State planners believed that they achieved great success.

Changes of that magnitude, however, came at a price. The former facilities were haphazard, and employees were encouraged to add personal touches. For example, at the end of a long corridor, a sign was painted on the wall:

> If you can see this sign you are walking in the wrong direction.
> This hallway doesn't go anywhere.
> Have a nice walk back to wherever you came from.

Another employee who worked in a windowless office painted a window on her wall and then put curtains up around it. Later, she added a window shade and a planter. Even employees who did not add such touches seemed to enjoy knowing that they could.

For years, there was a custom of taking new employees on a "tour" and then watching them as they wandered around, lost, during the first weeks on the job. All of this ended when the DAA moved to its new facility. Paradoxically, moving the DAA had a negative effect on many employees who felt that they "lost" something important: the benefit of being able to create their own space and to deal with space constraints creatively and with a sense of humor.

Changes in the Workflow Assignment System

Like all organizational systems, the state of New Essex moved increasingly since the 1980s toward reliance on technology to monitor its management, storage and retrieval systems. By 2002, shortly after the DAA's move to its new facility, a new state-of-the-art system became fully operational. This enabled DAA staff to monitor two of its most important and unwieldy functions: tracking the disposition of all licensed vehicles through their registered Vehicle Identification Number and ensuring that driver's licenses were renewed at the appropriate time.

There were, of course, other functions that required monitoring and tracking. For example, separate state inspections of vehicles for safety and environmental protection were required based on when the vehicle was initially registered. In addition, a mandatory road-use tax was put into effect in 1998 for commercial vehicles, and this required detailed follow-up since more than a third of the commercial vehicles operated in the state during any given year were, in fact, registered elsewhere.

For many years, the practice at the DAA had been for the 11 associate directors to meet with the director for a "brown bag extravaganza" at noon on Mondays. Associate directors would report on the anticipated workflow for the week, especially at times in which heavy volume was expected. Some times were easily understood and predictable, such as the end of each quarter (March, June, September and December), when automotive dealers were required to submit VIN information on all vehicles sold. The associate directors would then informally agree on having some staff in one department assist in other departments. These informal arrangements worked well because the DAA had many long-term employees who knew one another, who understood the operations of other departments and who enjoyed this variety in their jobs. "It was," as retiring director Foley said, "an arrangement that worked and that everyone responded to favorably."

With the new system "online," however, the informal arrangement was replaced by a sophisticated program called the "Induced Workload Planning Matrix" (IWPM). IWPM estimated workflow each week for the next week and then calculated how many people would need to be temporarily reassigned—and from which departments—to meet the DAA's needs. The program also calculated how many times personnel were assigned to other departments in the past year so that the assignments were equitable. The IWPM system was faster and more accurate than the "brown bag extravaganza" meetings had been. These improvements in efficiency, however, led to discontent among many DAA employees because they felt that discretion and choice had been removed. During an interview with Henderson, one of the associate directors, a 15-year veteran of the DAA, emphatically said: "The computer doesn't know whose husband is recovering from a heart attack, who is preoccupied with problems at home or who is playing a critical, but informal, role in a project under way and whose presence would be greatly missed, even for just a week."

Within a relatively short period, the temporary personnel reassignment went from being an informal and favorably received practice to one which was looked on with disdain and resentment.

Changes in the Perception of Autonomy

In his interviews, Henderson learned the DAA's biggest problem was the most elusive to define and describe. For as long as anyone could remember, each of the many state agencies and divisions operated with a good deal of autonomy and independence in establishing "operating procedures" for work to be done.

The roots of autonomy were core values to New Essex that had defined the three branches of state government as "self regulating and self governing entities" in the state's constitution. For more than two centuries, the branches of government established their own procedures and regulations. This had little effect on policy or on fundamental rights and principles but, for example, different agencies in the executive branch could establish their own hours of operation, subject to the governor's approval.

In early 2003, the state's attorney general issued a directive stating that the principle and tradition of self-regulation of the branches of government did not extend to compliance with federal laws or to laws which "materially affected the health and well being of citizens." Initially, few people understood the potential consequences of the change, but gradually changes were mandated that rankled many employees at the DAA. For example, although smoking was banned in state buildings for many years, several agencies and divisions created "smoking zones," usually in corridors near entrances and exits to the building. It made life more tolerable for smokers and did not seem to bother the nonsmokers. When the DAA was notified that the "smoking zones" had to be shut down, smokers and nonsmokers resented this intrusion on their autonomy.

A year later, the director and associate directors were notified that no job vacancies could be posted in the future unless an affirmative action/minority hiring plan had been approved by the Civil Rights Division of the attorney general's office. The combined African-American and Hispanic population of New Essex was 8 percent, but the number employed by the DAA was 15 percent, almost twice the state average. The ides of having to get state approval to do something that was already being done—and done well—was infuriating.

One of the associate directors told Henderson, "I know that I work for a state agency and that we are part of a large bureaucracy, but it felt so good to have a sense of autonomy. Look, we work hard and one of the rewards, especially for those of us who are 'lifers' in DAA, is feeling that we have some control over how we do things: others set the goals, but we have a say in how we achieve them."

Another associate director said, "All these small changes added up to a big change that affected everyone at DAA, starting from the top down. As we lost those intangible rewards we cared about so much, absenteeism increased, the paperwork that people took pride in finishing up before the end of the day or the week began to pile up and people just cared less."

Finally, The Story Comes Into Focus

Henderson thought he finally put the pieces together. It was not a scandal, and it was not a single bad decision that led to the metamorphosis of the DAA from an effectively running organization with high morale to one that was dispirited and inefficient. It was a chronic misunderstanding of what employees regarded as rewards for their efforts. Each incremental change in the "larger" system brought the DAA closer to disarray.

Henderson sat at his desk and turned on his computer. He had more than three dozen e-mails, and when he checked his voice mail, he had nearly as many phone messages. The next few days would be hectic and critical as he tried to explain to others what he had learned. He noticed a large envelope on his desk with the seal of the governor in the upper left-hand corner. He opened it and read the brief handwritten note from the governor.

Dear Mr. Henderson,

I would appreciate it if you would call my office as soon as possible so we can meet to discuss your articles about the DAA and your suggestions about how I should respond.

"Well," he thought to himself, "I wrote it and now I have to explain it."

Questions for Consideration and Discussion
'All the Intangibles Went Up Like Smoke'

1. What are some of the intangible rewards that employees at the DAA miss? To what extent are intangible rewards an important part of overall reward and recognition?

2. "Everyone expects a paycheck and everyone wants some intangible rewards, satisfaction and recognition." Do you agree or disagree with this statement? Why or why not?

3. What are some of the most significant intangible rewards that you have received from work? Why did you value these rewards? Under what conditions are intangible rewards more important than tangible ones?

4. Suppose you were hired as a consultant to advise the DAA on ways to improve reward and recognition practices. Given the resource constraints of state government, what might you suggest? How can managers motivate employees with intangible rewards?

5. How would you respond to an employee who simply says, "I don't care about anything else, just give me more money!" To what extent is this a worthwhile approach to employee motivation and satisfaction? What are the potential pitfalls of simply giving employees more money?

Chapter 10:
Work-Life Balance

Introduction: What do We Mean By 'Work-Life Balance'?

Work-life balance involves the ability of HR professionals to assist the organization by creating approaches for employees to balance personal, work and community responsibilities; developing flexible approaches to work, as feasible; and managing stress, promoting wellness and avoiding employee burnout. The work-life component of workforce engagement reflects the extent to which employees perceive the organization as an environment that recognizes multiple commitments in an employee's life and structures the work environment to facilitate the meeting of individual and organizational needs.

Highlights from the 2004-2005 National Benchmark Study on Workforce Engagement

Many managers, supervisors and HR professionals know that losing some employees could have been avoided, in part, if the organization could have figured out a way to provide them with more balance in their personal and work lives. These individuals know, intuitively, what the *pan* study uncovered in its analysis: Work-life balance is a top-five driver of workforce engagement for individual contributors in an organization ... and companies do not do a good job of providing for it.

Less than half of all employees in the *pan* study agreed that their company is sensitive to the needs of employees, while 20 percent disagreed. Of concern is the notion that employees' perception of this sensitivity decreases as the age of the employee increases. In the world of work-life balance, as employees get older, get married, have children and look at the possibility of taking care of their parents, they become more critical of their employer. While two-thirds of 18-to 24-year-olds agree that their organization is sensitive to employee needs, only 39 percent of those employees older than 45 feel the same.

One of the interesting findings in the *pan* study related to work-life balance is the difference between those employees who have at least one child living at home and those employees who are caring for a loved one *other than a child*. In each of the individual attributes within the work-life balance component, employees taking care of a child are more positive in their assessment of their organizations' performance than are those taking care of a parent, sibling or other family member. This may be due to companies having a longer history of dealing with child-care issues, where the problems faced by the baby boomer and the "sandwich generation" (those employees who are taking care of their children and their parents) increase. Adult-care benefits are one of the fasting-growing benefits under the work-life umbrella.

The adage *"Employees quit a boss, not a company"* is alive and well in the area of work-life balance. It is usually the employee's direct manager or supervisor that grants (or turns down) an employee's attempt to find flexibility with the job. In the **pan** study, four in 10 employees could not agree that their manager recognizes the importance of their personal and family life. Similar patterns as seen before in the **pan** study emerge when reviewing these specific data points:

- As employees get older, their perceptions become less positive and more negative.
- Companies with less than 1,000 employees are perceived more positively than those organizations with more than 1,000 employees.
- There is no difference in the results based on the gender of employees.
- Employees who travel internationally for work are significantly more positive than employees who do not, however, employees who always commute more than 50 miles to work are less positive than those that often, seldom or never commute that distance.
- Part-time workers are slightly more positive than full timers.
- Employees who have children living at home are significantly more positive (and significantly less negative) in their assessment than employees who are not caring for children. However, there are no significant differences, positively or negatively, when reviewing employees who are caring for a loved one other than a child.
- Executives are significantly more positive in their perceptions than middle managers, supervisors or individual contributors.
- Perhaps due to increased sensitivity of this issue, employees in HR positions are only slightly more positive than the lowest-rated area of the company, operations, where just half of all employees agree and one-quarter disagree that their manager understands the importance of their personal and family life.

One of the struggles related to work-life balance is the fear that employees will hinder their potential career progression if they attempt to balance their work life and their responsibilities at home. Whether true or not, one in seven employees in the *pan* study believes that his or her career progression has been hindered due to work-life balance issues; another one-quarter neither agreed nor disagreed.

A deeper look at this question provides insight into the pressures employees feel. Employees who have children living in their home are significantly more positive about achieving this "noncareer threatening" work-life balance than employees who do not have children in the house. However, employees who are caring for a loved one other than a child are significantly less positive than employees who are not caring for a loved one. Based on those results, employees will choose to "honor thy mother and father" over their career progression if forced to choose.

As the likelihood that employees have to commute more than 50 miles for work increases, the ability of finding this balance without hindering career progression decreases. Not surprisingly, employees who travel internationally are 50 percent more pessimistic in their ability to find this balance than employees that do not travel internationally. Although more than three-quarters of 18-to 24-year-olds felt able to achieve this balance, the number drops to two-thirds of 25-to 34-year-olds and less than six in 10 of those employees older than 35. Again, as responsibilities at home increase, their ability to find an adequate balance decreases.

Perhaps a surprise to many readers of the *pan* study, women are significantly more positive in their assessment of finding this balance without hindering career progression than men (65-percent positive versus 58-percent positive). Perhaps due to societal expectations, women may find it easier to "demand" or "request" this balance, whereas men as the traditional "bread-winner" of the family may find it more difficult to balance or demand this balance from a manager. Employees in manufacturing, retail trade and the leisure/hospitality industries were most negative, with more than one in five not able to attain that balance.

Finally, employees want their employer to provide family-friendly benefits, whether it is adequate health care, adoption assistance, on-site or reduced cost child care or even services that assist employees with referrals for elder care. Although benefits can unintentionally trap an employee into staying with an organization, providing these kinds of benefits can lessen the worry of many employees. Of concern to the customer contact workforce, employees in sales/client development were the most negative when reviewing the *pan* data by department/area of the company, perhaps due to the amount of time spent away from home.

Finally, employees who have children living at home were significantly more positive about having family-friendly benefits than were childless households and were more positive than employees who were taking care of a loved one other than a child. Individual contributors were significantly less positive and significantly more negative in their perceptions than supervisors, middle managers and executives. There was no difference in the perceptions of family-friendly benefits when reviewing union versus nonunion affiliation and very little difference when reviewing the age of the employee or the size of the company.

Highlights from the 2006-2007 National Benchmark Study on Workforce Engagement

A secondary driver of workforce engagement in 2004-2005, work-life balance is not considered a key driver of workforce engagement in 2006-2007. As explained earlier, this does not mean that providing work-life balance is not important to employees—all 13 workforce components are "important," which is why they are in the causal model of engagement.

Only four in 10 of all employees in 2006-2007 believe their organization *is sensitive to the needs of employees*, while three in 10 disagree, slightly worse than the results of the 2004-2005 benchmark study. Work-life balance is another area in which experience with the company weakens an employee's perception over time:

- 51 percent of new employees agree the organization is sensitive to employee needs.
- 47 percent of one- to two-year employees agree.
- 40 percent of three- to five-year employees agree.
- 32 percent of six- to nine-year employees agree.
- 38 percent of 10-year-plus employees agree.

This "U-Curve" pattern is consistent throughout the national benchmark results, with the highest levels of agreement coming from the newest employees.

Less than six in 10 employees in 2006-2007 agree *their managers recognize the importance of their personal and family life*, a significant decrease from 2004-2005 levels. In addition, while one in six employees disagreed with the statement in 2004-2005, the number of employees who do not believe their managers recognize the importance of their personal life jumped to one in four (24 percent):

- One-third of employees with their organization for more than 20 years feel negatively (34 percent).
- More than four in 10 unengaged employees disagree with the statement (44 percent).
- One-third of employees with just a high school education disagree (35 percent).
- Full-time workers are significantly more negative than part-time workers (26 percent negative versus 15 percent).
- One in 12 executives disagrees with the statement, while one in four middle managers, supervisors and individual contributors feels the same.

Finally, roughly half of all employees agree their company provides *family-friendly benefits and their manager pays attention to how people feel at work,* while one in five disagrees. Again, company performance as measured by the employee has slipped from 2004-2005 levels, a continuing and dangerous trend.

Why is Work-Life Balance Important?

Get up. Make breakfast. Pack lunches. Get the kids ready for school. Pick up refreshments for a morning meeting. Network with clients. Make a doctor's appointment. Finish a work report. Prepare for a business trip. Meet with the boss. Volunteer at the community center. Write a paper for school. Pick up the dry cleaning. Visit a sick relative. Get the car repaired. Walk the dog. Pay the bills. Go to bed. Repeat again the next day.

While perhaps a bit exaggerated, the activities described above are representative of the busy, complicated lives led by many employees. Their ability to juggle work, personal, family and community responsibilities has a direct impact on how well they can perform their work. To maximize employee attendance, productivity and satisfaction, there are a number of strategies organizations can employ to assist with work-life endeavors.

Work-life balance involves organizational approaches to identifying, addressing and monitoring concerns employees have about managing their work and personal lives. Beyond a mere fad, work-life balance plays a critical role in creating a work environment that is respectful of individual employee needs, while also maximizing their contributions to organizational success. Measures such as attendance, productivity, satisfaction, retention and medical-claims experience are all bottom-line-oriented reasons for why and how work-life balance has received so much attention in recent years.

For work-life balance to be realized in organizational settings, it requires that all employees know why work-life balance is important. It is also necessary to develop specific approaches to work-life balance and to implement and manage, on an ongoing basis, the work-life initiatives within an organization.

Work-Life Balance is Important Because:

- A diverse workforce requires diverse workplace solutions.
- Changes to work results in new challenges and opportunities.
- Reducing absences, minimizing stress and avoiding burnout saves money.
- Employees appreciate organizations that are concerned about their holistic well-being.

A diverse workforce requires diverse workplace solutions

The workforce is incredibly diverse, and employers are confronted with managing this diversity. Specific organizational policies and practices, especially as they relate to work-life balance, can aid in meeting the needs of a diverse workforce. In any given organization, the following types of employees are present:

- Women and men
- Minority and immigrant workers
- Disabled workers
- Older and younger workers
- Contingent and part-time workers
- Single, married, divorced and widowed individuals
- Dual-career couples
- Gay, lesbian, bisexual, transgendered individuals
- Varying levels of educational attainment and socioeconomic differences
- Religious, lifestyle, personality and work-style differences
- Single parents
- Individuals caring for children, elderly parents or other relatives at home
- Individuals working multiple jobs
- Individuals pursuing educational opportunities while working
- Individuals with varying ease of transportation access to the workplace.

While not all-inclusive, the previous list highlights how diversity, in its many forms, provides challenges and opportunities in meeting the needs of diverse employees. Thus, new, innovative solutions must be continually created, implemented and evaluated to find, keep and motivate employees who require different things from the work experience.

Changes to work results in new challenges and opportunities

There are numerous changes that have impacted the nature of work in the past 25 years, all of which have presented new challenges and opportunities to employers and employees in the management of work-life balance. Technological changes have sped up work in many instances and have permitted employees to be "on call" or available to work anytime, anyplace and on many devices, literally on a 24/7 basis. As a result of technology, among other factors, many companies have adopted flattened organizational structures. This has provided more autonomy and accountability for individual work efforts and has, in many instances, reduced the managerial scope of control. This means that some managers and supervisors may have 10, 20 or more direct reports, limiting the personal attention that can be paid to each employee.

Another increasing trend is an emphasis on project-based, client-centered and team-interdependent work. This type of work results in pressures to get the job done to satisfy customer demand, regardless of the impact on one's personal life. All successful, high-performance organizations have demanding expectations for employees. This translates into a continuous tension for an employee who must balance the strong demands from employers against the desire for a well-balanced lifestyle. Additionally, many firms are increasingly reluctant to hire additional "permanent" staff. That has resulted in many organizations requiring workers to do more with less. This is further exacerbated by increased competition and minimal profit margins that have increased pressure for production and cost containment in many industries.

Reducing absences, minimizing stress and avoiding burnout saves money

Creating work-life balance approaches also helps manage and/or reduce absences. Employees want to work in an environment that recognizes the myriad of life circumstances that individuals face and provides them with appropriate latitude in dealing with these circumstances. Concern for employee well-being contributes to enhanced productivity. The flexibility, resources and monitoring of employee behaviors, among other things, afforded under work-life initiatives helps discourage abuses to leave and attendance policies.

Employers should also provide mechanisms to minimize stress in the workplace. This can be accomplished, in part, by outlining expectations and giving clear directions with a reasonable timeline for completion. Allocating the right tools, technologies and resources to perform the work is essential. Providing an environment free of fear and intimidation and encouraging open, candid communication can promote a professional, respectful workplace. Finally, ongoing monitoring of the work environment for hazards and minimizing or eradicating those hazards contribute to employee well-being.

Burnout is a condition in which an employee literally becomes physically, emotionally or intellectually exhausted to the point in which he or she chooses not to participate in the job or organization. Organizations can help employees avoid burnout by encouraging them to regularly take advantage of accrued leave opportunities and by reasonably maintaining consistency of work schedule, pace and assignments. Other ways burnout can be minimized or avoided include providing access to EAPs or other mental health professionals, as warranted. Also, encouraging employees to seek additional help from supervisors, peers and others in the organization when they become overloaded is one simple way to help employees manage job-related stress and avoid burnout.

Employees appreciate organizations that are concerned about their holistic well-being

The proper creation, implementation and ongoing evaluation and improvement of work-life approaches can signal to employees the organization's commitment to their holistic well-being. To achieve this, however, work-life balance has to be viewed as an organizational priority, and matters pertaining to work-life balance, including the availability of resources, need to be explicitly communicated to the workforce. Managers and supervisors must also realize that employees have a life beyond the workplace. When employees feels stressed and overwhelmed due to issues in their personal life, managers and supervisors should adjust work schedules, make referrals to counselors, listen to employees, etc. Of course, managers and supervisors must learn to recognize the differences between an isolated incident and a pattern of behavior.

What are Some Approaches to Work-Life Balance?

Some Approaches to Work-Life Balance Include:

- Flexible work arrangements
- Health and wellness programs
- Specific interventions to address employee needs
- Personal development and enrichment activities
- Convenient services and solutions for employees.

Flexible work arrangements

To meet the needs of individuals and organizations, companies can provide flexibility in areas such as scheduling and the nature of work. From a scheduling standpoint, there are several options to facilitate work-life balance. First, flex time is an approach that permits variable start and finish times for employees, usually with a requirement of a minimum number of core hours worked per day and a minimum number of required hours per week. For example, employees might have the option of arriving between 6 a.m. and 9 a.m. and departing between 3 p.m. and 6 p.m., with the core hours of work between 9 a.m. and 3 p.m. Closely related to flex time is the compressed workweek, in which workers can work four 10-hour days, three 12-hour days or another compressed schedule. Finally, annualized hours allow for employees to accumulate a minimum number of total hours per year, largely on their own schedule. This works well in large organizations, or where the needs of employees span many hours of the day and week.

The nature of work can also impact work-life balance, and there are some specific work arrangements that organizations can employ. First, providing part-time employment can assist individuals and the organization. Individuals benefit from participation in the workforce, while working less than full-time hours. Organizations benefit from this approach as a means of labor-cost containment while providing more consistency with part-time employees than through contract, contingent or staffing-agency employees. Second, telecommuting permits employees to work from home or another remote location. This decreases congestion and other factors that impact commuting, while providing employees the flexibility to work from a distance either continuously, regularly or as necessary. Finally, job sharing entails employing two part-time people to split the work of one full-time job. The two employees typically work separate schedules, yet may have overlapping schedules on occasion to coordinate or discuss work. Job sharing works well when position duties and responsibilities can be reasonably divided into parts and when the organization, managers and peer-group members support and assist the job incumbents in making job sharing achievable.

Health and wellness programs

Another organizational approach to work-life balance includes emphasizing health, wellness and fitness programs for employees. Organizations are concerned about their workers' health for productivity and cost reasons. When employees are healthy, they tend to miss work less often, thus impacting productivity. From a cost-containment standpoint, healthy employees tend to have fewer medical insurance claims, something that ultimately impacts the amount of premiums the employer and employees pay. Some health-related programs sponsored by organizations include healthy living, smoking cessation, weight management, and exercise and nutrition programs.

Wellness of employees refers to their overall physical health and emotional stability. Organizations want to keep employees well for the same reasons as they want a healthy workforce. Wellness may be emphasized through preventive care measures; sponsored health screenings (e.g., blood sugar, cholesterol) and health fairs; literature and other resources for well-being; and access to an EAP. EAPs are typically administered by third-party providers that offer a variety of special, individualized interventions for employees. This could include marital counseling, coaching, addiction issues and recovery support and other psychological services. Finally, emphasizing an active, fitness-oriented lifestyle for employees can improve their overall health and wellness. Organizations can adopt varying degrees of fitness interventions, ranging from simple encouragement of fitness to subsidized or discounted access to area gyms and health clubs to the construction of on-site physical-fitness facilities.

Specific interventions to address employee needs

A diverse workforce requires specific interventions to meet the needs of employees. Depending on the employee population served by the organization, a number of interventions can be developed. Child-care assistance permits employees with young children to find affordable, quality care for children, and this is often subsidized (in full or in part) by the organization. Elder-care assistance provides many of the same benefits and services as child-care assistance, only with an emphasis on the unique care-giving and other needs of an employee's elderly parent or relative. Important is the fact that, increasingly, some employees find themselves as part of the "sandwich" generation, caught in the midst of providing child-care and elder-care simultaneously.

Additional specific interventions to address employee needs include providing financial assistance to employees in need. Usually administered in the form of low- or no-interest loans, grants or even donations, financial assistance can be made available to an employee following a qualifying event (e.g., house fire, mounting medical bills, other hardships). Another approach is offering employees the ability to buy, sell, bank or donate time off. This permits individuals to customize their time-off arrangements within guidelines and limitations and, in some cases, allows workers to sell or give away time off to other employees who need or value this benefit. Finally, involvement in a variety of community activities (e.g., walks/races to benefit a certain cause, donating to local food pantries) are ways to signal to employees and other stakeholders the organization's philanthropic side, while also encouraging employees to "give back" to the community, in some cases on company time.

Personal development and enrichment activities

The availability of personal development and enrichment activities can also go a long way toward encouraging work-life balance. Holding courses, seminars and workshops of interest to employees can help them in acquiring the knowledge and skills necessary for improved life management. The following are types of educational programs that organizations may sponsor or offer for the aid and benefit of their employees:

- Financial management
- Retirement planning
- Child-care and elder-care

- Home buying and improvement
- Personal safety and self defense
- Returning to school
- Improving communications (e.g., Toastmasters International).

In addition to personal-development courses, organizations can offer ways for employees to network and socialize such as employee picnics, recognition and appreciation events, games and other employee-involvement activities. Finally, the ability to personalize and customize workspaces, as appropriate, can aid in employees' overall enjoyment and satisfaction from their physical work environment.

Convenient services and solutions for employees

In many medium to large organizations, approaches to work-life balance include infrastructure enhancement designed to bring convenient services and solutions to employees. The following are examples of such services and solutions:

- Employee cafeterias and break rooms
- Concierge services (large companies)
- Sundry stores/newspaper stands
- Banking ATMs available on site
- Physical fitness facilities available on site
- Direct-deposit programs
- Access to resources for professional and personal use (e.g., laptops, Internet access)
- Special discounts for employees.

At first glance, it might appear odd for an organization to invest in these seemingly nonwork-related expenditures. It may make sense, however, for medium to large organizations to spend money in these areas. The sheer volume of employees can make such investments pay off through enhanced employee retention and satisfaction. Additionally, these (and other) services and solutions assist individuals in managing their work-life balance by bringing to the workplace those things that can ease or reduce the burdens and distractions of employees, thus increasing their punctuality, attendance and productivity.

How are Work-Life Programs Implemented and Managed in Organizations?

Organizations Can Implement and Manage Work-life Programs By:

- Making the business case for work-life initiatives

- Assessing current approaches, surveying employees and benchmarking with other organizations

- Clarifying and prioritizing work-life approaches

- Implementing, evaluating and improving work-life activities.

Making the business case for work-life initiatives

To secure broad organizational buy-in and support, from senior leaders to individual-contributor employees, it is necessary to make the business case for work-life initiatives. A sound business case will begin by determining the demographic profile of employees: who is employed in the organization, for how long and to what extent, if any, are there differences to the frequency and nature of turnover for particular employee groups? Answering these and other questions helps identify the causes of employee turnover, which can also be translated into hard and soft costs of replacing workers. A sound business case also includes data on the costs and consequences associated with health-, wellness- and stress-related medical claims. Additionally, feedback from employee opinion surveys (or other communication vehicles) provides information about what employees want and desire from work. All of this information can be collected, analyzed and reported in the business case, along with the corresponding activities, costs and expected benefits of work-life initiatives proposed.

Assessing current approaches, surveying employees and benchmarking with other organizations

To determine what work-life initiatives are needed in an organization, it is necessary to assess current approaches, survey employees and benchmark with other organizations. This involves identifying, describing and documenting current approaches, as well as the cost and real or perceived benefit of each approach. Next, surveying employees to find out what they need and want from work-life initiatives is necessary. It is important to ensure that a true representative sample of employees is queried. Finally, identifying and benchmarking with other organizations to find out about effective work-life practices can help the organization see how it compares. This information can be useful in determining industry norms and what best-in-class organizations—within the industry or elsewhere—are doing concerning work-life initiatives.

Clarifying and prioritizing work-life approaches

While all approaches to work-life balance are worthwhile, it is impractical and unnecessary to initiate and implement all approaches. Thus, it is necessary to analyze the results of the data-gathering process and to determine which activities are most important to the workforce. Prioritizing work-life interventions based on time and cost matrix is helpful (time: immediate, short-term and long-term interventions; cost: no-cost, low-cost and moderate-to high-cost interventions). The ability to link interventions to the work-life business case and overall organizational strategic directions can aid in marshalling support and securing resources for these activities.

Implementing, evaluating and improving work-life activities

Implementing work-life initiatives can begin after the business case for work-life has been made, data collected, activities prioritized and resources secured. When this occurs, it is important to communicate changes to the workforce as programs are implemented. The continual and explicit availability of work-life information can assist in equipping managers and employees with a greater awareness and understanding of the programs, resources and guidelines available to them.

As work-life programs are implemented, it is necessary to monitor progress and make adjustments accordingly. Ultimately, an evaluation of the impact that work-life initiatives have had on the organization must occur. Performance indicators or measures used to determine work-life program effectiveness include the following:

- Employee satisfaction
- Turnover rates
- Medical claims experience
- EAP usage statistics (at the aggregate, not individual-employee, level)
- Absenteeism/tardiness occurrences
- Productivity targets
- Employee complaints and feedback.

Finally, improving approaches to work-life balance should be an ongoing goal. It creates an environment that signals to employees and candidates that the organization is concerned with their overall well-being. This helps the firm find, keep and motivate its increasingly diverse workforce, while meeting individual and organizational needs.

Summary

Work-life balance is important for organizational success because of the increasing diversity of the workforce and the changes brought about by the nature of work. Work-life initiatives have an impact on employee productivity, medical claims, turnover and satisfaction. There are a variety of approaches to work-life balance, including flexible work arrangements, health and wellness, specific interventions to meet employee needs and, in some cases, the availability of convenient services and solutions. To be effective, work-life programs should have a business case, use appropriate methods to gather and analyze data, effectively clarify and prioritize approaches and, ultimately, implement, monitor and evaluate the effectiveness of work-life initiatives. The case study that follows, *"Different Person, Same Story,"* examines how organizational responsiveness—or lack thereof—can positively or negatively impact work-life balance for employees.

Case Study:
Work-Life Balance and Workforce Engagement
'Different Person, Same Story'

Matt Zacharias looked up from his desk as Jennifer Fowler-Ely entered his office. Zacharias, the president of Mather and Co., the fifth-largest textbook manufacturer in the United States, had an easygoing and relaxed style, and his senior staff had access to him. He and Fowler-Ely, the vice president for Field Sales, worked together for eight years, and they respected and admired one another. "Jenn," he said, "I know that look. Who is it this time?" She smiled. "Am I that transparent? You better make sure I never negotiate with any of our authors. This time, it's Hank Washington. He feels that he isn't making progress on his MBA, and he's invested too much money and time to stop now."

She sat down and said, "Matt, we have been over this so many times. We have to figure out how to stabilize the field sales staff. The unit is demoralized by so many new faces every year, and I'm having problems meeting my revenue goals. And, we are spending almost twice as much time on hiring and training as we did five years ago. Every month or so, it's a different person, but the same story."

Zacharias looked out the window and appeared to be deep in thought. When he turned back to his colleague he said, "OK. You're right. We can't continue playing musical chairs with our salesforce. If there's a solution out there, let's find it."

Mather and Co. was a successful and dynamic college and university textbook publisher. Like most companies working in this competitive market, Mather employed "field staff representatives" to meet with faculty members, department chairpersons and bookstore managers, and it was the first major publisher to enable field staff representatives to use the Internet to place and monitor orders. That meant the representative could place an order from the faculty member's office and provide specific information about when the books would arrive on campus.

Mather also encouraged its representatives to be entrepreneurial and paid commissions to them if they successfully arranged for a faculty member pen a book. This was somewhat unusual in the profession and was lucrative for its representatives. Although they were well compensated, the representatives worked hard, traveled a great deal and worked under pressure from competing publishers.

The most difficult parts of the job were the travel schedule and the pressure to get faculty members and others to adopt Mather books. In a state like Ohio, where there were many colleges and universities, representatives typically drove and could usually get home most evenings. In states with fewer schools, representatives had to cover large geographic regions and were on the road several days a week during the busy ordering season.

The travel schedule and long hours created problems for many of the representatives. The publishing industry had long attracted younger people, and 80 percent of Mather's workforce was younger than 40. The conflict between work life and personal life intensified as people began to make life choices, either going to graduate school, getting married or having children.

When Zacharias and Fowler-Ely began working together, they treated the relatively high turnover among field representatives as part of the cost of doing business and did not regard it as a significant problem. Over time, however, it became apparent that there were costs associated with high turnover and a loss of "institutional memory" as new people joined the organization. Furthermore, when new people began working for Mather, they had to meet and establish relationships with faculty members, and that took time.

What had once appeared to be anecdotal stories about a small group of employees emerged over time to be a pattern of employee behavior that was markedly different from the behavior of other employees.

Mather and Co. was organized into four divisions.

Mather and Co.—Operating Divisions			
(1) Editorial Assistance	(2) Advertising & Marketing	(3) Field Staff Representatives	(4) Administrative Services

The first three divisions tended to attract a similar employee pool: college graduates, relatively young, in first professional positions, with strong motivation to succeed. Gradually, however, the demographic characteristics of the four divisions began to diverge, as illustrated in the following summary:

Basic Demographics for Divisions 1, 2 and 3
(Mather and Co.)
2001—2003

Demographic Variable	Editorial Assistance & Advertising & Marketing	Field Staff Representatives
Average age	36	31
Average years employed	7 years, 2 months	4 years, 5 months
Mean performance rating*	4.9	5.2
Reason for leaving: Family and school	22%	54%

* Rating Scale: Unsatisfactory=1, Outstanding=6; Score is *mean for last two years.*

When Zacharias and Fowler-Ely reviewed the data, they concluded that there was tension between work life and personal life as a field staff representative that resulted in increased turnover and shorter length of service with the company. They could find no easy solution to this dilemma, but both observed that it was cost ineffective to do nothing. Every few months, Fowler-Ely would ask Zacharias what interventions they could pursue, but he usually said that he would have to think about to do next. Nothing happened.

Fowler-Ely left Zacharias' office and walked back toward her own. Although they had this conversation many times before, she felt that he was more serious this time and that he really wanted her to come up with ideas to alleviate the problems that had become so disruptive to the company.

Exhibit A:
Stated Reasons for Leaving Mather and Co.—
Field Staff Representatives 2001—2003

Reason for Leaving	Number	Percent
Family	4	31%
School	3	23%
New job	2	15%
Internal	1	8%
Relocating	1	8%
Unknown	1	8%
Personal	1	8%
TOTAL	13	100%

Questions for Consideration and Discussion
'Different Person, Same Story'

1. What are the central problems and challenges facing field sales representatives at Mather? To what extent are these issues similar to or different from problems and challenges facing other employee groups at Mather?

2. Jennifer Fowler-Ely has been tasked with developing a series of interventions for employees at Mather. What, specifically, should she do? With which employee group should she begin and why? How will she know if she is successful in her efforts?

3. To what extent does an organization need to be concerned about the work-life balance issues facing employees? How can the organization meet its business obligations while also tending to the needs of its employees?

4. Whose responsibility is it to address work-life issues in an organization? How might individual employees, managers, human resources and others engage in discussions, plans and policies concerning this subject?

5. To what extent is the notion of work-life balance a lofty goal versus a sound business practice? What are reasons why people might support a culture of work-life balance, and what are reasons why people might resist such an idea?

PART IV

Operational Components in Workforce Engagement

Performance Management

Tools and Technology

Opportunities for Advancement

Daily Satisfaction

Chapter 11:
Performance Management

Introduction: What do We Mean by 'Performance Management'?

Performance management includes the ability of managers and supervisors to identify relevant dimensions of employee performance; set challenging and meaningful expectations; monitor and evaluate performance; and provide regular and constructive feedback to employees. The performance-management component of workforce engagement reflects the extent to which employees perceive that the company holds people accountable for results. This component also includes the fairness and timeliness of job appraisals and how well managers clearly define appropriate work performance and expectations.

Highlights from the 2004-2005 National Benchmark Study on Workforce Engagement

Based on the results from the *pan* study, four in 10 employees do not believe that their supervisor adequately and clearly explained their performance goals and objectives, rising to six in 10 employees with 10 or more years of tenure with their company. Clearly, supervisors and managers should not assume that employees who have been with their company for more than a couple years can do without ongoing performance-related feedback.

According to the PAN study, only half of all employees (53 percent) agree that their supervisors provide information that helps them work more efficiently, while nearly one-quarter disagree (23 percent). The length of time an employee has been with the company or in a job shows the greatest variance in results. In fact, employees who have been with their company 10 or more years are more than twice as likely to disagree that supervisors provide needed information than are employees with their company less than one year. This level of disagreement doubles for those with their organization more than one year, showing that supervisors and managers are failing in this regard with the vast majority of their employees. Remember, supervisors and managers tend to spend time with two groups of employees: new ones and those that are underperforming. Remember that employees with three to five years' experience, those most vulnerable to take their skills to another company, expect this same feedback.

Only six in 10 employees in *pan*'s national benchmark study agreed that their supervisor set goals and objectives that were realistic and achievable. The age of employees plays a role in how they react to their goals and objectives. Seven in 10 employees ages 18 to 24 agree that their goals pass the "RUMBA" test (Reasonable, Understandable, Measurable, Believable and Attainable), dropping to roughly six in 10 of 35-to-44-year-olds and just more than half of those older than 45. Tenure again plays into this issue, with seven in 10 employees with their organization less than one year feeling goals were realistic, dropping to just more than half of those employees with their organization more than 20 years.

Not surprisingly, employees who received work-related training or education were significantly more likely to feel positively (68 percent), versus those who were not given additional training (52 percent). Employees in sales/client service were the most negative employees in any department, with one in five employees disagreeing that goals were achievable. Again, knowing the importance of workforce engagement with salespeople, this is a serious concern for today's employer.

In *pan*'s national study, two-thirds of all employees felt their organization held people accountable for results, the most positive results in the area of performance management. While 86 percent of executives believed that there was accountability for results, only 70 percent of supervisors and 64 percent of individual contributors felt the same. As employees gain more experience with their company, their perceptions of this accountability decrease, a familiar pattern in the area of performance management and across the study as a whole.

Many of the issues surrounding performance management center on a lack of open, honest communication. In the *pan* study, only half of all employees felt that their organization encouraged open, candid communication, while more than a quarter disagreed. As employees' tenure with the company increased, their perceptions of communication being open and candid dropped significantly. Of equal concern, senior management is significantly more likely to be satisfied with the communication than are individual contributors (71 percent positive versus 47 percent positive), even though the majority of the communication is directed at those individual contributors.

Highlights from the 2006-2007 National Benchmark Study on Workforce Engagement

Based on the 2006-2007 benchmark study, seven in 10 employees believe their *company holds people accountable for results*:

- Three quarters of employees who work for companies employing less than 1,000 workers agree, while just two-thirds of employees in larger companies feel the same (74 percent versus 66 percent).
- Nonunion employees are significantly more positive than union employees (73 percent versus 60 percent).
- Only six in 10 education employees agree with the statement (62 percent), compared to 85 percent of leisure/hospitality employees.

The current survey uncovered continued weakness in a key supervisory function: *my supervisor gives clearly defined performance goals and objectives*. Only six in 10 of all employees agree with the statement. Other key findings include:

- Information-services employees are the least positive (49 percent), while nearly three quarters of leisure/hospitality employees and seven in 10 health services workers feel the same (74 percent and 70 percent).
- Part-time workers are significantly more positive than full-time workers (70 percent versus 57 percent).
- As an employee's tenure in a company increases, positive perception of the supervisor's performance drops. Seventy-two percent of employees with their company less than one year feel they are given clearly defined goals, dropping to 60 percent of one- to five-year employees and 53 percent of six-plus-year employees.
- Employees who are fully engaged are twice as likely to agree with the statement as employees who are unengaged (77 percent versus 38 percent).

The importance of ethics can also be seen in the *performance management* workforce component. The percentage of employees who agree *ethical issues are clearly communicated in this organization* showed a significant decline in 2006-2007, down to less than six in 10 of all employees (58 percent). One in six disagreed (17 percent). Additional findings include the following:

- In one of the few differences noticed in the benchmark results, women are significantly more likely than men to agree that these ethical issues are clearly communicated (63 percent versus 55 percent).
- Eight in 10 executives agreed with the statement. However, this percentage drops to 56 percent of individual contributors. As individual contributors deal with the majority of the ethical issues, this communication is vital with this group, as well.

- Nonunion employees are significantly more likely to agree with this statement than union employees (60 percent versus 47 percent).
- Perceptions are most positive in highly regulated industries (71 percent of health-services employees agree, and 69 percent of financial-services employees agree), while least-positive employees work in state/local government (52 percent) and manufacturing (50 percent).

Why is Performance Management Important?

To truly engage employees and to compel employees to perform to their highest potential, it is necessary for managers to define, monitor and evaluate performance on an ongoing basis. Additionally, performance expectations and outcomes should be articulated in such ways for employees to understand how their performance is aligned with, contributes to and is an outgrowth of the strategic directions of the organization.

In reality, performance management represents a "bookended" process, one that begins with hiring an employee and ends with broader career-development activities. Pre-employment assessments may be used to test for the types of knowledge, skills, abilities, competencies, dispositions and/or behaviors required for the specific job, thereby ensuring that the right person is chosen for the right job.

Performance management also extends to activities beyond merely evaluating individual employee work outcomes. An important way to create feelings of accomplishment—critical to the strongest driver of workforce engagement, daily satisfaction—is through career-development activities. Promotion from within, succession planning (evaluating the internal workforce and preparing employees to move up the hierarchy) and mapping career paths (outlining actual paths taken by those who are at the top) can also help. Thus, to recognize what occurs between the bookends of recruitment and promotion/career development, it is important to understand some principles of effective performance management.

What are Some Principles of Effective Performance Management?

> **Principles of Effective Performance Management Recognize:**
>
> - Performance management is a process, not just an appraisal of employee performance.
> - Performance management is related to other HR activities and organizational initiatives.
> - Performance management is, primarily, the ongoing responsibility of the employee's direct manager.
> - Performance management should be aligned with the broader strategic directions of the organization.
> - Performance management relies on appropriate information about work outcomes.

Performance management is a process, not just an appraisal of employee performance

Many managers and employees view performance management as a synonym for the performance appraisal. In reality, performance management encompasses a number of activities under one umbrella, under which performance appraisals reside. A performance-management process begins with understanding the organization's philosophy toward individual performance. That is, to what extent are individuals expected to contribute in substantive, meritorious ways to the achievement of results? In some high-performance organizational cultures, a tremendous emphasis is placed on responsibility and accountability in individual performance. In other, collective-oriented cultures, greater emphasis might be placed on the broader performance of the work team, department or organization. The performance-management process continues with establishing performance expectations, communicating those expectations to employees, monitoring employee performance, evaluating and providing feedback on performance, formally appraising performance and developing approaches to improve or sustain performance.

Performance management is related to other HR activities and organizational initiatives

Because performance does not occur in a vacuum, performance-management activities should be directly related to other HR activities and organizational initiatives. Two areas closely related to performance management are training and development and rewards and recognition. Training and development activities serve to contribute toward the maintenance and improvement of employee knowledge, skills and competencies. Thus, performance-management activities should inform, in part, the training and development agenda within the organization. Increasingly, many organizations explicitly link employee performance with tangible rewards and recognition. As a result, performance-management activities, most notably the formal employee-performance appraisal, should address how, why and by whom compensation decisions related to performance are made.

Finally, there are likely numerous other HR and organizational initiatives that impact—and are impacted by—performance management. Some examples include a change in corporate strategic direction (which potentially changes performance goals for individual employees), updates to technology (which potentially changes the nature of employee work) and customer feedback or operational data (which potentially changes the emphasis on certain aspects of work or internal business processes). Thus, managers and employees should be mindful of the fluidity surrounding performance management and the impact that broader activities and initiatives have on daily performance.

Performance management is, primarily, the ongoing responsibility of the employee's direct manager

One of the most central and important tasks a manager undertakes is monitoring and evaluating the performance of his or her direct reports. Even when employees (and others) are directly involved in setting goals and evaluating performance (e.g., 360-degree feedback systems), it is the manager who, ultimately, has the responsibility for the performance-management process. In this context, performance should be managed regularly, with the manager providing feedback, guidance and resources for employees on an ongoing basis.

The annual or semi-annual performance-appraisal meeting, while necessary to document performance, does not replace the day-to-day management of employee performance. Managers have a responsibility to give employees information about the positive and negative aspects of performance when such performance occurs, not weeks or even months after the fact. Providing measures to correct performance deficiencies when they occur can go a long way toward ensuring employees are given the ample information and time to improve their performance. Thus, when properly managed, employees should never be surprised by the information conveyed to them during the formal performance-appraisal meeting.

Performance management should be aligned with the broader strategic directions of the organization

Aligning individual performance with the broader strategic directions of the organization is necessary to realize business results and to provide appropriate context-setting for employees. Simply put, an employee needs to know how his or her job directly connects to the bigger picture of the organization's mission and strategic intent. This can provide a frame of reference for how work is performed and can serve to educate employees about how the inputs and outputs of their work impact others within the organization. Again, managers can play a crucial role in providing information to employees about how individual performance is related to the broader strategic directions.

Performance management relies on appropriate information about work outcomes

For employees to view performance management as credible and important, supervisors and managers must ensure that appropriate information about work outcomes is used in measuring and evaluating performance. Using valid, reliable and timely information is one way to improve performance-management effectiveness. Validity refers to the extent to which performance measures accurately reflect the nature of work performed. Reliability refers to the extent to which performance measures produce consistent results over time. Finally, timely information acknowledges that, for employees to be effective in their jobs, feedback on performance should be given as regularly and feasibly as possible.

What Activities are Involved in Performance Management?

Typical Performance-Management Activities Involve:

- Identifying performance dimensions for a job
- Conducting a performance-expectations meeting
- Monitoring performance to provide ongoing feedback to employees.

Identifying performance dimensions for a job

One of the first steps in performance management involves identifying performance dimensions for a particular job. Job analysis, the task of gathering specific, detailed information about a job, can serve as the principal means to provide the organization with a framework for understanding work. Typically, job analysis yields information such as the knowledge, skills and abilities used in performing the job; other characteristics or dispositions needed to be successful in the job; primary duties and responsibilities of the job; reporting relationships in the job; and any unusual or unique working conditions associated with the job.

Information from job analysis makes several important contributions to performance management. First, job-analysis outcomes are typically translated into a job description, a narrative summary of job-related requirements. This informs other components of workforce engagement, including workforce selection, organizational orientation, training and development, and rewards and recognition. Second, job analysis provides the basis by which to evaluate the relative worth of all jobs in the company, thereby producing an understanding of how each job fits into the broader structure of the organization. Finally, job analysis gives managers the information needed to set performance expectations for individual employees who occupy the job. These expectations, therefore, should be communicated to employees through a performance-expectations meeting.

Conducting a performance-expectations meeting

To provide employees with an adequate understanding of the nature of their work, managers should initiate a meeting with employees to outline the expectations for job performance. For newly hired employees, this meeting should be part of the organizational orientation and onboarding process. For existing employees, this meeting should be a natural outgrowth of the annual performance-appraisal meeting, in which past performance was reviewed and evaluated and future performance expectations are outlined. Using information from the job analysis and job description as a basis for the discussion, managers should use performance-expectations meetings to discuss three broad components to performance: key result areas, organizational values and strategic initiatives.

Key result areas include the major areas of responsibility for the job. This is the essence of job performance and delineates the expectations for performance on a daily, weekly, monthly, quarterly or annual basis, depending on scope and nature of work. Key result areas may also identify any physical, financial, human or other resources over which an employee has direct responsibility, with corresponding performance goals developed for each.

While key result areas typically focus on what employees produce in the performance of their job, organizational values focus on some of the *processes used* by employees in doing their job. Organizational values, therefore, are typically translated into performance expectations that are expressed as the behaviors or attitudes that are expected of employees enterprisewide, regardless of job title or function. Examples of such values include teamwork, customer service, ethical decision-making, pursuit of quality and fiscal stewardship. Increasingly, these organizational values are branded as broad competencies that all employees are expected to embrace and model and can serve as a way of attempting to institutionalize the corporate culture through performance management.

Finally, strategic initiatives are the components of job performance that connect individuals with the broader work of the organization. While most jobs have relatively stable and constant performance expectations, many workplaces have certain organizationwide or departmentwide benchmarks for performance that are outlined for the quarter or year. For example, a furniture store may have as its strategic initiative to increase its customer base by 15 percent for the year. Although it is highly unlikely that any one employee would be charged with accomplishing this goal, it is nevertheless important to, whenever possible, acknowledge and integrate relevant strategic initiatives into the performance expectations for individual employees. This tactic can go a long way toward helping employees realize how their work is aligned with—and derived from—the broader strategic direction of the organization.

A performance-expectations meeting, therefore, should highlight important job components (key result areas) as well as the unique aspects of work (organizational values and strategic directions). Too often, too little attention is given to employees in setting the context for which subsequent performance will be expected and evaluated. Thus, to provide a platform from which workforce engagement can be enhanced, conducting an explicit and intentional performance-expectations meeting should be a central component in the performance-management process.

Monitoring performance to provide ongoing feedback to employees

After identifying relevant dimensions of job performance and conducting a performance-expectations meeting, a manager should properly monitor performance to provide ongoing feedback. This includes allocating sufficient resources for employees to accomplish tasks and for giving feedback that is timely, honest and drawn from valid and reliable measures of employee performance. Doing so ensures that employees are given the appropriate conditions to improve their performance prior to the formal performance-appraisal meeting.

As noted, information conveyed during a performance-appraisal meeting should never be a surprise to the employee. Conducting a formal annual or semi-annual review of employee performance is, perhaps, one of the most important tasks a manager will undertake in the manager-employee relationship. These meetings can typically be enhanced by setting aside an appropriate amount of time to discuss performance, involving the employee in rating his or her own performance and focusing on resolving problems through improvement-oriented approaches, such as training, mentoring or coaching.

The performance-appraisal meeting is a reference point that serves to document and encapsulate an employee's performance over a period of time. The outcomes of such a meeting serve to provide the basis for future performance, and often these meetings entail clarifying the dimensions of a job and articulating the expectations for subsequent performance. It further reinforces the ongoing and cyclical nature of performance management.

Finally, while it may be championed by senior leaders and HR professionals, performance management is, principally, the responsibility of managers who have direct oversight of employees. This responsibility also extends to the related operational-level workforce engagement components of tools and technology, opportunities for advancement and daily satisfaction. The relationship an employee has with his or her manager is often one of the most salient determinants to his or her retention, commitment and performance. Therefore, attending to these workforce engagement components needs to be a managerial priority.

Summary

Performance management is an important component to workforce engagement, even though it is not a top driver. Employees dislike role ambiguity and ill-conceived approaches to evaluating their performance. This chapter provided a perspective about performance management as a process, not just a yearly appraisal activity. Responsibility for performance management, including specific suggestions for managers, was provided. Additionally, some activities associated with performance management were outlined. The following case, *"One Job, Too Many Bosses,"* highlights a situation where conflicting information and differentiated performance expectations adversely impact an employee's ability to truly be effective.

Performance Management and Workforce Engagement
'One Job, Too Many Bosses'

Molly Fitzgerald was furious. As she waited for the elevator, she could feel the tension in her arms and back. "If I had stayed there for another minute," she thought, "I would have told her what I really think of her, her forms, her 'helpful suggestions' and her lack of understanding of how this business works."

As she reached her desk, she saw that a large floral arrangement had been placed there. It was beautiful. She looked at the card:

> *Molly,*
> *Thank you again. We could not have completed the biggest sale of the year without your help. You are a star!*
>
> *Ben, Meredith and Rachel*

Despite her anger, she could not help but smile as she thought of the irony of getting flowers from three of the brokers right after that session with the director of operations, who had told her that her performance on the job was inadequate. "What a crazy world," she thought. "I only have one job, but too many bosses."

After more than 40 years in business in the Seattle area, McNulty Brothers Real Estate Co. merged with Dream Homes For You, a national realty company with operations in more than 30 states. McNulty is one of the most successful and visible real-estate companies operating in the metropolitan Seattle area. With the retirement of the third (and last) of the brothers who founded the firm, it seemed like a good time to affiliate with one of the growing number of nationally linked real-estate operations. The merger agreement permitted the use of the name "McNulty Brothers/Dream Homes" for 10 years so that the McNulty reputation could be associated with the new corporate entity.

Initially, there were few evident changes in the operations of the "new" company. Nearly three-quarters of the McNulty employees stayed in their jobs, and the working environment remained the same. During the next three years, however, some changes became evident. Business increased, partly because Dream Homes For You had a national referral system so people in, for example, Baltimore, who were moving to the Seattle area, could "shop" over the Internet, and partly because the Seattle office was now listed in "Dream's" highly visible national advertising promotions.

There were also a few "new" procedures required from the national office, but these were, for the most part, manageable. The biggest changes were the loss of informality as the company grew and the adherence to "consistency across the company," which was reinforced through a series of "functional training seminars" for all those with similar job titles in the offices throughout the company. In any given year, Dream Homes For You might offer six to eight seminars for specific job functions: office managers, comptrollers, HR coordinators, training specialists, performance-appraisal specialists, customer relations, etc. Similar training seminars were held for rental agents, brokers, underwriters and appraisers.

In 2004, one of the longest-serving McNulty employees, the director of operations, retired. Senior management wanted to find someone who could "modernize" some of the antiquated procedures at McNulty. They hired Marjorie Woodright, who earned a master's degree in human resources and worked for 10 years as associate director in the state's Office of Real Property Services and Compliance. She appeared to be an ideal choice for the job because she understood the real-estate business and had training and experience in human resources. She was energetic and friendly and said that she wanted to be a "listener" rather than a "doer" in her new job. In her second year, however, she began making significant changes in the existing systems and became more assertive in her interactions with those who reported to her. Woodright believed that the success of a large real-estate business was, to a large degree, dependent on effective systems, carefully monitored and consistently followed. To achieve this, she implemented a process-improvement system that tracked all business transactions, ensuring everything was done in proper sequence.

In many ways, a sequential process made sense in the real-estate industry because getting to a settlement with the buyer and seller required many steps, some dependent upon completing a previous one. There were credit checks, title searches, premise inspections, review of tax and utility records, underwriting, internal "quality audits" and final review by in-house legal counsel. Each sale was assigned a "routing number," and Woodright routinely examined completed transactions, reviewing the cover page to see how long each step took to complete and whether or not they were done in the proper sequence.

Fitzgerald was senior title officer at McNulty, a post she retained after the merger. She had been at McNulty for 12 years, seven as senior title officer. She was well liked, respected for her "getting-the-job-done" attitude and had a reputation for being resourceful and responsive to the needs of other employees. The title operations at a large real-estate organization with residential and commercial sale and rental activities were complex and multifaceted, with serious financial and legal risks if there were errors or omissions. Fitzgerald always said she "never let the ball drop." When nervous brokers, agents and attorneys called to make sure that everything was ready for an upcoming settlement, she always said, "Unless I win the lottery, I'll be there with all the paperwork in order."

There were, inevitably, glitches, changes and unanticipated circumstances that had to be addressed. An attorney for a buyer, for example, might have to travel suddenly, and the settlement had to be held two days earlier than expected. Or a "release of lien" from the state comptroller's office did not arrive and could not be located. There were many stories of Fitzgerald working on a Sunday, working through the night, calling bankers and lawyers at home and—once—flying round trip from Seattle to Portland to secure a power of attorney and then rushing to a settlement meeting only 15 minutes before the agreement "lock" expired.

All of these efforts and the stories surrounding her determination to meet necessary deadlines earned her the admiration of her colleagues. Numerous people throughout the company claimed that without her help their closings would not have taken place. People who knew her well thought that Fitzgerald liked the role of "rescuer" more than any other part of her job.

Woodright understood and appreciated the need to operate "outside the box" from time to time, and she was aware that people with Fitzgerald's energy and commitment were hard to find. Still, she was resentful of Fitzgerald making decisions to give one project priority over others, or changing schedules, or ignoring the operating guidelines of the company without consulting her or even informing her of changes. Fitzgerald, she thought, always had a ready explanation or excuse: "I didn't know how to reach you," "I didn't want to bother you on a weekend," "I needed every minute to get everything done so we could meet the deadline."

In addition, Woodright secretly thought that Fitzgerald liked the "urgency" and the last-minute pleas to help avert disaster and that she could have avoided some of the emergencies that occurred. Fitzgerald, for her part, believed that she was a team player and that she did not object to the procedures Woodright put in place. She felt, however, that in operational matters she needed the autonomy to ignore or change the existing procedures.

After being on the job for about nine months, Woodright sent a memo to Fitzgerald that said, "I have a suggestion that may be very helpful as we plan ahead. If you move 'Settlement File B' ahead of 'Settlement File A' for title follow-up, you should add an addendum explaining why it was necessary to do that. I will then have an idea of what kind of unforeseen circumstances can occur and that will facilitate planning." In passing, Fitzgerald mentioned to Woodright that she received the memo.

Several months later, Woodright again wrote to Fitzgerald: "I keep seeing a number of 'lapses' in title procedures where you appear to change the order in which you act on files. There are probably good reasons for this, but, as I have suggested previously, you need to put those reasons in writing so I know why you are making changes in what we have both agreed is a fundamentally good system." This time, Fitzgerald wrote back, "It would take up too much valuable time for me to justify and explain each change. When I make a change in which files are handled first it is always because someone has indicated a problem exists that must be dealt with. If you have specific questions about a particular file, let me know and I will explain it to you."

The time was approaching when Fitzgerald was due to have her semiannual performance review with Woodright. In the section of the self-appraisal form where Fitzgerald had to write about her accomplishments in the past six months, she wrote, "I believe that my department operates efficiently and that we are able to respond quickly to the many requests we have from brokers, agents, attorneys and banks. As business has grown, so too, have the pressures on us to be prompt and efficient. In the last year, almost a third of the files moving through the title office have required some 'exception' to procedures and schedules. Despite this, we have not had a single failure in having everything ready for settlement."

At their meeting, Woodright commented on some other sections of Fitzgerald's performance and made a point of praising her for the stability and performance of her staff. She paused and then said, "I am concerned that you have not responded to my suggestions about explaining why it is necessary to circumvent our procedures so often. I have tried to give you leeway, but why haven't you followed through on my suggestions?"

"Believe me, I would if I could, but it just isn't practical," Fitzgerald replied. She continued, "These brokers and agents are my friends, and I see them every day. If a broker calls and says he has screwed up and forgotten to get a copy of something and the whole deal may fall apart, I want to help, and I think it's my job to help. Don't you agree?"

Woodright said, "I admire you for wanting to help, but remember, you work for the company, not for them. They need to learn the procedures, and you're not helping them. If you have to make an exception in one of 25 situations, that is fine, but you're making it a routine matter. People end up not caring about getting things in on time because they know you will save them. I want you to stop doing that. I am making that your top priority for the next six months."

The flowers were beautiful and several people stopped by and asked Molly who sent them and why. Someone said, "Ben told me that the deal he, Meredith and Rachel had been working on would have been down the sewer if you hadn't jumped in and saved the day." Someone else said, "Molly, who did you bail out this time?" Molly sat at her desk, confused and dispirited. Did she work for the people around her who turned to her for help, or did she work for Marjorie Woodright and "the company?"

Questions for Consideration and Discussion
'One Job, Too Many Bosses'

1. What advice would you give Molly Fitzgerald in this case and why? What advice would you give Marjorie Woodright and why? To what extent are there truly different views of performance?

2. How might performance expectations be best communicated to employees to avoid misinterpretations, miscommunications and frustrations? Whose responsibility is it to define, monitor and evaluate performance?

3. To what extent does an organization need to be concerned about performance management? In what ways can performance management enhance productivity and effectiveness? In what ways can performance management impede productivity and effectiveness?

4. What are the advantages and disadvantages of having managers evaluate employee performance? What are the advantages and disadvantages of having employees evaluate their own performance? What are the advantages and disadvantages of having other stakeholders (e.g., customer, subordinates, business partners) evaluate employee performance?

Chapter 12:
Tools and Technology

Introduction: What do We Mean By 'Tools and Technology'?

Tools and technology refers to the ability of managers and supervisors to allocate resources necessary for employee work; provide tools and techniques for job performance; ensure ergonomically correct work environments; and structure workflow, interactions and processes appropriately. The tools and technology component of workforce engagement reflects the extent to which employees perceive the company adequately equips them to perform their job and is interested in providing them the appropriate resources to do good work.

Highlights from the 2004-2005 National Benchmark Study on Workforce Engagement

According to the *pan* study, one-third of all employees could not agree that the tools and technology provided by their company were straightforward and easy to use, slightly worse for the MIS/IT employees who tend to be responsible for these same tools and technology.

As we have seen repeatedly, executives were significantly more positive than those holding other positions in the company, this time in their perceptions of tools and technology. Nearly nine in 10 executives felt positively about the tools and technology their company provided. However, just six in 10 of the day-to-day employees felt the same, a common pattern found throughout the *pan* study. In fact, while only one in 16 senior managers disagreed that their tools and technology were easy for employees to use, twice as many contributors disagreed. Not surprising, as front-line employees are the biggest users of the company's tools and technology.

Managers and supervisors can also play a part in their employee's perceptions in this area. While three-quarters of the employees in the *pan* study indicated that they were given enough authority to get the job done (73 percent), only two-thirds felt they were given the freedom to make their own decisions at work (68 percent) and less than six in 10 were encouraged to try new ways of doing things at work (57 percent). Further review of these issues shows similar patterns to other *pan* data:

- Employees with their organization for less than one year or in their job for less than one year were most positive.
- Younger workers (those younger than 35) felt better about technology than did older workers, a significant finding for those companies struggling with technology.
- Employees who received job-related training and development were significantly more positive in their perceptions than employees who were provided with training.
- Employees working in operations tended to be most negative, while employees in administration and finance tended to be most positive.
- Union employees were significantly less positive than nonunion employees.
- Perceptions of employees in smaller firms (fewer than 500 employees) were generally more positive than those employees who worked in larger firms (1,000 plus).
- As an employee's position in the company moved up the corporate ladder, positive perceptions of tools and technology decreased.
- Employees who participated in a company-sponsored social event were significantly more positive about their perceptions of tools and technology than employees who did not participate.
- State/local government employees had the lowest scores related to tools and technology, while employees in education and health services tended to have more positive perceptions.

Moreover, one in four operations employees (23 percent) in the *pan* survey disagreed that they had control over the resources they use to do their work. While, 85 percent of senior leaders felt they controlled their own resources, just slightly more than half of the individual contributors felt the same (53 percent), while more than one in five (22 percent) disagreed.

New employees seem most positive about having control over these resources (63 percent). However, this level of agreement is never again reached by employees of any tenure, showing the same fall-off in performance as was seen in reviews of other portions of the *pan* survey. It is not until the employees take off those "rose-colored glasses" that they see the true picture, and according to employees, the picture they see is not a pretty one.

Highlights from the 2006-2007 National Benchmark Study on Workforce Engagement

Showing no improvement over 2004-2005 results, less than six in 10 employees in 2006-2007 believe *they have control over the resources they use to do their work*, while one in five disagrees (59 percent versus 19 percent):

- Employees who received work-related training are significantly more likely to agree with this statement than employees not receiving training (66 percent versus 53 percent).

- Nonunion employees are significantly more positive than union employees (60 percent versus 49 percent).

- Two-thirds of leisure/hospitality workers agreed with the statement (66 percent), while slightly less than half of all retail workers felt the same (47 percent).

- Although nine in 10 senior executives agree with the statement (88 percent), just over half of individual contributors feel the same. Remember, it is these front-line employees who handle 85 percent to 90 percent of customer contact, so equipping them with the right tools and technology is critical.

Only six in 10 employees in 2006-2007 agree they *have the freedom to make their own decisions at work*, a significant decrease from 2004-2005 levels. The three- to five-year employees, those who tend to get the least attention from supervisors and managers, are least positive and most negative regarding the ability to make their own decisions, even though these are often the same people most counted on to create and exceed customer satisfaction.

Employer performance slipped during the last two years related to employees being *encouraged to try new ways of doing things at work*, down in 2006-2007 to slightly more than half of all employees (53 percent), and dropping to less than half of all individual contributors (49 percent). Employees who have participated in work-related training or education are significantly more likely to receive this encouragement (61 percent), compared to those not receiving the training (46 percent). In addition, nonunion employees are significantly more positive in their perceptions than union employees.

Finally, employees need to make sure they are given *enough authority to get the job done* and, as seen in 2004-2005, only 12 percent of employees in 2006-2007 disagree with that statement. While there are no executives/senior managers who feel they are not given enough authority to get the job done, one in nine individual contributors feel that way, as do one in eight supervisors and one in seven middle managers.

Why are Tools and Technology Important?

Aside from the physical plant, labor costs are typically the largest expenditure in an organization. Thus, it is critical for all employees to have the resources they need to perform meaningful work and make important contributions to the organization's effectiveness daily. These resources include having the right technology and equipment, the proper training, an adequate amount of time to complete the task/assignment, the right number of people on the team and the authority to make their own decisions. Thus, it is necessary to understand the types of tools and technology available to employees and other conditions needed to maximize productivity and performance.

What Types of Tools and Technology are Typically Available to Employees?

Types of Tools and Technology Typically Available to Employees Include:

- Physical Resources
- Financial Resources
- Human Resources.

Physical Resources

Physical tools and technology include the materials regularly needed, inventory often used and manuals frequently consulted in performing the routine nature of work. Many jobs also require employees to use specific hardware, interact with specific software and have access to specialized databases or data sets to research issues, solve problems and accomplish tasks. Finally, workspaces need to be sufficiently designed to provide adequate space. Providing comfortable chairs, ergonomic work stations and proper lighting can go a long way in proving to employees their value inside the organization. Increasingly, organizations are attending to these environmental needs of employees by ensuring that ergonomically correct, safe and pleasant work conditions are constructed, maintained and improved.

To be effective in performing their job, individual employees need to have appropriate access to tools and technology, an understanding of how the tools and technology are to be used and the ability to request additional tools and technology to enhance overall work processes and productivity. The manager or supervisor bears the responsibility for identifying, locating, sourcing, allocating and maintaining tools and technology for an employee to use at work.

The basic supplies and equipment needed to perform work should be easily available to the employees or, if not, these resources should be able to be acquired with a minimum amount of effort. Going through a long ordering and approval system can create a negative impression for employees, forcing them to potentially use substandard or out-of-date equipment in their job. When inevitable equipment breakdowns occur, repairs should occur quickly and, whenever feasible, temporary replacements should be made available.

Financial Resources

Clearly, not every employee will have responsibility for fiscal matters in the workplace. However, employees need to understand the financial resources available to them, based on their position and including any limitations that preclude the ability to secure tools and technology in performing work. Issues of budgetary responsibility, purchasing power and spending authority need to be identified, clarified, communicated and reinforced to employees on a regular basis.

It has often been said that "time is money." Related to time, employees should be given reasonable deadlines for accomplishing work. Making unrealistic demands, giving an unreasonable number of projects and unnecessarily overloading or burdening employees to get a job done quickly may force them to consider putting speed before quality—something that might have adverse consequences for the employee, customers and the organization. Impossible deadlines do happen, but they should be the exception, not the rule.

Human Resources

Beyond physical and financial resources, many jobs require employees to work with others in carrying out duties and responsibilities. Thus, it is important for organizations to ensure that there are enough people to do the job and, more importantly, that the organization has the right employees with specialized skills and abilities to accomplish tasks. Employees should know about staffing practices and the matrices in place that indicate when it is necessary to hire additional employees (and, conversely, when it is necessary to downsize).

It is important to equip employees with an understanding of the human resources that are available to them to enhance and maximize performance. Some positions will require an employee to have span-of-control and managerial or supervisory responsibility over other employees. In these instances, it is necessary to delineate how work outcomes are realized and the specific duties and responsibilities required of each direct report.

For positions that do not involve managerial or supervisory responsibility, it is important to identify other human resources that are available to an employee. These include an understanding of the appropriate and needed access to supervisors, co-workers and other departments within the organization; subject-matter experts and specialists; vendors, suppliers and business partners; and other external stakeholders in the industry, profession or community.

What are Other Considerations for Enhanced Work Performance?

Other Considerations For Enhanced Work Performance Involve:

- Policies and procedures that make sense
- Discretion and autonomy in performing work
- Access to ongoing training and development opportunities.

Policies and procedures that make sense

Every organization needs certain policies and procedures to state how work is performed. Indeed, policy and procedures manuals are examples of a physical resource that employees can access to aid in job performance. To be truly effective, however, policies and procedures need to make sense, given the nature, context, changes and challenges employees face every day. Thus, there are often competing and coexisting tensions to balance consistency versus flexibility in the development and interpretation of work-related policies and procedures.

Effective policies and procedures serve to enhance the workplace and employee productivity by providing a framework against which decisions can and should be made. Good policies and procedures have a sound "business case" behind their creation and have often been developed by individuals with first-hand knowledge of successful and unsuccessful past practices.

The need to standardize approaches to work increases as organizational scope and complexity grow. A challenge, therefore, is balancing the need of standardization with the ability to make individual, unique accommodations to the interpretation of organizational policies and procedures. Employees need to be given guidance on the extent to which certain policies and procedures are set in stone or are able to be modified. A system to regularly review and revise policies and procedures needs to be established. Finally, employee input about the validity and utility of policies and procedures should be sought regularly. Presumably, many employees often have a more realistic vantage point concerning how such policies and procedures work in daily practice.

Discretion and autonomy in performing work

Of all the tools and technology available to employees, perhaps the one most valued is also the one most intangible: discretion and autonomy in performing work. Given the complexities associated with knowledge- and service-based work, it is vital that employees be permitted to have reasonable control over their jobs. This includes the ability to make judgments concerning the routine and *ad hoc* aspects of work and the freedom to make reasonable changes to deadlines, approaches and processes.

With discretion and autonomy, however, come risks and responsibilities. Managers may risk giving up control over certain matters, something they may be reluctant to do if they feel threatened by a subordinate's capabilities. There is also a risk that employees may abuse their positions or make decisions that have a negative financial, quality, customer or reputation consequence. Employees bear the responsibilities for the decisions they make, although the manager may be the one ultimately held accountable for employee actions. Establishing clear boundaries to decision-making, giving employees training on how to make decisions and judgment calls and installing in employees trust and confidence can go a long way toward minimizing risks and promoting responsible approaches to the use of discretion and autonomy in performing work.

Access to ongoing training and development opportunities

Because tools and technology associated with work regularly change, it is logical that an organization provides ongoing training and development. The ability for employees to have access to ongoing training and development opportunities is an additional consideration for enhanced work performance. As discussed in prior chapters, there are, indeed, a variety of approaches to training and development. Employees need to be made aware of such opportunities, need to be afforded the time and resources to attend such opportunities and need to have managerial and peer support for implementing the learning that results from such opportunities.

Summary

Employees represent intellectual capital that can be harnessed for competitive-advantage purposes. Every manager should have as a primary goal the maximization of individual employee effectiveness in creating and sustaining value-added contributions at work. Thus, it is necessary to allocate tools and technology such as physical, financial and human resources to carry out work. Additional considerations include the thoughtful use of policies and procedures, discretion and autonomy in work performance, and access to training and development opportunities. The case that follows, *"Caught in the Middle,"* identifies the challenges inherent in standardization versus flexibility in one key aspect of work: decision-making.

CASE STUDY:
Tools and Technology and Workforce Engagement
'Caught in the Middle'

Sharon Fein-Green watched her 9-year-old son Jonathan as he stood at first base, ready to run if his teammate hit the ball. She thoroughly enjoyed watching him play, not so much for his skill, but for his enthusiasm. No matter what happened, he loved playing the game, being involved and engaged. His teammate hit a grounder that got by the first baseman, and Jonathan started to run. Out of nowhere, the right fielder scooped up the ball and tossed it to the second baseman. It was a classic squeeze play, and Jonathan was caught in the middle with the two basemen slowly closing in on him. He ran one way, then the other, but he was going to be tagged and he knew it. That ended the inning, and as his passed his mother he said, "Mom, wasn't that great? I almost made it." She smiled as she thought of him out there stuck, but trying to get by one player and then the other and maintaining his optimism until the very end.

"He's a lot like me," she thought. "I go to work every day, caught in the middle between two looming forces, but I give it my best shot and then the next day, there I am again, trying just as hard."

Fein-Green was vice president for human resources at Harvest Table, an upscale chain of gourmet supermarkets. Harvest Table had 17 stores in two states and had four more under construction or scheduled for construction within the next six months. Two of the stores were in an adjacent state, and there was speculation within the retail grocery market that the new stores were the vanguard of stores to expand the chain regionally. In addition to being a vice president of the corporation, Fein-Green was also a confidante and adviser to Barbara Cooperwaite, Harvest Table's CEO. Cooperwaite's creativity and energy led the company to significant growth in revenue, stores and profits. She relied on Fein-Green for more than the oversight of the HR department; frequently, she involved Fein-Green in discussions about corporate strategy and a variety of management issues.

Fein-Green earned a master's of business administration in HR, was active in the state association of HR executives and, within the last year, had been the subject of a feature story about women executives in one of the area's largest newspapers. Among the most difficult challenges in her job was maintaining consistent polices in each of the separate stores, and she had become adept at permitting flexibility whenever possible, requiring adherence to existing policies only when absolutely necessary. Apart from the issues relating to decentralization, Fein-Green had to deal with two other major problems that characterized the supermarket industry:

1. More than 60 percent of Harvest Table's employees were in jobs classified as "unskilled" or "entry level." These included tasks such as warehouse, maintenance, shelf stacking, "bagging" purchases, simple food handling (e.g., washing produce, packaging meat and poultry) and bar coding inventory and sale items. Turnover was very high, and the average length of employment in these positions was only eight months.

2. It was an industry standard that individuals could not be promoted into management-level jobs without having served in a supervisory capacity in at least four of the operating divisions of the business, such as the butcher, dairy, produce, cooked-food preparation, bakery, food staples, household goods and special promotions. To ensure that there would be a steady pool of employees eligible for advancement into midlevel management positions, it was necessary to maintain an ongoing rotation system among the various divisions. While people understood the necessity of the rotation system, the continual movement of supervisors from one division to another inevitably caused discontinuity.

These issues, however, were well suited to a person of Fein-Green's temperament. She was a good listener and was comfortable in interpreting the company's policies flexibly if that was necessary to get a job done. Two years earlier, she solved a problem that had caused great friction in the warehouse operations. Company policy precluded paying overtime on a "regular, scheduled basis." In one of the stores, however, produce deliveries came late in the day, and it was impossible to unload and store everything without paying overtime. Fein-Green approved the payments and maintained careful records of when the deliveries arrived and why it was necessary to make an exception to policy. When the company's internal auditors noticed the overtime payments, she was able to explain and document her decision. She acknowledged that her approach was "unconventional" but said she demonstrated the validity of her action.

In another situation, she intervened to lengthen a supervisor's work in one division by four months and to shorten the next rotation by the same amount of time because the employee would not have been able to complete the courses he was taking at a local community college if had to start a new rotation then.

She knew there was a potential downside to being a problem solver and for trying to make the rules elastic: the more she succeeded with individual situations, the more people expected her to be able to solve *their* problems. It was probably inevitable, she thought, that people working in human resources were expected to enforce the rules and create the exceptions to them. When she had requests from managers, the requests were often framed in terms of goals and objectives; when they came from the working staff, the requests were frequently personal, sometimes heartbreakingly so.

Despite the difficulties she experienced in trying to be responsive and positive, while also attempting to run the HR operation effectively, she did her job well, and her interventions generally had positive results. In her mind, she could distinguish between living within the rules, broadly construed and interpreted, and operating outside of normative and acceptable behavior. She could not put it into words, but she felt that she understood the boundaries. Once, a manager allowed someone to start working as a cashier without having gone through the mandatory criminal-background check. When Fein-Green found out, she was furious. The manager's defense was that he was trying to solve an immediate problem just as he knew she attempted to do. "The difference," she said pointedly, "is that I know the boundaries and you don't."

As she continued to navigate between stated policies and pragmatic practices, she concluded that strict adherence to policies could lead to organizational rigidity, but management by exception could lead to organizational disarray. From time to time, she shared her thoughts with other HR personnel, and there was consensus that the middle ground was elusive.

There was no doubt that Fein-Green was a well-respected and effective HR executive and that for the most part, she balanced the competing demands she regularly faced. This might have continued indefinitely had there not been changes in Harvest Table's strategic plan. Under Cooperwaite's leadership, there was a goal of increasing the number of stores from 21 to 35 during the next five years, nearly three new stores a year.

Cooperwaite told Fein-Green, that she would need to build an internal capacity to identify and train twice as many managers as were now in the company's training program, expand recruiting initiatives for entry-level workers and develop "operating practices" personnel manuals for the new stores. It was a great professional opportunity for Fein-Green, and she was excited about the expanded responsibilities and new challenges. At the same time, she was acutely aware that the nature of her job would change, as would the way in which she allocated her time.

Fein-Green's mind was racing with questions. Could she continue to be an effective intermediary between policy principles and practice priorities? How would a host of issues that could potentially disrupt company operations be dealt with if there were no exceptions, no "broad interpretations" and no expedient solutions? She knew that part of her success could be attributed to her skills, but an equally important part was based on her role and title as a vice president. If she did not broker these transactions, they would probably fail. "I've been in the middle for so long," she thought, "I do it on auto pilot. How can we find someone who will know what to do and have the clout to get it done?"

Questions for Consideration and Discussion
'Caught in the Middle'

1. In what ways do organizational policies and procedures influence individual behaviors? Why are these tools necessary? To what extent do you feel employees are motivated or unmotivated by policies and procedures?

2. Under what conditions, if any, do you feel policies and procedures should be relaxed to accommodate an individual employee's circumstance? What are the potential positive and negative consequences to doing this?

3. How can an organization deal with the seemingly contradictory reality of seeking standardization and consistency with employees while balancing the unique situational and flexible interventions needed to find, keep and motivate the workforce? What advice would you give a manager "caught in the middle" of these two ends of the continuum?

4. How can employers create a culture that ensures fairness in the workplace? How does fairness extend to the interpretation and administration of polices and procedures?

Chapter 13:
Opportunities for Advancement

Introduction: What Do We Mean By 'Opportunities for Advancement'?

Opportunities for advancement refers to the ability of managers and supervisors to promote from within or provide lateral mobility to employees; identify, develop and, in some cases, release marginal, difficult or improper-fit employees; and effectively handle downsizing, outsourcing or discontinuation of work. The "opportunities for advancement" component of workforce engagement reflects the extent to which employees perceive that the company provides opportunities for advancement. This includes promoting from within as well as supporting career development. In addition, this component includes how the organization deals with poor performance.

Highlights from the 2004-2005 National Benchmark Study on Workforce Engagement

The *pan* national benchmark indicates employers do not understand the impact opportunities for advancement can have on the engagement of their workforce. A top-five driver of workforce engagement, opportunities for advancement are most critical for those employees younger than age 35, those that are "climbing the corporate ladder." Remember, the average employee has seven jobs by the time he or she is 30, so these younger employees are searching for those advancement opportunities.

Employees who are age 35 to 54 also consider advancement opportunities critical to their engagement level, but not surprisingly, those employees who are 55 and older are more interested in work-life balance than they are in future advancement opportunities. These employees are looking at winding down their career, not ratcheting it up.

Only half of all employees feel their organization provides opportunities for advancement, while one-half disagree. Considering the importance of advancement opportunities to most employees in an organization (senior leaders did not consider this to be a key driver of their engagement for logical reasons), companies need to find situations in which employees can not only learn new skills (training and development), but put those new skills to use.

As seen with previous survey data, financial-services employees rated this area highest, but only six in 10 employees felt positively in this area. Operations employees were most negative, with more than one in four (26 percent) feeling they are not given opportunities for advancement. Tenure is a recurring theme-perceptions of employees related to advancement opportunities fall as employees gain more experience with their organization. Ratings are highest with the newest employees (67-percent positive) and lowest with those employees that have been with the organization for more than 20 years (46 percent). There is a strong correlation with tenure and the age of the employee. Again, as employees get older, their positive perceptions fall, and negative impressions increase.

As expected, employees who receive training and development are significantly more positive about advancement opportunities than employees who did not receive work-related training or education in the last year (59 percent versus 42 percent). However, the difference is more striking in looking at the flip side: employees who have not received training and development are nearly twice as likely to disagree (31 percent) than those employees who received training in the last 12 months (17 percent).

Surprisingly, the employees' education level does not strongly impact their overall impressions of advancement opportunities. Those with college degrees are no more positive in their impressions than employees with only a high-school education, and those who have completed some college are no more negative than those who completed graduate school.

Another interesting finding relates to the full-time/part-time comparison in the *pan* study. As previously mentioned, part-time workers tend to feel more positively about the relationship they have with their organization, and the same pattern emerges with the opportunities for advancement workforce component. Part-time workers are significantly more likely than full-time workers to believe their organization provides opportunities to advance. Is this because these part-time workers have less interaction with their supervisors and managers, so it takes them longer to become disillusioned with their organization? Might this also be a reason why they are more positive about effective senior leadership and ethics, diversity and safety?

So, why are part-time employees more positive about whether or not their job performance has been judged fairly? The answer may lie in the types of jobs part-timer workers normally conduct. Due to their reduced schedule and the types of industries that usually employ part-time or seasonal workers, part-time workers tend to be much more task-specific in their jobs, with much clearer roles and responsibilities than full-time workers, who tend to have a much longer job description that includes the "all other duties as assigned" component as well. Because full-time workers tend to have broader responsibilities, they may feel that their performance review is more subjective (less fair), whereas part-time workers may feel their review is more objective (and therefore more fair).

Younger workers and those with less tenure are again more positive in their impressions of the fairness of their performance reviews. However, impressions become more negative as employees' experience grows in the company. Those who received work-related training are again much more positive in their impression than employees who were not provided training/education, and the largest-sized companies (those with more than 5,000 employees) tend to be weakest in this area.

Most concerning in this workforce component, only four in 10 employees believe that they have opportunities for promotion within their own division or department (42 percent), while more than a third disagree (36 percent). Nearly six in 10 senior executives agree with this statement (58 percent); however, this drops to less than half of middle managers and supervisors (46 percent), and less than four in 10 individual contributors (38 percent). As mentioned before, special care must be taken with the individual contributors, those employees who do the day-to-day work and have the vast majority of customer contact. Sales/business-development employees are most positive (49 percent agree, versus 28 percent disagree), with HR employees being most negative (37 percent agree, versus 35 percent disagree). Age and tenure repeat similar patterns, as does participation in training and development.

Employees who were given a pre-employment test or assessment were significantly more positive in their impressions about all aspects of opportunities for advancement than employees who were not. Employees (correctly) feel that if organizations take the time to ensure that there is a good fit between the skills and abilities of an applicant and a job, and the company understands that *recruiting* is finding the "right person at the right time for the right job," then the company is interested in ensuring that employees are given opportunities to grow and develop.

Highlights from the 2006-2007 National Benchmark Study on Workforce Engagement

Employers showed no progress in providing advancement opportunities to employees since the 2004-2005 national benchmark study. Slightly more than half of all employees (52 percent) agree their organization provides *opportunities for advancement*, while nearly one-quarter disagree (23 percent). One of the interesting findings in the 2006-07 national benchmark is the fact that senior management is fully aware of the issue. Less than six in 10 senior executives agree their organization gives advancement opportunities to employees, meaning more than four in 10 cannot agree with the statement. These percentages hold true for middle management and supervisors, as well. Only individual contributors are more negative in their perceptions.

Thus, managers have to give the employees an opportunity to move up or move over, or the employees are going to move out. Only four in 10 employees believe they have *opportunities for promotion within their department or division*, while one in three employees disagrees. As noted earlier, there is a direct linkage between the tenure of the employee and perceptions of opportunities for advancement. We again see a common "U curve" when reviewing the results:

- 50 percent with their organizations less than one year feel they have opportunities for promotion.
- 48 percent with their organizations for one to two years feel the same.
- 46 percent with their organizations for three to five years feel the same.
- 30 percent with their organizations for six to nine years feel the same.
- 36 percent with their organizations 10-plus years feel the same.

In addition, less than half of all employees (47 percent) believe their organization does a good job of supporting employee career development. Somewhat surprisingly, there is no significant difference in the opinions of full-time or part-time workers, employees in all sizes of companies, union or nonunion employees or across all industries. However, senior executives are significantly more likely to agree they provide good development support (62 percent) than are middle managers, supervisors or individual contributors (47 percent). And as noted earlier, employees in the East South-Central (Alabama, Kentucky, Tennessee and Mississippi) are significantly more positive than any other geographic census region. In fact, they are more positive across all of the *opportunities for advancement* questions in the national benchmark.

Finally, 55 percent of all workers agree *qualified employees are usually allowed to transfer to better jobs*, while nearly one in five disagree (18 percent). Although supervisors may not understand the benefits of letting their best employees move to a different department or division, it is certainly better to have those employees move somewhere else inside their organization than to take a job outside it. Perhaps most telling, when employees are fully engaged, they are nearly four times as likely to agree with this statement than unengaged employees (72 percent versus 19 percent).

Why are Opportunities for Advancement Important?

For some employees, advancement opportunities may be more important than money. For these employees, then, it is important for them to know that they will not be "held back" by their boss if they are eligible to transfer to a different department or division inside the organization. Employees want an advocate, someone who supports and even encourages their development internally.

Employees need to know they can move up or move over, or they will move out. However, it makes sense that some managers and supervisors are reluctant to let their employees move to a different department. Managers and supervisors are often rated on their ability to hold on to their people—to keep them "retained." It is also in their best interest to keep their best people, those who have proven their abilities to perform their duties and responsibilities. If a manager "loses" an employee, even if that person goes to another internal department or division, the manager must go through the selection and orientation process with a new employee. This replacement employee will likely not be as initially productive or efficient as the "lost" employee.

In cases where a manager serves as an advocate for the employee's opportunities for advancement, these managers should be rewarded for having their employee transfer somewhere internally. After all, the company is not losing intellectual capital or company history by allowing that employee to go to another organization. Instead, it is promoting from within, giving an employee the opportunity to grow and advance in the company and more than likely giving another employee the opportunity to get ahead, as well.

Just as important as providing employees with career-development opportunities, companies need to take appropriate action when individual employees are not performing up to expectations, especially those who interact with customers and could potentially harm the organization's reputation. Unengaged employees may have a negative impact on customers and co-workers. Thus, in this context, opportunities for advancement entail activities beyond simply promoting an employee.

What do Opportunities for Advancement Entail?

> **Opportunities for Advancement May Entail:**
>
> - Moving Up
> - Moving Around
> - Moving Out
> - Moving Back.

Moving Up

Upward mobility via advancement is still widespread, and several organizations actively adopt a "promote-from-within" philosophy to staffing decisions. To be effective for individual and organizational needs, moving up requires several actions.

First, employees need to know their promotion potential, in terms of opportunities for advancement, types of positions available, time-in-job requirements and knowledge, skills, abilities and competencies needed for the future. The employee's direct manager should provide this information, although career development is, ultimately, the employee's responsibility.

Second, in organizations that actively promote from within, an infrastructure and process must exist to announce vacancies to employees, seek nominations or applications from interested parties and select the most desired and qualified candidate. This is generally architected by HR professionals, with suggestions from hiring managers and others directly impacted by promotion decisions.

Third, an explicit link between performance management, training, rewards and opportunities for advancement needs to be established. Managers rating employee performance must do so by considering present and future job needs and by evaluating an employee's potential for advancement. This impacts the training and development an employee receives. It also might result in a re-examination of rewards offered to an employee—based on increased skill set or scope of responsibilities.

Finally, in dealing with promotion-from-within situations, organizations must be willing and able to explain to employees who are not selected for advancement why and how the decision was made. Providing a candid assessment of an employee's strengths and weaknesses can go a long way toward soothing hurt feelings and retaining, engaging and encouraging an employee to seek future advancement opportunities.

Moving Around

Unlike moving up, moving around refers to lateral moves that afford employees with the opportunities to increase their value to the organization by acquiring additional knowledge, skills, experiences and competencies. Lateral moves have become a more common form of "advancement" in the last two decades, largely because flattened organizational structures have limited upward moves.

For lateral moves to be successful for the individual and the organization, several conditions must be satisfied. First, lateral moves should be encouraged by the organization as an attractive form of advancement for employees. This should be communicated in clear terms to employees. Second, as employees increase their cross-functionality, employers should pay for the value-added knowledge, skill and/or competence the employee possesses. Finally, lateral moves should be used as an excellent technique to enrich and re-engage reluctant or unengaged employees.

Moving Out

Sometimes, opportunities for advancement require an employee to leave his or her present employment situation. While turnover is a concern for any employer, the fact remains that it is impossible, impractical and even undesirable to retain every employee. Moving out recognizes that, for a variety of reasons, an employee may voluntarily elect to leave the organization. When this happens, the organization should seek to determine why an employee is leaving (e.g., exit interview) and determine what, if anything, the organization could have done to prevent the employee from leaving. Voluntary turnover trends should be noted, and corrective actions should be initiated by the organization as conditions warrant.

In discussing opportunities for advancement, it is also necessary to acknowledge that employees often leave an organization by involuntary means. These include downsizing or a reduction in force brought about by changing economic, competitive or strategic conditions. Outsourcing, automation or discontinuation of work may also compel involuntary departures.

When conditions such as these arise, organizations should, whenever possible, offer outplacement assistance and severance pay to the employee who is being dismissed. By treating exiting employees with dignity and respect, remaining employees will see that the organization cares about the well-being of all its workers, even those that are being let go. Often, under circumstances such as these, it is the remaining employees who are asked to "do more with less;" therefore, it is critical to make sure the "survivors" stay engaged with the company.

Another dynamic faced by some managers is the need to encourage select employees to "graduate" from the organization and move on to fulfill personal, academic or professional endeavors elsewhere. Managers are often in the best position to understand the true hopes, dreams and desires of their employees. Managers are also in the best position to help employees assess whether staying with the organization is in the employee's long-term best interests. Thus, a truly selfless manager might best help an individual employee "engage" in his or her true avocation by pursuing advancement opportunities elsewhere.

Finally, moving out may be necessitated because of continued poor performance by an employee. Typically, an underperforming employee's performance would be noted through the performance-management process, and adequate interventions and accommodations to improve performance would be made. In the case of continued poor performance, however, the "opportunity to advance" would mean, in this context, activating progressive discipline—a series of increasingly serious oral and written warnings—to facilitate the employee's removal from the organization. To truly provide effective opportunities for all employees to advance, managers must ensure that marginal, difficult or "improper fit" employees are identified, developed and, in some cases, released from the organization.

Moving Back

Often viewed as the inverse of advancement, moving back, in this context, refers to a couple of unique phenomena employees and managers may experience in the organization. Moving back could refer to an employee taking a former position, perhaps at a lower level. This might be self-initiated, such as a new parent wishing to relinquish managerial responsibility in favor of becoming an individual contributor with a more fixed work schedule. Another reason for an employee taking a former position might be organizationally initiated, in the form of a demotion or as a result of restructuring. In these instances, great care and attention should be afforded the employee with regard to the financial, emotional and professional toll such a move would likely have on that person.

Moving back could also refer to a "retread" employee, an increasingly common dynamic where someone has left the organization in search of advancement opportunities elsewhere, only to seek a return to his or her job in the former organization. These employees are often able to "hit the ground running" and may, in fact, provide a useful perspective to dissuade employees from leaving in search of "greener pastures" elsewhere. Regardless of circumstance or dynamic, there are some approaches that organizations can undertake related to opportunities for advancement.

What are Some Approaches Related to Opportunities for Advancement?

> **Approaches Related to Opportunities for Advancement Include:**
> - Individual employee ownership of career-development matters
> - Leadership-development experiences
> - Coaching and mentoring
> - Job experiences
> - Delegation and special assignments.

Individual employee ownership of career-development matters

Simply put, the organization is not the employee's parent. In years past, however, many companies created, perhaps unintentionally, "paternalistic" cultures of employee dependence. This resulted in the organization actively managing an employee's career, providing the employee with long-term employment and guaranteeing economic security. For many employees, those days are long gone.

Savvy organizations now instill in their workforce a sense of individual employee ownership over career-development matters. Organizations have a responsibility to provide the time, tools and training for employees to be successful in their jobs; however, the ultimate responsibility for career development rests squarely on the employee's shoulders. Employees need to recognize that they must keep themselves viable on the open market and that, by doing so, they also remain valuable, contributing members of their own organization—something that may provide for them future advancement opportunities internally.

Leadership-development experiences

To develop executive capacity and to ensure that the organization's talent pipeline is populated with individuals ready to assume positions of greater authority and responsibility, many organizations engage certain high-potential employees in a variety of leadership-development experiences. These experiences are usually a blend of a variety of training, development and performance-improvement initiatives. Typically, leadership-development experiences involve some formal training program, either in house or off site. Employees in these programs are frequently exposed to senior executives and may be assigned to work on issues of strategic importance to the organization. They may also be asked to attend specialized seminars, take a variety of leadership assessments or inventories and engage in self-study of popular business, leadership and trade books and articles. Finally, many leadership-development experiences encourage involvement with leaders in other settings, something frequently accomplished through networking in professional associations or through community involvement (e.g., serving on boards of directors for local not-for-profit organizations). However leadership-development experiences are organized and structured, the goal is to equip the organization with capable, talented employees who are poised for new opportunities in the upper echelons of the company.

Coaching and mentoring

In addition to leadership-training programs, coaching and mentoring are also widely used approaches to prepare employees for advancement opportunities. Coaching entails having a peer, manager or external source work with an employee to develop skills and provide reinforcement and feedback. Coaching can be very specific, used on an ad hoc basis (e.g., to assist a salesperson in improving closing techniques) or can be an ongoing, long-term relationship (e.g., senior leaders who use outside coaches as a sounding board for problems).

Mentoring programs are formal relationships that are typically established and sanctioned by the organization. A mentor is an experienced employee who helps a less-experienced employee through a long-term developmental relationship. The mentor assists the protégé by providing information about the organization, including the resources and opportunities available to the employee, often for the purpose of assisting the employee in career-development matters. Coaching and mentoring are interpersonal skill-building approaches that can augment other training and development approaches and can assist in providing a basis for opportunities for advancement.

Job experiences

Certain job experiences can equip employees with skills useful for advancement. Beyond the day-to-day performance of typical duties and responsibilities, there are three other ways to enhance the work experience and contribute to improved employee engagement: job enlargement, job enrichment and job rotation.

Job enlargement, sometimes referred to as horizontal loading, involves giving the job incumbent additional duties that require the same level of skill, effort or responsibility as those currently performed. The additional duties should be a natural outgrowth of current duties, and enlarging a job permits an employee to learn additional skills and become cross-trained on other functions.

Job enrichment, sometimes refereed to as vertical loading, gives a job incumbent additional duties that require more complex levels of skill, effort or responsibility as those currently performed. Enriching a job permits an employee to acquire higher-level skills, permits the supervisor to determine whether the employee is a candidate for promotion and can aid in succession planning.

Finally, *job rotation* involves giving the job incumbent additional duties that require different levels of skill, effort or responsibility as those currently performed. Rotated jobs should relate, in some manner, to the current job. Rotating jobs permits an employee to increase skills, develop a big-picture perspective, alleviate boredom from performing the same job and add greater value to the organization.

Delegation and special assignments

In addition to the job experiences of enlargement, enrichment and rotation, employing delegation techniques and assigning special projects are additional ways to develop employee capabilities for advancement.

Delegation involves assigning duties, granting authority and installing responsibility in an employee, all while the manager or supervisor retains ultimate accountability for the tasks that were delegated. There are numerous reasons to delegate work to employees, including developing the knowledge, skills and abilities of employees; being able to get more accomplished; building trust and confidence between managers and employees; and aiding in succession planning. To delegate effectively, the manager or supervisor must define the task, identify and select employees as recipients of delegation, inform and instruct recipients, follow up with support and communication, and review and evaluate the work outcomes. Delegation works best when dirty work, trivial work or boring work is minimized and when the employee is not overloaded.

Project, task force or team-based work is another way to equip employees with different experiences and development opportunities. Many organizations have either standing committees or task forces or ad-hoc groups that meet to tackle a particular problem or issue. Assigning an employee to represent the department at one of these meetings is a way of exposing employees to other areas of the business. Additionally, employees can network with other organizational members and can make contributions beyond the scope of their job or department. In some instances, organizations might assign or permit an employee to engage in work with another organization, such as a community-based not-for-profit organization, a customer or a vendor, supplier or business partner. Whatever the special assignment arrangement, the goal is to provide additional opportunities, beyond just attending training programs, for employees to develop to their fullest capabilities to be poised for advancement opportunities.

Summary

Opportunities for advancement are highly valued by talented employees. The extent to which an organization can provide such opportunities can either facilitate or impede workforce engagement. This chapter highlighted a variety of circumstances and situations that might result in opportunities for advancement, along with some specific approaches that managers and others can provide employees seeking advancement options. The case study that follows, *A Perfect Plan,*" profiles the challenges in restructuring jobs and retraining employees in a changing business climate, both of which have implications for employee-advancement opportunities.

Opportunities for Advancement and Workforce Engagement

"A Perfect Plan"

Milton Guthrie entered the room and moved quickly to the head of the table. Without a word of introduction or welcome, he said, "OK. This is it, right? We finally get to discuss your proposal about what needs to be done before the new machinery is up and running, and the production line is ready to start operations."

The woman to Guthrie's right, Amelia Stewart, the company's director of human resources, said, "Well, yes, assuming that we have sufficient lead time to develop and implement the new training program." The man sitting to Guthrie's left, Larry Caldwell, the company's director of operations, said, "It should be a slam dunk, now that we have the lost production time down to eight working days."

Guthrie said, "Let me summarize where we are. We have sufficient capital to pay for a substantial portion of the 'clean room' equipment, and amortizing it over seven years will be good for our bottom line. Beyond that, the two of you are proposing a five-part strategy: we develop a training program for the 60 percent of current production workers who will be able to handle the new work; we offer retirement and outplacement packages to about 25 percent of current production workers; and we move and retrain 15 percent into other nonproduction jobs here. We then go out and find, hire and train as many new production workers as we will be retraining from our current workforce. Then, as we near completion of the training program, we shut down production for eight days while we make the transition to the new equipment and production procedures. Is that it?" They nodded their assent.

He paused and then said, "It's a perfect plan. Clear. Logical sequences. Addresses the big issues. Perfect." He stood up, walked to the other end of the table, paused and then said, "Except," another long pause, "it isn't practical, feasible or affordable. For starters, how are you going to train the present employees who will be staying on? How will you train the new workers? How will you deal with the dissatisfaction of employees in other parts of our operation as they see their friends lose jobs? How much will all this cost to develop and implement?"

Stewart and Caldwell looked stunned and remained silent as Guthrie's face showed his frustration. "I've waited a long time to hear your plan, and we don't have much time left. I want a leaner and more cost-effective plan on my desk in a week." He turned and left the room.

After decades of steady growth, Bander Industries was one of the three largest manufacturers in the United States of cash registers with networking capabilities. Bander produced more than a dozen models, from one-user types to complex registers that could be used by eight people simultaneously and could also manage inventory control. By using "composite modules," registers could be produced that had specific capabilities, such as use in hotels, restaurants and supermarkets. Eighty percent of Bander's business came from customers buying more than 150 machines at a time.

Bander used an assembly-line production system that had not changed very much over the years. The manufacturing operation consisted of a standard "four line" assembly:

Station 1-shell assembly

Station 2-machinery and keyboard assembly

Station 3-drawer(s) and spring assembly

Station 4-finishing and inspection station.

The first three stations did not require sophisticated technical skills, although the more experience workers had, the more efficient they became. The work was routine, and very little training was needed.

To a limited degree, each station required different types of manual dexterity. Those who worked at Station 1, for example, had to lift and move components with a total weight of 25 pounds. Those who worked at Station 3 had to make sure that 12 screws were perfectly flush with the drawer sides so that the drawers opened and closed smoothly.

Throughout the 1990s, number of factors caused Bander to make changes and to consider implementing others. The first big change came in 1994, when the company found that it could have the shell assemblies manufactured in China and shipped to the United States fully assembled. This made it possible to move the fully assembled shells from the warehouse directly to the assembly line. What had been Station 1 became an inspection station to make sure none of the shells had been damaged in transit.

The second change was the result of improvements in microchip technology applied to cash registers. Cash registers typically operated with a series of cylinders which "clicked" when a key was pressed, moving a "pointer" across notches arranged in rows of 10. Microchips were faster, more compact and could be calibrated to different currencies. That technology, however, required a "clean" environment, and workers were trained to insert and stabilize the chips. Bander could not utilize this improved cash-register technology unless it abandoned its assembly-line operation and retrained (or hired) new workers who had the technical skills needed.

The third change had to do with the market for Bander's products. At one time, more than 90 percent of Bander's products were sold in the United States. The surge in international trade and the growth of multinational organizations meant that Bander might receive an order for 2,000 registers from a clothing chain but some were to be calibrated for dollars, pounds, euros, etc. Although the first step in "customizing" a register would occur with the insertion of the microchips, the next steps involved tailoring the keyboards and space for bills in the drawer to the specific currency. The traditional assembly-line operation did not work well for this part of the manufacturing process because there were different requirements for different countries and a host of details and adjustments with which to deal.

By 2002, it became clear that Bander would need to change its manufacturing procedures. Guthrie, the grandson of the company's founder, was a blunt "bottom line" executive whose main interest was "getting the job done." As someone said of him, "Beneath his gruff exterior there lies a gruff interior." Guthrie was not worried about finding the capital to make the production-line changes. He knew the company could afford it, and he was convinced that the two biggest changes—having the shells produced and assembled abroad and using microchip technology—would eventually reduce costs. He worried about how to manage the transition from the present system to the new one, what the impact of that would be on present employees and whether the company would be able to find and train the people needed to do the jobs that would be created when the change took place.

Characteristically, he did not want to involve himself with details. He told Stewart and Caldwell that he wanted them to develop a plan to make the changes "operational." He told Stewart to "figure out" what to do with the workers who would have to be let go, and then develop a plan for new hires. He told Caldwell to minimize the "lost time" when the switchover occurred. "I'd like to leave here at 6 p.m. one night and come in at 8 a.m. the next morning, and everything would be done," he said.

After a few months, Stewart and Caldwell met with him and told him that it was a harder job than they originally envisioned. There would need to be some down time in terms of production, and it might be as much as 15 days. Their initial inquiries indicated there may not be enough qualified workers in the area to fill the technical jobs that would be created. Moreover, they told him, there would likely be serious morale problems among the remaining workers if no provisions were made to offer retraining to some of the assembly-line workers whose jobs would now be eliminated.

Guthrie said, "I didn't ask you to bring me a list of your problems. I told you to bring me a plan about how to make these changes. Now go do it and come back when you have a plan." It took them almost six more months to develop a list of goals, a timeline, proposed actions, contingency plans, costs and benchmarks. The result was a strategic plan, not an operational one, but they thought that if Guthrie bought into their goals, they could then figure out the time and costs. Believing that they had done what he wanted, they gave him a copy of the report and asked to meet with him.

Stewart and Caldwell looked at one another helplessly. Guthrie had just trashed months of work and given them a nearly impossible deadline to come up with a new and detailed plan of action. Stewart said, "It's obvious now that he wants more details: what kind of training, what strategies for retraining, which outplacement services, which new job descriptions? We better focus on that."

Questions for Consideration and Discussion
'A Perfect Plan'

1. What impact will the proposed changes to production processes at Bander International have on each of the following groups of current employees: (a) current production workers who will be retrained to handle the new production work (b) workers who will be offered early retirement and/or outplacement and (c) workers who will be moved and retrained into other nonproduction jobs at Bander?

2. Suppose you were hired as a consultant to assist Amelia Stewart and Larry Caldwell in planning and implementing the changes highlighted in the case. What, specifically, would you suggest? How might this change process be communicated to employees? What actions would be required from Guthrie, Stewart, Caldwell, managers and employees?

3. In times of rapid change, downsizing and redesigned business processes,

how can organizations best stabilize their workforce? What are specific things that managers can do to help employees anticipate, embrace and manage change on a regular basis?

4. To what extent is it feasible or necessary to retrain existing employees for new work methods? Under what conditions should organizations initiate layoffs of exiting employees and hire new employees? What are the ramifications of such a practice?

Chapter 14:
Daily Satisfaction

Introduction: What do We Mean By 'Daily Satisfaction'?

Daily satisfaction refers to the managers' and supervisors' ability to recognize what motivates employees to come to work daily; ensure working relationships are positive; allow for autonomy and discretion in job performance; show respect to employees and maintain a high-performance, enjoyable workplace. The daily satisfaction component of workforce engagement reflects the extent to which employees perceive the company as cultivating an environment that regularly produces enjoyment, fulfillment and commitment in workers.

Highlights from the 2004-2005 National Benchmark Study on Workforce Engagement

Daily satisfaction is a main driver of workforce engagement; study after study comes to the same conclusion. Not surprisingly, the *pan* study came to the same conclusion: Daily satisfaction is the strongest driver of workforce engagement, far surpassing any other workforce engagement component. Through an analysis of the various demographic segments in the *pan* study, daily satisfaction is either the strongest or second strongest driver of workforce engagement across all industries, regions of the country, position in the company, employee age, tenure, gender, educational attainment, department/division, etc.

The good news? Daily satisfaction is considered an employer "strength," as 71 percent of employees in the *pan* study indicated their job was satisfying to them. If a company is going to perform well in one of the 13 components of workforce engagement, it is best focusing attention on the strongest impact of engagement and the kinds of behaviors and actions it counts on from employees. Taking a closer look at the *pan* data, recurring patterns emerge:

- Employees who had received work-related training or education were significantly more satisfied with their job than employees who did not receive training.

- Employees who were given a pre-employment test or assessment were significantly more satisfied in their job than were employees who were not given a test.
- Human resources and finance rated satisfaction highest, while employees in research and development and operations rated satisfaction lowest.
- Employees who participated in a company-sponsored social event were more satisfied than employees who had not participated.
- As the age of the employee increased, so did daily satisfaction.
- As employees moved up the "corporate ladder," their daily satisfaction increased. In fact, nine of 10 executives felt their job was satisfying. However, this dropped to eight in 10 middle managers, seven of 10 supervisors and just more than six in 10 individual contributors.

What many companies have failed to realize, even after the "fun and games" that took place during the technology boom of the late 1990s, is that being satisfied with a job does not mean that employees jump out of bed in the morning excited about going to work. In fact, four in 10 employees could not agree that they enjoyed coming to work. Those who had not received training, had not participated in company-sponsored social events, worked in companies with more than 10,000 employees, had not been promoted in the past three years, worked in operations and were "individual contributors" were the least positive in their assessment of enjoying going to work.

One of the strongest drivers of daily satisfaction is ensuring a good fit between employees' skills and interests and their job. Again, employers seem to be performing well in this area, with more than seven in 10 employees agreeing with this statement. There is a significant decrease in perceptions after an employee has been with the organization for more than a year, and again, those who received training were significantly more positive in their beliefs than those who had not received training and development. Interestingly, employees who worked for smaller companies (less than 1,000 employees) performed significantly better in this area than larger companies. One bad hire can impact a smaller company much more than one bad hire in a company of 10,000.

However, the same pattern related to "position in the company" emerges while reviewing this data. Indeed, nine in 10 senior managers feel there is a good fit between their skills and their job, not like the one-third of individual contributors who could not agree with the statement.

Another strong driver of daily satisfaction is the relationship employees have with their supervisor. In fact, *employees quit a boss, not a company.* Given the high scores employees gave the overall measure of daily satisfaction, it is not surprising that eight in 10 employees indicated a positive relationship with their immediate supervisor. New employees (with the company and/or in their job) are the most positive in their assessment of their supervisor, because supervisors and managers give attention to two groups: new employees and bad employees. Once the "new" employee goes through onboarding, the attention received from managers decreases. In fact, the lowest scores come from the three- to five-year employees, consistent across the majority of the *pan* study.

As stated in previous chapters, employees who received work-related training or education are significantly more positive in their perceptions of the relationship they have with their supervisor, as are employees who have participated in a company-sponsored social event, trends that are seen in other parts of the *pan* survey. One interesting trend relates to the educational attainment of the employee. As an employee's level of education increases, his or her satisfaction with his or her immediate supervisor decreases significantly, with one in nine employees with an advanced degree dissatisfied with the relationship he or she has with the boss.

Employees who have taken a pre-employment assessment are significantly more positive in their perceptions of the relationship they have with their supervisor, perhaps because the supervisor knows they are getting a better-quality hire. Finally, part timers have a stronger relationship with their bosses than full-time workers. This is perhaps due to having less interaction with them. Senior management is no more positive about their relationships with their immediate supervisor than are middle management, supervisors or individual contributors. It is one of the few questions in the survey that shows little difference in perceptions across position in the company.

Highlights from the 2006-2007 National Benchmark Study on Workforce Engagement

By far the strongest driver of workforce engagement across nearly every demographic category, even stronger than two years ago, the overall performance as perceived by the employees is more negative than it was. In fact, daily satisfaction is no longer considered a strength to leverage, but instead is an opportunity for improvement.

In two of the most critical aspects of daily satisfaction, *My job provides me a feeling of personal accomplishment* and *There is a good fit between my skills/interests and my job*, there was a significant weakening in employer performance. In fact, both these items moved from strengths in 2004-2005 to opportunities in 2006-2007. The third driver of daily satisfaction, *I enjoy coming to work,* was agreed to by six in 10 employees and disagreed with by one in six.

Continuing a trend witnessed in the 2004-2005 benchmark study, nonunion employees in 2006-2007 are more positive than union employees on every aspect of daily satisfaction. In fact, while nearly two-thirds of nonunion employees enjoy coming to work, only half of union employees feel the same.

Another important consideration from the 2006-2007 benchmark study is the importance of job-related training and education to daily satisfaction. In every measure of daily satisfaction, employees who received job-related training and education were significantly more positive in their impressions than employees who did not receive this training or education in the last 12 months:

- My job provides me a feeling of personal accomplishment: 73-percent positive versus 62-percent positive.
- I enjoy coming to work: 67-percent positive versus 56-percent positive.
- There is a good fit between my skills/interests and my job: 76-percent positive versus 59-percent positive

Training and education are investments that pay themselves back very quickly. Employees who have been trained and developed over time will stay longer, work harder for customers and help out other members of their team.

Important stakeholders (employees, customers, suppliers, competitors) need to be regarded more strongly in those areas that most impact their particular engagement and loyalty. In terms of daily satisfaction, while its impact on engagement has gotten stronger over the last two years, the performance of employers has, regrettably, weakened.

Why is Daily Satisfaction Important?

For most of us, we will spend more of our waking hours per week involved in work than in any other activity of our lives. Many employees have jobs that require working specific hours, at specific places and with specific people. To retain, motivate and, ultimately, engage workers to the highest level of personal and organizational effectiveness, it is important for employees to, generally, look forward to coming to work. Thus, it is necessary to understand concepts such as these: what employees want from their manager; ways to make work more satisfying; additional approaches to employee satisfaction; and the likely results of satisfying, engaging work.

What Do Employees Want from Their Managers?

Employees Respect and Appreciate Managers Who:

- Act with integrity.

- Display competence.

- Demonstrate fairness.

- Pursue excellence.

- Inspire innovation.

Employees respect and appreciate managers who *act with integrity*

Managers—whether they are called managers, supervisors, team leaders, etc.—need to be viewed by employees as acting with a high sense of personal and professional integrity. This means that managers should identify, describe, communicate and monitor ethical conduct in the workplace. Ethics goes beyond mere compliance. Instead, a culture of ethical conduct and decision-making starts with managers who have strong personal and moral convictions about right and wrong business practices and then illuminates those convictions throughout their department or work team.

Employees respect and appreciate managers who *display competence*

Managers need to be viewed by employees as being competent about matters concerning the organization, its customers, the industry and general principles of leading people. Knowledge of the organization includes issues around products and services, employee needs and capabilities and the history, culture and future direction of the business. Knowledge of customers includes the ability to identify, anticipate and fulfill customer needs, wants and desires in a timely manner and to understand the different types and segments of customers served by the organization. Knowledge of the industry requires bosses to be engaged in environmental scanning activities; to understand competitive pressures, emerging trends and public policy issues confronting the industry; and to understand other challenges and opportunities inherent as a participant in the industry. Finally, managers need to be knowledgeable of basic principles and practices of leading people. Employees inherently expect individuals who occupy managerial positions to understand leadership issues from a broad perspective, and successful bosses must invest time in their continued personal and professional leadership-development agenda.

Employees respect and appreciate managers who *demonstrate fairness*

While the goal of equity is to treat everyone the same, regardless of personal circumstance or characteristic, the concept of fairness inherently treats different people uniquely. Employees want to trust that their organization's leaders will treat them fairly. In this context, fairness includes how information is shared, how performance is rewarded, how decisions are made, how resources are allocated and how opportunities for advancement are determined. Thus, managers are challenged to exhibit the appropriate balance between equity and fairness in their dealings with employees.

Employees respect and appreciate managers who *pursue excellence*

Because managers are, generally, in positions of influence, they help set the tone for how their employees will perform. The pursuit of excellence is a hallmark of successful organizations. Managers in these environments are not content with the status quo, nor do they aspire to achieve only mediocre performance. Instead, they seek excellence by setting the bar high for employees, benchmarking with other organizations on effective practices, keeping up to date with trends impacting the industry and continuing to work to improve products, processes, services and relationships with employees, customers and business partners. Employees, in turn, can be challenged and inspired by managers who pursue excellence.

Employees respect and appreciate managers who *initiate innovation*

In the past decade, much attention has been paid to reinventing and re-engineering business processes in an attempt to streamline operations and improve speed of delivery and service to customers. Much of these initiatives have, in fact, yielded innovative solutions to solving organizational problems and bottlenecks. Managers who look for new ways of doing business and who take appropriate risks in this pursuit are often viewed as innovative. A culture of innovation encourages "thinking outside of the box" and seeks input and ideas from all levels of the organization. 3M has long been heralded as an organization that values creativity and innovation. In fact, 3M encourages employees to take a portion of their workweek to devote to innovative endeavors, with the hopes of yielding new offerings. The success of its products, most notably Post-It notes and accessories, is a testament to leadership practices that cultivate innovation among employees.

Recognizing what employees respect and appreciate in their manager—namely, their ability to act with integrity, display competence, demonstrate fairness, pursue excellence and inspire innovation—is one step in enhancing daily satisfaction. The subtle and explicit actions bosses take can also contribute to an environment that either enhances or impedes the employee's real and perceived experiences at work and his or her resulting motivation and satisfaction in the workplace. The next section further describes some approaches to motivate employees.

How Can Managers Make Work More Satisfying?

How Managers Can Make Work More Satisfying:

- For the Employee
- Through Job Responsibilities
- In the Work Environment.

Making Work More Satisfying *For the Employee*

Managers can make work more satisfying for the employee by emphasizing identity, significance and opportunities to improve skills and interests during the performance of the job. *Identity* involves letting individual employee know what his or her specific job responsibilities entail, what outcomes his or her work is expected to produce and how his or her work is related to other jobs. *Significance* permits individual employees to realize why the work they undertake is important, how their job impacts the larger scheme of the organization and the consequences (positive or negative) their work has on a product, a service, a customer, a business process or a solution. Finally, *opportunities to improve skills and interests* focus on providing employees with information about the present and future skills needed by the organization; ways to acquire, practice and improve additional skills; opportunities to broaden work experiences and contributions beyond one's immediate job; and the ability to integrate personal and professional interests, as appropriate.

Making Work More Satisfying *Through Job Responsibilities*

Managers can make work more satisfying for employees by including variety, autonomy and pay for performance as part of job responsibilities. *Variety* requires that job responsibilities should include an array of activities that draw upon and develop employee skills and interests; a rotation of tasks to avoid monotony; depth of assignments to increase understanding, proficiency and expertise; and breadth of assignments to increase cross-training capabilities and flexibility. *Autonomy* requires that job responsibilities should provide appropriate discretion in managing workflow; decision-making authority consistent with the scope of work performance expected; individual access to tools and resources necessary to perform the job; and sufficient discretion to determine communications across departmental and/or organizational lines. Finally, *pay for performance* requires that job responsibilities should reward high-quality work outcomes, meritorious contributions from individual efforts, and the acquisition and use of value-added knowledge and skills.

Making Work More Satisfying *In the Work Environment*

Managers can make work more satisfying for employees by ensuring fairness and equity, feedback and pleasant physical workspaces and positive relationships in the work environment. *Fairness* treats unequal people differently (for example, individuals performing the same job and producing different levels of output or quality). *Equity,* however, treats different people the same (for example, providing equal opportunities to all qualified candidates and employees). *Feedback* provides employees with guidance on what constitutes excellent, satisfactory and poor performance; timely and accurate examples of how their work is viewed by peers, managers/supervisors and customers; and information on changes within the industry, the organization and their unit/department. *Pleasant physical workspaces* include safe and ergonomically correct work stations; well-maintained, up-to-date and properly functioning equipment; and an aesthetically pleasing and enjoyable work experience. Finally, *positive working relationships* encourage open, cordial and candid communication between employees, managers and other stakeholders; constructive feedback on ways to improve work experiences; and respect for individual contributions and differences.

What are Some Additional Employee Satisfaction Approaches?

Employee Satisfaction Approaches Include:

- Understanding why each employee chooses to work for the organization
- Treating employees with dignity and respect
- Frequent interactions between managers and employees
- Involvement in organizational change and improvement endeavors.

Understanding why each employee chooses to work for the organization

A fundamental premise of the "Employer of Choice" philosophy is rooted in the notion that talented employees have a myriad of options when it comes to where they earn a living. These individuals make a concerted, conscious choice to work for a particular organization. They recognize that, as high-performing individuals with knowledge, skills and competencies in demand by other employers, their ability to find gainful employment elsewhere is, for many, a constant reality.

Faced with this reality, it is incumbent upon managers to understand why each of their direct reports chooses to work for the organization. In other words: what motivates these employees to stay with the organization? While employee opinion surveys provide useful information, perhaps the most salient, relevant data source comes from the employee. Thus, managers need to spend time trying to truly understand the motivations employees have for working in the organization and to work with each individual employee to ensure that his or her specific needs are met.

Treating employees with dignity and respect

A fundamental ingredient in employee motivation and satisfaction is having managers and co-workers treat each individual in the workplace with dignity and respect. This means that every person, regardless of position, tenure and station in life, should be afforded common courtesy in interpersonal interactions. Managers can model behaviors that support dignity and respect by listening to employees; acknowledging their presence and contributions to conversations and meetings; and treating people as individuals. Managers can also indicate to employees that they matter by taking individual personal needs seriously and by providing flexibility and understanding as the circumstance warrants. Finally, managers can hold other employees accountable for not treating co-workers with dignity and respect. This means that offensive individuals can and should be coached and counseled and that acceptable behavior is expected, and unacceptable behavior is subject to corrective actions—up to and including terminations. Creating an environment that encourages and fosters dignity and respect for all individuals can facilitate an employee's motivation to continue working in the organization, thus saving turnover costs and enhancing productivity.

Frequent interactions between managers and employees

While the old adage says that children should be seen and not heard, this is not the case for managers. Employees need to frequently see and hear managers. This requires employing a management style commonly referred to as "management-by-walking-around." As the phrase implies, this activity encourages managers to mingle regularly with their direct reports and to seek out employees to discuss work issues, seek input, share information and, in general, understand the department's or team's work climate. By having frequent interaction with employees, by "walking around" or through individual or department meetings, managers can involve their employees in decision-making and become involved in assisting employees with any challenges they face.

Another strategy for employee involvement and motivation is the establishment of open-door policies. This approach encourages employees to proactively and regularly seek out the manager; in theory, the manager's door is always open to receiving, hearing from and interacting with employees. To work effectively, "open door" policies must be more than mere lip service. Instead, managers must actively cultivate one-on-one relationships with direct reports and create an environment that makes the employee feel comfortable seeking out the manager for advice or to share information or suggestions. Both "management-by-walking around" and open-door policies can be effective in involving, motivating and satisfying employees in the workplace.

Involvement in organizational change and improvement endeavors

Employees are often an excellent source for ideas on improving products, services, solutions, customer experiences and business processes. Thus, one way to capitalize on this expertise, as well as create an environment that motivates employees, is regularly involving staff in organizational change and improvement endeavors. In an era frequently characterized by external accreditation standards (e.g., ISO certification), employee involvement makes good business sense. Task forces, committees, ad-hoc groups and project teams are all ways to seek regular input from employees. Involvement in these activities helps the organization by leveraging knowledge from key internal informants, while also further recognizing and developing the employee's capabilities. Less structured ways, such as suggestion systems, discussions or employee opinion/feedback surveys, can also facilitate employee involvement in matters pertaining to organizational life.

As organizations continue to anticipate, embrace and manage change, involving employees can yield new insights and secure buy-in as the change unfolds. The "what's-in-it-for-me?" questions associated with organizational change can often be anticipated and answered by early and continuous involvement of employees who will be impacted by the change. Using a variety of formal and informal involvement approaches can positively influence an employee's interest in, commitment to and satisfaction from the workplace.

What Actions Result from Satisfying and Engaging Work?

> **What Actions Result from Satisfying and Engaging Work:**
>
> - Financial Outcomes
> - Reputation Outcomes
> - Quality Outcomes
> - Relationships Outcomes.

Financial Outcomes

When an organization engages employees through satisfying work experiences, this typically translates into improved productivity, efficiency and retention. Additionally, employees who have a high personal attachment to the organization and who are committed to their work will generate enhanced relationships with customers. This typically yields greater revenue per employee, higher profitability and increased market share for customers. Finally, engaged employees will behave in ways that exercise stewardship over the organization's resources. Abuse of policies, "shrinkage" and employee theft and questionable medical, workers' compensation and other similar claims will tend to decrease. Thus, the extent to which employees are engaged in performing meaningful work has a bottom-line impact.

Reputation Outcomes

Organizations that employ workers who actually enjoy their work are often viewed as excellent employers. This is evidenced by the fact that employees will have a high likelihood to recommend the organization as a good place to work and as a good place with whom to conduct business. This leads to an enhanced ability for the organization to attract the type of talent it needs to be successful. In some instances, positive reputations have led to external recognition (e.g., "Best Company to Work For") of excellent employee-centric practices. Finally, employees who are engaged in their organizations tend to doubt negative information heard about the organization in the press or elsewhere and are willing to support the organization in times of crises.

Quality Outcomes

Organizations that have workforces who care about how work is performed, products are produced and business processes are maximized will tend to have environments characterized by high quality and an emphasis on excellence. This is evidenced by measures such as error rates, product defects, product returns and customer complaints received. Additionally, a quality-minded culture unleashes creativity among workers, leading to an increased ability to innovate products, services and processes, and to adopt and implement a continuous-improvement mindset and culture.

Relationships Outcomes

When employees are engaged in satisfying work, the relationships they have with co-workers, supervisors, customers and business partners tend to be enhanced. In such environments, employees tend to be willing to work harder, go the extra mile to ensure customer satisfaction and perform work beyond the minimum level of acceptable performance. Enhanced relationships among and between stakeholders can also positively impact the other outcomes of meaningful work: finances, reputation and quality.

There is a compelling business case for the creation of engaging, satisfying work experiences for employees. Some of the likely actions that might result from a workforce that is not engaged include, but are not limited to, the following: employee turnover; customer dissatisfaction; poor financial performance; lack of innovation; theft and unethical practices; conflict between management and labor; and poor or diminished quality or service. Thus, there is the need for organizations to continuously identify, implement, monitor, evaluate and improve specific practices that contribute to workforce engagement.

Summary

This chapter acknowledges perhaps the most paramount finding from the National Benchmark Studies on Workforce Engagement: daily satisfaction is the No. 1 driver of workforce engagement. More importantly, daily satisfaction is largely informed by the nature of work experiences and relationships that managers create. The specific aspects of what employees want from a manager were highlighted. Ways that managers can provide satisfying work experiences, coupled with additional employee-satisfaction approaches, were also profiled. Finally, some of the likely outcomes of satisfying, engaging work were presented. The case that follows, *"The Man Who Knew Too Much."* examines how pressures and stresses in the workplace impede one employee's ability to fully realize daily satisfaction from his job.

CASE STUDY:
Daily Satisfaction and Workforce Engagement
'The Man Who Knew Too Much'

To casual and careful observers, Nelson Syms looked like the prototype of a happy, successful and engaged employee. He was praised by his supervisors, admired by those who worked for him and respected by both groups for his command of information, systematic planning and capacity to remain focused on the task at hand, even when the unexpected occurred.

Syms' work routine began and ended each day with his "checking in" with those with whom he worked most closely, interspersing casual queries and quips about their lives, families and interests with some focused questions about progress on work tasks, attempting to gauge what had been done and what still needed to be done. At a surprise luncheon the year before to celebrate his 50th birthday, he said that he liked his work and co-workers.

In the fluid, occasionally volatile environment of a startup company in a highly competitive market, calm demeanor and focus on task were valuable assets, and Syms appeared to have it all. Few, if any, of those he worked with could imagine—or believe—that he drove to and from work each day with his hands gripping the steering wheel of his car, the visible manifestation of a person filled with stress, overwhelmed with tension.

Syms was director of finance at RXServices, a mail-order prescription-distribution center serving a consortium of businesses that had 35,000 employees, nearly two thirds of whom used RXServices for individual and family prescription needs. Because of the escalating costs of health insurance, many employers had become aggressive in seeking the lowest bidder for a variety of health services. The prescription drug business was a highly competitive one in the region: 10 years earlier, there was one such company; five years ago, there were seven; today, there are 11. All these companies offered the same basic product: prescription drugs at prices lower than were available at local pharmacies.

What made some mail-order prescription distribution centers "better" than others were small differences in cost, in processing orders and in resolving problems. There was little need to advertise because marketing was done at the corporate level, with companies annually issuing requests for proposals. It was common for companies like RXServices to submit bids for new business that were less than the true estimated costs because this gave the company a foot in the door.

One of the strategies RXServices used to make its proposals more attractive was to permit employers to "float" costs for a business quarter. This meant that the employers could deduct the health-insurance payments from employees weekly or monthly, but they did not have to submit their payments to RXServices until the end of the business quarter.

This was a competitive business operating with a small profit margin, and the history of such businesses indicated that if companies could survive for six or eight years and build up the volume of business, they could be profitable. RXServices was nearly five years old. Although growth had not been as strong as the initial business plan estimated, the company was making slow, steady progress toward viability. Although the company had not yet had a profitable year, its deficits had decreased each year. Company projections indicated no loss in year five and a small profit in year six.

RXServices operated with five divisions (finance, operations, human resources, strategic planning and information resources), each headed by an associate vice president who reported to the company executive vice president. As director of finance, Syms coordinated all of the company's financial affairs. He used to say, "I pay the bills, write the checks, lick the stamps and go to the bank to make deposits, just like most people do in their homes. And, just like most people, I'm usually broke at the end of the month."

That was really the problem. Syms felt as if he lived in two worlds: the world of anticipated growth and success and the world of not enough money to cover expenses. Like the other division heads, he was often exhilarated by the optimism of the employees and the ambitious goals of the senior executives and board of directors. High morale and optimism about the future were important ingredients to a new venture's success, and so Syms kept his concerns and reservations to himself. He just was not going to puncture the balloon of optimism so many employees of RXServices felt.

Still, he faced monthly challenges of juggling which vendors to pay, and he still needed to access the company's line of credit four or five times a year, essentially as often and as much as had been done since the company started doing business.

There was a note due in two years to liquidate the line of credit, and it had not been possible to put any money aside, ever, to use when the note became due. As a new company, RXServices had been given a five-year "startup" exemption before it had to capitalize its retirement fund for employees. That was less than a year away. The company's production effectiveness was due to its expensive automated sorting—counting—packaging system, capable of sorting 20,000 pills and tablets daily. Five years old, the equipment was nearing the end of efficient operation. New equipment would cost twice as much as the original equipment.

Syms also had to deal with relatively low employee turnover. He found it ironic that the optimism, confidence and success which the company consciously perpetuated kept turnover low. People liked their jobs. The more seniority people had, the more the payroll grew.

There was a particular incident Syms thought was the moment when he realized that there was the "real" world he lived in and another world that made people happy, but was far from real. When RXSystems opened its doors for business a week ahead of schedule, after an extraordinary effort by the new employees, the president and executive vice president had presided at a company celebration and the president said expansively, "I promise you this: When we begin year six of our operations I will give every one of you a bonus of two weeks' pay. That's my way of saying thanks." A year ago in a strategic planning and budget preparation meeting, he said that he intended to distribute the bonuses on "day one of year six."

Syms spoke up. "I don't know if we can afford that. It might be more prudent to wait until we have had a profitable year." "Nelson," the president said, "there is no one better than you to move things around, squeeze a bit, juggle and delay when you need to. This company is succeeding because people are satisfied and happy, and they appreciate all the things we have done. Keeping our employees happy is the best insurance policy we can have to make RXServices successful."

Driving home, Syms began to feel the familiar tension in his arms. He could juggle, sure. He could move things around so today's bills were paid, but sooner or later there probably would not be enough money. He remembered that the president had said to him, "You know it all. Where it is and where it needs to go, who has to be paid and who can wait."

Syms thought it was true. He did know all of that and a lot more. He thought about the uncertainties of the future and said to himself, "Maybe that's the real problem. Maybe I know too much."

Questions for Consideration and Discussion
'The Man Who Knew Too Much'

1. Many of the employees at RXSystems do not appear to have a grasp on the precarious financial state in which the organization operates. To what extent should employees know of such details? How can leaders share this type of information without giving employees too much confidential or proprietary information?

2. What do you believe are the factors that are motivating employees to work at RXSystems? Do you feel many of them are maintaining their loyalty to the organization because of the promise of future success?

3. What advice would you give to Nelson Syms for him to improve his daily satisfaction at work? What advice would you give Nelson's boss?

4. To what extent is it necessary for leaders to be concerned with the level of daily satisfaction felt by their employees? How might leaders best gauge the level of satisfaction in the workforce? What evidence might suggest if employees are satisfied or dissatisfied in the workplace?

PART V

Enhancing Workforce Engagement

Making Workforce Engagement Work

Chapter 15:
Making Workforce Engagement Work

Introduction: What do We Mean By 'Making Workforce Engagement Work'?

Making workforce engagement work refers to the commitment by leaders, HR professionals, managers and even individual-contributor employees to assessing, clarifying and prioritizing workforce issues in organizational settings. There are several steps involved in this process, along with numerous diagnostic questions that can be used to gauge organizational effectiveness concerning workforce engagement practices.

Why is Making Workforce Engagement Work Important?

As we have discussed, employees represent the intellectual capital of an organization and can provide the basis for long-term, competitive sustainable advantage in the marketplace. By bringing knowledge, skills and competencies to bear in the performance of their jobs, employees can help deepen relationships with customers, develop new products, services and solutions and innovate or improve business processes. An organization's payroll can be as high as 70 percent of the firm's total costs, making the workforce a principal, strategic expense. Beyond merely a cost, however, employees represent an investment in the organization's future. Thus, many organizations must remember that workforce engagement is an ongoing process, not merely a once-a-year or one-time endeavor. This requires the continuous introduction, refinement and improvement of workforce engagement practices that have consistently been acknowledged as effective in finding, keeping and motivating employees.

How Can Organizations Make Workforce Engagement Work?

> **Steps Involved in Making Workforce Engagement Work:**
>
> - Secure senior leadership buy-in to workforce engagement.
> - Assess current state of employee perceptions and organizational practices.
> - Identify and involve relevant stakeholders in the improvement and implementation process.
> - Communicate changes to the workforce.
> - Make responsibility for workforce engagement part of everyone's job every day.

Secure senior leadership buy-in to workforce engagement

In reality, workforce engagement matters will not become—or stay—a priority unless senior leaders have support for the philosophy and approach. There are, indeed, likely several leadership teams for whom workforce engagement matters are already a priority. In settings where workforce engagement is, presently, a low priority, senior leaders might be compelled to take a more proactive role in such matters by making the "business case" for workforce engagement activities. Such a business case should focus on the cost and revenue variables associated with workforce engagement.

On the cost side of the equation, there are soft and hard costs associated with employee turnover. *Soft costs* include lack of production during the "predeparture" phase of an employee who has given notice; the lost productivity of a vacant position; the potential lower morale of remaining employees; the lower productivity of a new hire; and the additional supervision time required for a new hire. *Hard costs* of turnover (typically those more quantifiable than "soft" ones) include separation processing (e.g., continuation of benefits, severance); co-worker burdens such as overtime or added shifts; headhunter or executive search firm expenses (which can range from 25 percent to 75 percent or more of an employees' annual salary); advertising and other recruiting costs; interviewing, reference checking and other selection tests, including drug, criminal and psychological testing; and orientation/onboarding and on-the-job training costs. Indeed, depending on the industry and nature of the position, turnover costs might be as high as 18 months' worth of an employee's salary.

On the revenue side of the equation, there exists evidence to suggest that having a stable, committed and engaged workforce promotes customer satisfaction and retention and overall firm performance. For example, in his books *Loyalty Rules* and *The Loyalty Effect*, author Frederick Reichheld notes that a mere 5-percent increase in employee loyalty can yield as much as a 50-percent increase in profits (because, in part, of the soft and hard costs employers avoid, thanks to retention). Studies—from Walker Information, Watson Wyatt, Sears and *pan*, among others—all suggest that organizations that invest in employees tend to realize greater productivity and profitability as a result. Thus, from a revenue and profitability and cost-savings perspective, workforce engagement matters deserve the attention of senior leaders.

Assess current state of employee perceptions and organizational practices

With senior leader acceptance, the next step is to assess the state of employee perceptions and organizational practices related to workforce engagement. Recall that employee perceptions include the priorities an individual places on work (something an employer may have little control over), along with that person's attitudes, behaviors and intentions (things an employer may have more control over). Assessing employer perceptions can be done informally through the daily interactions between managers and employees. Or, perceptions can be measured formally through employee opinion surveys, focus-group research, analyses of performance-management problems or commercial products such as *pan*'s Workforce Engagement Assessment (from which the National Benchmark data profiled in this book was derived). Understanding how employees perceive the organization's commitment to workforce engagement is needed to more fully target organizational resources to better recruit, retrain, reward and retain talent.

Assessing organizational practices involves, among other things, inventorying what the organization is doing in the workforce engagement area, determining the practices that are lacking, benchmarking with other organizations and reviewing the research, professional and trade literature for useful ideas and strategies. Because all organizational resources are inherently constrained, it is necessary for decision makers to determine which organizational practices are likely to yield the greatest ROI or other impact on the workforce. This can be informed, in part, by analyzing findings from the assessment of employee perspectives.

The experiential case study at the conclusion of this chapter also provides the reader with more than 70 diagnostic questions aimed at determining the extent to which certain organizational practices are effective in contributing to workforce engagement.

Identify and involve relevant stakeholders in the improvement and implementation process

As internal organizational champions seek to improve and implement workforce engagement practices, it is wise to involve all relevant stakeholders. First, change-management theories hold that individuals are more likely to support decisions when they have been involved in crafting those decisions. Second, managers and individual-contributor employees, especially, are likely to be an excellent source for providing information about the true value and likely impact of proposed changes or improvements to workforce engagement practices. Third, for workforce engagement to be sustainable, employees at all levels must understand and accept the concepts and approaches. The "business case" made to senior leaders may also be useful for employees at other levels of the enterprise.

Communicate changes to the workforce

Ironically, many organizations institute some well-intentioned and sound practices aimed at improving workforce engagement ... only to have those practices go virtually unnoticed by busy managers and employees. Thus, it is vital that intentional, explicit and continuous communication about the ways in which the organization is taking actions to enhance the climate, nature and culture of work be communicated to the workforce. Intranets, e-mails, employee newsletters, posters, payroll' advice inserts, training programs and department meetings are some of the many ways to regularly "get the message out" and keep internal organizational stakeholders informed.

Organizations that do a good job of communicating to their employees about workforce engagement initiatives recognize a couple of things. First, such messages send a signal to employees that workforce engagement is an organizational priority and that employees really do matter. Second, one of the frequent complaints employees articulate is that feedback provided via employee opinion surveys and other means is largely ignored (or, at the very least, that is the perception many employees hold). By following up on employee suggestions with explanations and action items and communicating this information back to employees, organizations can send a signal to employees that their voices were, indeed, heard. Finally, when it is time to collect additional feedback from employees—in the form of employee opinion surveys, etc.—employees are more likely to remember information that has been intentionally, explicitly and continuously communicated to them. Thus, employees may be more likely to participate in the process and provide candid, fair feedback on what works well and what is in need of further refinements and improvement.

Make responsibility for workforce engagement part of everyone's job every day

Although individual-contributor employees play a role in providing feedback on their perspectives concerning workforce engagement practices, their role does not end there. Indeed, organizations need to make responsibility for workforce engagement part of everyone's job every day. Individuals and departments at all levels of the organization bear responsibility for workforce engagement.

Data from both of **pan**'s national benchmark studies on workforce engagement shows employees expect senior leaders to act with integrity as they advance the organization's strategy. This also necessarily involves shaping and managing the organization's reputation; making ethics, diversity and safety central to the organization's culture; and regularly taking the organization's temperature through ongoing stakeholder input.

HR professionals are likely to be the lead champions of workforce engagement within organizations, something rather ironic because none of the core HR processes were drivers of workforce engagement. Nevertheless, workforce selection, organizational orientation, training and development, rewards and recognition and work-life balance all support efforts to recruit, retrain, reward and retain talent.

Managers and individual-contributor employees are, perhaps, the most important players in workforce engagement. Recall that daily satisfaction is the No. 1-driver of workforce engagement. This means that managers and individual-contributor employees play a key role in creating environments that are enjoyable and productive for employees on a daily basis. After all, employees do not necessarily quit a bad job, they leave a poor working relationship—and bosses and co-workers are often the reasons cited for why and how relationships at work are poor. Given the cost and revenue implications of workforce engagement, therefore, it is important to educate managers and individual-contributor employees about these issues—and to hold them accountable, in part, for variables such as employee retention, satisfaction and productivity.

Summary

This chapter provided advice and steps about making workforce engagement work. Central to this concept is a commitment from senior leaders, coupled with a realistic and ongoing assessment of employee perspectives and organizational practices. There is also a paramount need to prioritize action items, involve key stakeholders in implementing changes, communicate those changes to the workforce and make responsibility for workforce engagement part of everyone's daily job. The case study that follows is a departure from the norm and actively invites the reader to truly make workforce engagement work in his or her organization.

Case Study:
An Experimental Approach to Making Workforce Engagement Work

Unlike previous end-of-chapter case studies, this chapter issues a "call to action" and involves the reader in an "experiential case study" assessment of organizational practices contributing to workforce engagement. To accomplish this, the reader is encouraged to use his or her own organization (or a unit therein) to assess current strengths to leverage and opportunities for improvement—and to develop specific recommendations—as they relate to workforce engagement.

Begin by identifying key informants (a mix of senior leaders, HR professionals, managers and individual-contributor employees) who are knowledgeable about the organization, its history and its workforce-related practices. Using the "Critical Questions" framework on page 306, ask key informants about all of the components of workforce engagement, drawn from the framework of 13 organizational practices contributing to workforce engagement.

After collecting the information, analyze the findings, identify common themes, and synthesize and summarize the results. Then, share this information with the key informants who initially provided the answers to the questions. Finally, involve colleagues who can assist you in these activities: (1) brainstorm possible recommendations for improvements; (2) develop specific strategies and a timeline for implementation; (3) identify indicators of performance (e.g., reduced turnover, enhanced employee satisfaction, lower absenteeism); and (4) assign action items or responsibilities to people or departments who will champion or implement the recommendations.

Strategic Issues

To demonstrate *effective senior leadership*, how well does our organization ...

- Articulate a meaningful strategic direction (mission, vision, values,
  goals, etc.)?
- Recognize the relationship between workforce engagement and organizational success?
- Leverage employees as a strategic choice to competitively differentiate the
  organization?
- Identify and model leadership behaviors that support workforce engagement?
- Cultivate a high-performance culture and meaningful work environment
  through effective organizational practices?

To develop strong *reputation management*, how well does our organization ...

- Shape and manage the organization's reputation with all stakeholder groups?
- Communicate the organization's value proposition?
- Identify and describe strengths of the organization's products, services and
  solutions?
- Exercise corporate social responsibility (e.g., being a good corporate citizen)?
- Ensure that employees understand how the organization is competitively
  differentiated?
- Establish an employment philosophy and brand?

To create an environment that values *ethics, diversity and safety*, how well does our
organization ...

- Create, implement and nurture a culture of ethical conduct and decision-
  making?
- Comply with laws, regulations and organizational policies?

- Develop and implement fair and consistent disciplinary, grievance and dispute-resolution procedures?
- Respect, cultivate and manage diversity?
- Ensure a safe work environment?
- Monitor, evaluate and improve organizational approaches to ethics, diversity and safety?

To fully develop the organization's capabilities through *stakeholder input*, how well does our organization ...
- Seek regular feedback from customers, business partners and other stake-holders on how well the organization is meeting their needs?
- Benchmark with other organizations on effective practices?
- Measure employee perceptions about the organization through formal and informal ways?
- Evaluate internal work experiences, assessing strengths, weaknesses, opportunities and threats?
- Identify internal champions (beyond HR) to conduct "organizational temperature taking" and provide feedback?
* Develop strategies for improved experiences that meet the needs of employees and the organization?

Core HR Processes

To realize effective *workforce selection*, how well does our organization ...
- Design meaningful job and work experiences?
- Adjust staffing levels appropriately to meet the requirements of the organization?
- Outline hiring criteria and competencies needed for success?
- Develop effective recruitment sources and methods?
- Establish and implement selection processes, approaches and practices that ensure the right fit?
- Evaluate and improve the utility and yield ratios of selection processes and practices?

To maximize *organizational orientation*, how well does our organization ...
- Link planning, recruitment and selection to organizational onboarding and orientation?
- Design processes/programs for employee integration into the organization?

- Indoctrinate employees in organizational values and business practices?
- Involve relevant stakeholders in orientation activities?
- Develop successful mentoring and coaching programs?
- Evaluate and improve the effectiveness of organizational onboarding and orientation initiatives?

To provide effective *training and development*, how well does our organization ...
- Assess needs and establish priorities for employee training and development?
- Design performance-improvement approaches (including nontraining interventions)?
- Develop training, development and other experiences for employee growth?
- Implement activities for improvement, change and effectiveness?
- Evaluate the outcomes of training, development and other experiences?

To effectively utilize *rewards and recognition,* how well does our organization ...
- Reward performance through cash, noncash and other approaches?
- Pay for the acquisition and application of new knowledge and skills?
- Recognize employee contributions to organizational achievements?
- Identify and reward employees who contribute to a high-performance, meaningful work environment?
- Ensure equitable treatment of employees in reward and recognition practices?
- Develop, implement and encourage employee-involvement activities?

To permit employees to achieve *work-life balance*, how well does our organization ...
- Explain the business case for work-life balance?
- Create approaches for employees to balance personal, family and community obligations?
- Develop flexible work schedules and options, as feasible?
- Manage stress, promote employee wellness and minimize burnout?
- Monitor and evaluate the impact of work-life balance initiatives on employee satisfaction, retention and performance?

Operational Components

To provide effective *performance management*, how well does our organization ...
- Identify relevant dimensions of employee performance?
- Set challenging, meaningful and achievable expectations for employees?
- Implement procedures to monitor and evaluate employee performance?

- Involve stakeholders in measuring and managing employee performance?
- Conduct regular and effective performance-feedback meetings?
- Develop plans and approaches for improved employee performance?

To equip employees with appropriate *tools and technology*, how well does our organization ...
- Identify and allocate the resources (physical, technological, financial, human, etc.) necessary for meaningful work experiences?
- Provide time, tools and techniques required for understanding and performing the job?
- Ensure ergonomically correct work environments?
- Structure workload, workflow and interactions with people, processes and technologies appropriately?

To retain talented employees and release marginal employees through *opportunities for advancement*, how well does our organization ...
- Broker employee talent internally and (in some cases) externally?
- Promote from within and provide lateral mobility, whenever possible?
- Identify, develop and (in some cases) release marginal, difficult and improper fit employees?
- Avoid perpetuating a "paternalistic" culture of employee dependence?
- Encourage employees to keep themselves viable on the open market?
- Anticipate, embrace and lead change in the workplace?
- Handle downsizing, outsourcing and discontinuation of work effectively?

To create a work environment that leads to *daily satisfaction*, how well does our organization ...
- Recognize what motivates employees to come to work each day?
- Ensure that relationships with supervisor and peers are positive?
- Remove barriers and bottlenecks that inhibit meaningful work performance?
- Create an environment of open, candid communication?
- Show respect for employees as individuals?
- Allow appropriate autonomy and discretion in performing work?
- Maintain a high-performance, enjoyable workplace?

Selected References

Armitage, Amelia. 2004. "Overcoming the 'Elephant Problem': Creating Value with Corporate Performance Management Through Strategic Alignment and Engagement." *WorldatWork Journal*, Third Quarter, 35-45.

Baumruk, Ray. 2004. "The Missing Link: The Role of Employee Engagement in Business Success." *workspan*, November, 49-52.

Belliveau, Paul L. 2004. "Feeding the Sandwich Generation." *WorldatWork Journal*, Fourth Quarter, 25-31.

Blackburn, Jan; Bremen, John M. 2003. "From Exporting to Integrating: Optimizing Total Rewards for a Global Sales Force." *WorldatWork Journal*, Fourth Quarter, 72-79.

Bond, James T.; Galinsky, Ellen; Hill, E. Jeffrey. 2005. "Flexibility: A Critical Ingredient in Creating an Effective Workplace." *workspan*, February, 17-22.

Bradley, Gibson J.; Jones, Blair; Hatfield, Clare. 2005. "Proctor & Gamble's Balanced Approach to Long-Term Incentives." *WorldatWork Journal*, First Quarter,

Brown, Duncan; West, Michael. 2005. "Rewarding Service? Using Reward Policies to Deliver Your Customer Service Strategy." *WorldatWork Journal*, Fourth Quarter, 22-31.

Burchman, Seymour; Jones, Blair. 2006. "Executive Compensation as a Support for a Growth Strategy." *WorldatWork Journal*, Third Quarter, 39-46.

Burchman, Seymour; Jones, Blair. 2004. "The Future of Stock Options: From Starring Role to Ensemble Player." *WorldatWork Journal*, First Quarter, 29-38.

Crandall, N. Frederic. 2004. "New Ways to Manage Pay: Upgrading Base Pay, Pay Progression, and Variable Pay Plans to Attract and Retain Talent." *WorldatWork Journal*, Third Quarter, 56-61.

Drizin, Marc. 2005. "Let's Get Engaged: Benchmarks Help Employers Drive Results." *workspan*, April, 47-49.

Ellig, Bruce R. 2002. "Executive Compensation 101: Considering the Many

Elements." *WorldatWork Journal*, First Quarter, 11-20.

Finesod, Rosalyn; Davenport, Thomas O. 2006. "The Aging Workforce: Challenge or Opportunity?" *WorldatWork Journal*, Third Quarter, 14-23.

Gebauer, Julie; O'Neal, Sandra. 2006. "Talent Management in the 21st Century: Attracting, Retaining and Engaging Employees of Choice." *WorldatWork Journal*, First Quarter, 6-17.

Giancola, Frank. 2006. "Toward a Deeper Understanding of Employee Commitment." *WorldatWork Journal*, First Quarter, 18-23.

Green, Gordon T. 2005. "Recognition and the Generational Divide." *workspan*, 10-11.

Greenberg, Richard; Shaffer, Aaron. 2006. "Employee Survey Advantage: The 'Rule of Twos' Helps Gain a Competitive Advantage." September, 57-59.

Gross, Steven E.; Nalbantian, Haig R. 2002. "Looking at Rewards Holistically." *WorldatWork Journal*, Second Quarter, 52-64.

Harter, James K.; Wagner, Rodd. 2006. "An Element Unto Itself: The Problem of Pay." *WorldatWork Journal*, Fourth Quarter, 77-84.

Heneman, Robert L.; Mulvey, Paul W.; LeBlanc, Peter V. 2002. "Improve Base Pay ROI by Increasing Employee Knowledge." *WorldatWork Journal*, Fourth Quarter, 21-27.

Heneman, Robert L.; LeBlanc, Peter V.; Reynolds, Tim L. 2002. "Using Work Valuation to Identify and Protect the Talent Pool." *WorldatWork Journal*, Third Quarter, 32-41.

Jesuthasan, Ravin. 2003. "Business Performance Management: Improving Return on Rewards Investments." *WorldatWork Journal*, Fourth Quarter, 55-64.

Kantor, Richard; Kao, Tina. 2004. "Total Rewards: Clarity from the Confusion and Chaos." *WorldatWork Journal*, Third Quarter, 7–15.

Lawler, Edward E. III. 2002. "Pay Strategies for the Next Economy: Lessons from the Dot-comp Era." *WorldatWork Journal*, First Quarter, 6–10.

Latta, Geoffrey, W. 2003. "Expatriate Compensation Policies and Programs - How Do You Measure Performance?" *WorldatWork Journal*, Second Quarter, 68-74.

Levine, Brian; Nugent, Kim. 2005. "Rethinking Careers to Enhance Business Performance." *WorldatWork Journal*, Third Quarter, 56-63.

Lingle, Kathleen M. 2005. "Employer of Choice is in the Eye of the Beholder." *WorldatWork Journal*, Third Quarter, 26-31.

Meyer, Kathryn. 2005. "Survival of the Fittest: Creating a Committed and Engaged Workforce." *workspan*, May, 47-51.

Mitchell, Kenneth. 2006. "Productive Aging: The New Life Stage." *WorldatWork Journal*, First Quarter, 62-72.

Mitchell, Kenneth. 2006. "Creating New Horizons: Productive Aging as a Corporate Strategy." *WorldatWork Journal*, Third Quarter, 6-13.

O'Malley, Michael. 2003. "What is Base Salary?" *WorldatWork Journal*, Third Quarter, 22-28.

Parus, Barbara. 2004. "Pump Up Your Flexibility Quotient." *workspan*, August, 48-53.

Parus, Barbara. 2003. "The Show Must Go On: Talent Management Sets the Stage for Business Success." *workspan*, July, 48-51.

Piktialis, Diane. 2006. "The Generational Divide in Talent Management." *workspan*, March, 10-12.

Platt, Rodney K. 2002. "A Strategic Approach to Benefits." *workspan*, July, 22-24.

Reilly, Mark. 2005. "Pay for Performance or Pay for the Masses?" *WorldatWork Journal*, Fourth Quarter, 16-21.

Richman, Amy. 2006. "Everyone Wants An Engaged Workforce – How Can You Create It?" *workspan*, January, 36-39.

Scott, K. Dow; Morajda, Dennis; Bishop, James W. 2002. "Increase Company Competitiveness: 'Tune Up' Your Pay System." *WorldatWork Journal*, First Quarter, 35-42.

Shafer, Paul; Fischetti, Virginia. 2005. "Rewarding Your Way to Double-Digit Growth." *WorldatWork Journal*, Fourth Quarter, 6-15.

Stettler, Donna. 2004. "Restricted Stock: The Option to Options?" *WorldatWork Journal*, First Quarter, 19-28.

Stoskopt, Gregory A. 2004. "Using Total Rewards to Attract and Retain Health-Care Employees." *WorldatWork Journal*, Third Quarter, 16-25.

Sung, Amy; Todd, Emory. 2004. "Line of Sight: Moving Beyond the Catchphrase." *workspan*, October, 65-69.

Tracey, Monica W.; Flinchbaugh, Jamie. 2006. "HR's Role in the Lean Organizational Journey." *WorldatWork Journal*, Fourth Quarter, 49-58.

Vallas, Sara. 2006. "Communicating is Key to Total Rewards Success." *workspan*, October, 25-27.

Verive, Jennifer M.; Delay, Nancy. 2006. "Measuring Telework ROI: Metrics

Based on the Employee Life Cycle." *WorldatWork Journal*, Second Quarter, 6-15.

Winter, Nadine. "Tuned In and Turned On: Keeping Employees Engaged in a Tumultuous Economy." *workspan*, 2003. April, 48-52.

WorldatWork Surveys (www.worldatwork.org/library/research/surveys)

Aligning Rewards with the Changing Employment Deal – 2006/2007 Strategic Rewards Report

Flexible Work Schedules Survey Brief – 2005

Bonus Program Practices Survey Brief – 2005

Trends in Employee Recognition Survey Brief – 2005

Variable Pay and Organizational Performance Survey Brief – 2004

WorldatWork Bookstore (www.worldatwork.org/bookstore)

Barton, G. Michael. 2002. *Recognition at Work*. Scottsdale: WorldatWork Press.

Bellingham, Richard. 2001. *The Manager's Pocket Guide to Corporate Culture Change.* Amherst: HRD Press.

Carsen, Jennifer A. 2003. *HR How-to: Employee Retention: Everything You Need To Know About Creating an Effective Employee Retention Program*. Riverwoods: CCH Knowledge Point.

Dychtwald, Ken; Erickson, Tamara J.; Morison, Robert. 2006. *Workforce Crisis: How to Beat the Coming Shortage of Skills and Talents*. Boston: Harvard Business School Press.

Gallagher, Richard S. 2003. *The Soul of an Organization: Understanding the Values that Drive Successful Corporate Cultures*. Chicago: Dearborn Trade Publishing.

Harris, Philip R.; Moran, Robert T.; Moran, Sarah V. 2004. *Managing Cultural Difference: Global Leadership Strategies for the Twenty-first Century*. St. Louis: Elsevier Butterworth-Heinemann.

Holbeche, Linda. 2005. *The High Performance Organization: Creating Dynamic Stability and Sustainable Success*. Engelwood: Elsevier Butterworth-Heinemann.

Horibe, Frances. 2001. *Creating the Innovation Culture: Leveraging Visionaries, Dissenters and Other Useful Troublemakers in Your Organization*. San Francisco: John Wiley & Sons.

Kaye, Beverly; Jordan-Evans, Sharon. 2005. *Love 'Em or Lose 'Em: Getting Good People to Stay*, 3d, San Francisco: Berrett-Koehler.

Ledford, Gerald E. 2003. *The 2003 Rewards of Work: The Employment Deal in a Changing Economy*. New York: Sibson Consulting.

Phillips, Jack J. 2003. *Managing Employee Retention: A Strategic Accountability Approach*. Englewood: Butterworth-Heinemann.

Phillips, Jack J. 2002. *Retaining Your Best Employees: Nine Case Studies from the Real World of Training*. Alexandria: SHRM.

Rosen, Corey; Carberry, Ed. 2002. *Ownership Management: Building a Culture of Lasting Innovation*. Oakland: National Center for Employee Ownership.

Wilson, Thomas B. 2003. *Innovative Reward Systems for the Changing Workplace*. New York: McGraw-Hill.

WorldatWork. 2002. *Best of Attraction and Retention*. Scottsdale: WorldatWork.

WorldatWork. 2005. *Cash Bonuses: Four Ways to Attract, Retain and Motivate Employees*, 2d. Scottsdale: WorldatWork.

Zachary, Lois J. 2005. *Creating a Mentoring Culture*. Hoboken: Jossey-Bass.

WorldatWork Courses (www.worldatwork.org/education)

B1: Fundamentals of Employee Benefits Programs

B5: Managing Flexible Benefits

T1: Total Rewards Management

T4: Strategic Communication in Total Rewards

T11: Fundamentals of Equity-based Rewards

C12: Variable Pay—Incentives, Recognition and Bonuses

Index